Crime Stoppers:
Unsolved Homicides -

Find
My
Killer

By
Cal Millar

This book is dedicated to my wife, Penny, and our family.

Acknowledgements

I would like to thank the various police agencies and Crime Stoppers units for making available information related to unsolved homicides in hopes of reaching people across North America and in other parts of the world who may be in a position to provide answers that will allow detectives to resolve some of the homicides portrayed in this book. In many cases police agencies are revealing facts about unsolved slayings in their files and asking for public assistance to help find those responsible so they can be brought to justice. A great number of media outlets, including newspapers in both the United States and Canada, have assisted police and Crime Stoppers units by publicizing appeals and bringing numerous unsolved murders to the attention of the public. The media sought assistance on behalf of police agencies and Crime Stoppers by encouraging members of the public to come forward if they know who committed any of these crimes or have clues that will put investigators on the track of the perpetrators. Information provided by police and Crime Stoppers as well as public appeals in various newspapers greatly assisted in providing details about the victims. Web sites set up by family members and friends to focus public attention on the murder of a loved one were invaluable and gave me the opportunity to show the true impact of this type of tragedy while at the same time giving a glimpse into who the victim was and the aspirations they had before their lives were ended so senselessly and with such violence. The photographs which were made public by police agencies and Crime Stoppers units as well as those posted on web sites in an effort to encourage people to come forward with information not only puts a face to what often become mere statistics, but also allows anyone reading the appeals in this book to think back and recall if they remember any of the individuals and if they can think of facts that will help investigators conclude the homicide cases with arrests. In addition, I would like to thank all police officers who have worked diligently on any of these investigations, the media who assisted with appeals to inform the public and the board of directors and police coordinators of the various Crime Stoppers programs who have posted rewards in hopes of catching these killers.

Copyright © 2009 by Cal Millar

(Most of the photographs depicting victims in this book were released by law enforcement agencies or Crime Stoppers units while others were made public by family members and posted on web sites in hopes of encouraging individuals to come forward with information that will assist in solving the various slayings.)

All rights reserved. No part of this book may be reproduced or transmitted in any form, including photocopying, recording or by any other information storage and retrieval system without permission in writing by the author.

ISBN/EAN13: 1448648769 / 9781448648764

Additional copies of this book are available from www.amazon.com

Find My Killer

Prologue

Each year across North America, on average, some 17,000 people are murdered. These are senseless killings, but the deaths don't directly affect the majority of those living in the United States or Canada. They are faceless victims and quickly become statistics remembered only by their families and the detectives who hope to someday make an arrest. Crime Stoppers programs in both countries appeal for information, but most victims of homicide receive mainly local attention and seldom capture international headlines. The purpose of this book is to highlight murder victims pulled randomly from the files of police departments and Crime Stoppers units on both sides of the 49th parallel. Rewards associated with the cases in this book total more than five-and-a-half million dollars.

Crime Stoppers programs offer rewards for tips that lead to an arrest and individuals don't have to wait for a conviction in order to collect their money. Those calling Crime Stoppers tip lines also remain completely anonymous since individuals providing information are never asked to give their name and no details are recorded that would allow any person to be identified. Although many crimes are solved through the dedicated work of investigators it is acknowledged that without direct assistance from the public, police would be stymied in their efforts to resolve numerous cases. Unfortunately in recent years a culture has developed, especially among people in certain communities, where cooperating with police is somehow wrong and this has greatly hampered investigators in their quest to bring criminals to justice. In addition, a degree of apathy has taken over society and people do not feel it is their civic duty to freely come forward with information they may possess that would allow authorities to identify those responsible for criminal activity. Crime Stoppers was developed as an avenue to encourage individuals to provide information to police without getting directly involved or being compelled to appear in court as a witness. Obviously detectives require those with direct information to testify under oath and provide the necessary evidence to convict those brought before the courts, but it is also necessary for investigators to have avenues they can pursue while hunting for individuals who have committed crimes, especially those involving homicide.

Initially in any murder investigation the search for the killer spreads out in a 360 degree radius and every trail or lead, spanning out like the spokes in a wheel, must be followed until the perpetrator is identified and taken into custody. A witness assists detectives by taking the guess work from the investigation and putting police on the path that leads directly to the killer. Tips from the public can save detectives countless hours of investigative time and assist in putting those behind bars who pose a risk to society.

Specifically in regard to this book, if you have any information that can assist investigators, please contact your local Crime Stoppers program, police department or law enforcement agency responsible for the case. It is important to study photographs included with some of the victims to determine if you remember the individual or have any recollection of something that might be helpful to investigators. The details included with each case could also trigger a memory that may seem extremely trivial, but could be the important piece of evidence that police have been seeking to bring closure to the case. Every piece of the puzzle is important and although you may feel it's insignificant, the detail you possess might hold the clue that has eluded investigators for years. It is important that you not evaluate the information, but provide it to police to allow them to determine its value to their investigation. Even though you don't live near where the homicide occurred there might be a few words or the description of a suspect that resembles someone now living in your community. Details on the various cases in this book came from police files, media accounts of the crime, appeals issued through Crime Stoppers and web sites developed by friends and relatives of some murder victims who are trying to help law enforcement bring the killers to justice. The messages in many of the personal appeals on web sites are poignant and reveal the character of the victims and dreams that will never be fulfilled. They also describe the deep feelings of family members and close associates of the victims who have been devastated with the loss and in many cases had their lives turned into living nightmares by the senseless act of a killer. At the same time the emotions they have expressed and the memories they have of those who were murdered provide an opportunity to give the victims a human face rather than allowing them to languish as a statistic on a police homicide report.

Anyone who has information regarding an unsolved case is urged to contact the police department directly involved with the investigation, but if for one reason or another, you want to remain anonymous, you can call any of the various Crime Stoppers organizations around the world. Details you provide will be forwarded by Crime Stoppers to the police agency responsible for investigating the homicide and detectives will follow up to determine if your information can advance the investigation and ultimately solve the case with an arrest. There are Crime Stoppers or similar programs, such as Silent Witness, Crime Solvers and CrimeLine, in all 50 states and the various U. S. territories as well as across Canada and in many other countries worldwide, including the United Kingdom, Australia, India, the Netherlands and throughout the Caribbean. Since the first Crime Stoppers program was originated in September 1976 in Albuquerque, New Mexico by Detective Greg MacAleese, programs on a global basis have received tips resulting in the arrests to date of more than 822,000 individuals, the clearing of 1.2 million cases, the recovery of some $1.9 billion in stolen property and the seizure of drugs with a street value of $6.9 billion.

There have also been tremendous advances in forensic technology; including DNA analysis, that has allowed police agencies to resolve cases that in some instances are decades old. During the research and writing of this book, some of the cases originally selected for inclusion were solved through DNA assessments that were not available when the crimes were initially committed. Many police departments have activated Cold Case Squads to review evidence collected by now retired detectives and submit evidence for specialized forensic analysis that wasn't available to investigators years earlier. This demonstrates the importance of providing police with information on suspects so today's technology can be utilized to confirm or eliminate their involvement with a crime. In many cases police have blood, hair, fingerprints and other physical evidence from a crime scene but don't have similar material from a suspect to make the necessary comparisons. Your tip could be the vital piece of information that solves one of these cases.

Through the years Crime Stoppers has relied on newspapers and the electronic broadcast media to promote unsolved crimes to the public. Appeals from local programs reached the circulation boundaries of the publications that gave them support or the broadcast range of radio and television stations. On a rare occasion and if the crime was spectacular enough, the Crime Stoppers appeal would merit coverage on network broadcasts or be highlighted by CNN's Nancy Grace or Greta Van Susteren and others on the Fox News network. Through the years there have been a number of most wanted shows such as the long running America's Most Wanted which copied the Crime Stoppers format and highlighted some cases to millions of viewers across North America. The advent of the Internet provided a worldwide reach to those visiting local Crime Stoppers computer home pages and sites such as Facebook and YouTube have allowed programs to broadcast reenactment appeals to people linking onto social network groups. The concept of publishing unsolved crimes in a book is a further advancement for Crime Stoppers and gives programs an unlimited reach and a resource that has never before been tapped by the worldwide crime fighting organization. Books are distributed across North America and around the world as well as being passed from person to person in a fairly short span of time. This initiative gives Crime Stoppers and law enforcement agencies in the United States and Canada a unique opportunity to appeal for assistance to an almost unlimited audience and could be utilized as an investigative tool for solving a variety of cases in the future.

The concept of publicizing unsolved crime obviously isn't new, but police agencies are always looking for methods to expand their reach when making appeals to identify suspects and obtain new leads that will assist them in solving crime. Quite early in my newspaper career, I became aware of the role the media could play in helping police to encourage individuals to come forward with information that is vital to successfully conclude an investigation. Apart from directly asking for public assistance in general news coverage related to criminal activity, I wrote the first series of Crime Flashback articles for the Toronto Sun in 1972 which brought forward information in a couple of cases that was extremely helpful to the investigators and eventually directly led them to the individuals responsible. When Crime Stoppers was developed a few years later, I was keenly aware of the importance of publicity in highlighting unsolved cases and became an ardent supporter of the program. The title of the book comes directly from an initiative of the Crime Stoppers program in Toronto and its then coordinator, Detective Jeff Zammit, who printed posters of homicide victims under the heading: Find My Killer.

Find My Killer

Chapter 1 – Acosta to Chia

Christopher Acosta

Christopher Acosta
Phoenix, Arizona

A young man was murdered in Phoenix, Arizona while trying to diffuse an argument during a street party. The victim, Christopher Acosta, was shot point blank in the chest at 1:20 a.m. on Sunday, September 12, 1999 in a field just off East Jones Avenue at 16th Place. Investigators were told things started getting out of hand after two women got into an argument at a block party organized by a teenager who'd been left alone while his parents were away for the weekend. The squabble escalated and some 100 or so partygoers made their way to the open field and fights broke out between members of two rival gangs. Twenty-one-year-old Acosta, a nearby resident who wasn't affiliated with a gang, tried to assist a man who was being beaten by four people. At that point at least two men pulled out guns. One person fired a shot into the air, but the other individual pointed his handgun directly at Acosta. His father, Ben, told investigators that Christopher put his hands in front of his face and said "no, no, no…" as the gunman fired a single shot from the .45 caliber weapon. The slug went right through him and Acosta was pronounced dead on arrival at the hospital a short time later. Police have an idea of who is responsible but need someone to provide specific information and confirm the individual was at the street party. The suspect is a Hispanic male between 19 and 21 years, 130 to 150 pounds and wearing a white muscle shirt and dark baggy pants. The Phoenix Silent Witness program is offering a reward of up to $1,000 for anyone who can assist police in identifying the killer.

Raymond Aguirre and wife, Mabel

Raymond Aguirre
Topeka, Kansas

An elderly couple was savagely beaten and left for dead by an intruder who broke into their Topeka, Kansas home. Eighty-two-year-old Raymond Aguirre died from his injuries a month after the attack which occurred sometime after 1 p.m. on Tuesday, September 19, 2000. His wife, Mabel, survived but lost sight from one eye. Investigators discovered someone removed a rear bathroom window to gain entry to the house at 1900 SE Washington Street, near SE 19th Street, while the couple was away. When Aguirre and his wife returned to the home they were confronted by the assailant who demanded cash. After insisting he didn't have any money, Aguirre was left unconscious on the floor when struck several times with a blunt instrument. The attacker then grabbed Mabel's cane as she sat praying in the living room and beat her into unconsciousness. The suspect took several items including Aguirre's gold watch and a quantity of bank cheques before fleeing. The victims weren't found until the next morning when their son dropped by to check on them. The attacker was described as a black male in his late teens or early 20s, about five-feet, eight-inches and close to 160 pounds. He had short hair worn in an Afro style with little or no facial hair and was wearing a red shirt with a white collar.

Friends and neighbors described the victims as an outstanding couple who had recently celebrated their 60th wedding anniversary. One investigator said they were pillars of the community and salt of the earth people who had lived in the East Topeka area for many years. Police distributed posters with a photograph of the couple throughout the city in hopes of getting information to solve the crime, but no one came forward with information. Investigators said they are still hopeful someone knows something and will eventually provide the name of the killer. The State of Kansas has offered a $5,000 reward to encourage people to tell authorities what they know about the attack and Topeka Crime Stoppers is offering up to $2,000 for anyone wishing to provide information anonymously that will solve the case. Raymond died October 14, 2000 from injuries directly related to the beating and his wife passed away peacefully at the Topeka Retirement Centre in September 2006 days before the anniversary of the 2000 attack. Detectives have vowed to never stop searching for the killer.

Jamal Ahmad

Jamal Ahmad
Philadelphia, Pennsylvania

A man who had been indicted on federal charges in a multi-million dollar payroll tax scam was shot to death in a rear drive at his Philadelphia, Pennsylvania home. The body of Jamal Ahmad was found around 10:30 p.m. on Sunday, November 16, 2008 near the back entrance of his house on O Street near East Hunting Park Avenue. The 66-year-old victim was shot in the chest and pronounced dead at Temple University Hospital. Ahmad and his brothers owned and operated the Three Cousins Food Market chain in North Philadelphia where employees had been paid more than $3.6 million in wages under the table to avoid income tax payments. Some $7.7 million was also skimmed from the company's revenues, according to documents submitted to the court by federal investigators. Kheirallah

Ahmad, who served as the company's chief executive officer, was sentenced to 48 month in prison in January 2008 and ordered to pay $1.2 million restitution to the Internal Revenue Service for conspiracy and filing false tax returns. Homicide investigators were unable to determine a motive for the slaying and the state's Crime Commission has put up a $1,000 reward to encourage anyone with information to come forward. Ahmad, known as Jimmy to his friends, was a respected member of the city's Hispanic community and contributed to a number of charities. His family was shocked by the killing and has no idea who could be responsible for Ahmad's death.

Mandi Alexander   Mary Drake

Mandi Alexander & Mary Drake
Great Bend, Kansas

A newly-hired store clerk and a customer were killed after being confronted by an attacker at the Dolly Madison Cake-Discount Bakery in Great Bend, a community of 15,500 in central Kansas. It was on Wednesday, September 4, 2002 when Mandi Alexander, a 24-year-old mother of two young children who had worked at the store only three days, and a 79-year-old customer, Mary Drake, were violently stabbed during what police believe was a robbery. A delivery driver discovered their blood drenched bodies at 7: 55 p.m. in a rear office of the bakery. The front door was locked but the driver had a key for the back door to pick up and drop off packages after normal business hours. Cash register sales receipts show the last purchase was made around 6 p.m. at the store in an older building on the east side of Harrison Street just north of 10th Street. A witness told police about a seeing a man locking the front door and walking away from the store shortly before the bodies were discovered. The man was around six-feet to six-feet, two-inches, 188 pounds with light brown blondish hair and wearing cut-off denim shorts, a dark gray or black t-shirt and white socks.

Mandi Alexander, the daughter of Karen and Guy Sunderland, and mother of two children, Brianna and Kirsten, aged four and six months, started work at 3 p.m. the day of her murder. Great Bend is the epitome of small town America and considered a safe and quiet place to raise a family. She was very friendly and loved the idea she had found a job where she could meet people from the community. Mary Drake was a long-time resident who enjoyed getting out of the house and often after doing a bit of shopping or some banking would stop at the Dolly Madison bakery to pick up sweets. Investigators believe the two women were confronted by the attacker and herded into the back room. Police have never revealed the type of weapon that was used to kill the women other than describing it as a sharp object. They also said some money was missing, giving the appearance the attack occurred during a robbery. Alexander's relatives said there is also the possibility Mandi was the target of a murder plot because she had recently gone to the police to complain about some illegal drug activity in her neighborhood. A $17,000 reward was posted for information that leads to an arrest and police are convinced there are people who know who is responsible for the slayings.

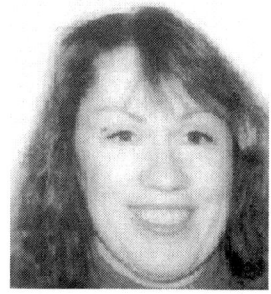
Sandra Allard

Sandra Allard
York Township, Illinois

A nurse who ran her own drug counseling business was stabbed to death and her townhouse set ablaze to cover up the murder in Oak Brook, Illinois. Sandra Allard was found dead on Sunday, October 3, 1993 in her bedroom after firefighters extinguished the flames at the home on Theresa Court just north of the Midwestern University campus. The 43-year-old woman, who also worked as a nurse at Elmhurst Hospital, had lived alone since getting divorced. An autopsy showed she'd received multiple stab wounds to the upper part of her body before a fire was set near her body. The DuPage County Sheriff's

Department has been unable to narrow the homicide investigation to one specific area and is appealing for people who might have information regarding a possible motive and who may be responsible for the Allard's killing.

Timothy Charles Allen
Highland Park, Michigan

Very few details have been released regarding the murder of a 40-year-old man in the Detroit, Michigan suburb of Highland Park. The victim, Timothy Charles Allen was found dead after being shot twice in the chest on Saturday, November 16, 2002. Born on July 7, 1963, Allen's wife, Terri, has posted several messages on web grief sites saying he's never forgotten and never alone. She described her husband as a good, kind, strong, gentle, trustworthy and compassionate man and said mere words cannot describe the pain of not having him in her life. Crime Stoppers of Michigan is offering a reward of up to $1,000 for information that helps solve this case.

Maricela Alvarez
San Jose, California

She came to the United States from Mexico at the age of 15 to live the American dream, but two years later she was dead. On Sunday, November 23, 2003, a Santa Clara County Park Ranger found  Maricela Alvarez seriously wounded in her car on Hellyer Avenue, just south of Highway 101. She had been shot 11 times. It was around 12:30 p.m. when the ranger spotted the victim's white two-door Daewoo sedan at the side of the road in the southbound lanes of the divided roadway near Coyote Creek Park. Alvarez lived with an older sister and her younger brother in Menlo Park, California and authorities have been unable to explain how she ended up at the remote spot on the eastern outskirts of San Jose. The victim was taken to the San Jose Medical Centre where she was pronounced dead about an hour later.

Alvarez was an exceptional student. When she came to the United States from her native Mexico, she couldn't speak English and didn't have any high school credits. She had attended classes at Menlo-Atherton High School on Middlefield Road but a month before she was killed transferred to Redwood High School on Old County Road in nearby Redwood City. Many students at the school were overcome with grief after learning their classmate had been murdered. Teachers described her as a gifted student who worked hard, had a full academic schedule and volunteered at the school. She also had a part-time job selling jewelry at a Mexican grocery store, Mi Rancho on Willow Road in Menlo Park between Chester Street and Durham Street. The money she earned helped pay for the apartment where she lived just around the corner from the store.

There was no hint Alvarez was in any danger the day she died. That morning she called her mother in Mexico to let her know she was doing fine and her studies were going well. Her goal was to go to university and the week before had made arrangements with Cañada College to participate in a specialized program that allows sophomore students to earn credit toward a degree. Attending community college while still in high school made her dream of graduating from Stanford University more of a reality. She brushed her hair after getting off the phone with her mother and left the house a short time later, telling her sister she was going to pick up some milk.

At that point there is a gap of about two-hours missing from the timeline in the life of the 17-year-old honor roll student. Investigators know approximately the time she left the apartment. They haven't indicted if she went to a store in the neighborhood to purchase milk. There is also no confirmation of the time she got into her car or if she was alone while driving the vehicle some three blocks from the Willow Road and Durham Street shopping district near her home to the entrance of Bayshore Freeway, an express route through Menlo Park for Highway 101 which runs from San Francisco to Los Angeles. It would take just over 40 minutes to drive the 35 mile distance to the spot in San Jose where she was found barely alive in her vehicle. She mumbled in Spanish to the English-speaking park ranger but interpretations of her final words didn't give any hint of who her killer might have been. There is also no clear understanding of how a trip to the store ended up at the side of a roadway that would have very little traffic on a Sunday afternoon.

She had dated a police officer from San Jose, but detectives were able to clear him of any involvement and the roadway where she was found was also nowhere near his home. Investigators questioned others who knew the girl, but didn't find anyone who might be responsible for her death. School friends described Maricela as an innocent person, one of those people you couldn't imagine ending up this way. They said she inspired them and never seemed to have any problems. She was just a nice person with a wonderful personality, always happy and always smiling. A $10,000 reward was offered for information on who killed Alvarez, but police said no one seems to have the answer. Ironically Alfonso Cuevas Gonzalez, the man she sold jewelry for at the Mexican supermarket in Menlo Park, was sentenced to life in prison for kidnapping, rape and conspiracy to commit murder after another store employee was abducted in June 2005 when she refused his sexual advances. Police did not link him to the Alvarez killing.

James Andrews

Kenneth Andrews

James Andrews & Kenneth Andrews
Sumter, South Carolina

A 50-year-old man and his 17-year-old son were shot to death shortly after closing their family owned convenience store for the night in Sumter, South Carolina. James W. Andrews and his son, Kenneth, were found dead around 11:15 p.m. on Friday, April 3, 1992 at their Kwik Fare store on Pinewood Road between Kolb Road and Clover Street. They normally closed at 10 p.m. and when they hadn't arrived home an hour later Jim's wife, Mary, called a woman who lived near the store to go over and see if everything was alright. The 28-year-old neighbor notified police moments later after finding the two victims sprawled on the floor. Investigation showed the gunman stood directly in front of James and shot him in the face. Kenneth appears to have been thrown to the floor while struggling with the attacker. His arm was broken and his shoulder dislocated. Investigation indicates the teenager maneuvered his way to the counter and used the heavy cash register to shield himself as the gunman approached. As Kenneth dropped to the floor with his arms extended upward the gunman went behind the counter and fired two shots into the back of his head. The killings occurred sometime between 10 p.m. and 11:15 p.m. which is when the neighbor arrived to make sure James and Kenneth Andrews were okay.

Deputies from the Sumter County Sheriff's Department found evidence indicating someone came to the store after closing. It's possible the victims recognized the individual and Kenneth unlocked the door to let him in. Initially the shootings appeared to have been committed during a robbery since some $800 was stolen, but further investigation fueled speculation the pair had been targeted for execution. Detectives have never been able to establish a motive but James had $3,000 in his pocket which significantly reduces the possibility robbery was behind the killings. Investigators learned the money Jim was carrying was from his son who had just paid off a loan his father had given him so he could buy a car. At some point, possibly after the gunman left, Kenneth tried to telephone for help but lost consciousness before completing the call. Forensic experts found his bloody fingerprints on the telephone keys. There was evidence a handgun was used, but police haven't positively confirmed the caliber of the weapon. The first police officers arrived at the shooting scene at 11:19 p.m. and found pools of blood beside both victims who were on the floor near the cash register. Detectives admit being puzzled by the deaths but are convinced there are some people who know why the victims were targeted for murder and who is responsible. His wife is also hoping someone will have the courage to come forward and tell police what they know. In an effort to persuade the person who can provide the key to solve the case, the local Crime Stoppers program is offering a reward of up to $1,000. At this point investigators have exhausted all possible leads and are just waiting for a caller to give them the piece that will solve the puzzle.

Preston Angelo
Greensboro, North Carolina

After sneaking out of the house in Greensboro, North Carolina, a 15-year-old boy was fatally shot. The victim, Preston Angelo, was taken to the hospital around 3 a.m. on Saturday, June 16, 2007 but investigations so far have failed to determine where and why the shooting occurred. Preston and his father, Paul, had spent Friday evening watching television until 11 p.m. when his son said goodnight and headed to bed. Paul Angelo went to his home office to do some work and had no idea his son had gone out until a group of teenagers came to the door of his home on Laramie Drive yelling that Preston had been shot. They said his son was taken to a friend's home after the shooting and the mother had driven him to the Moses Cone Hospital. Preston had already been pronounced dead when his father arrived at the emergency room. Only Preston and Paul were at home Friday night. His twin sister, Cassandra, was at a church camp, 150 miles to the west in the mountains at Montreat, near Asheville.

Detectives from the Greensboro Police Department were told Preston was well liked by people in the neighborhood where the family lived. He was a sophomore at Southern Guilford High School and was often seen outside his house skateboarding, biking or putting a basketball into the hoop. He would also sometimes just sit and read. There was no suggestion he was involved with gangs or drugs, but police said they have to keep an open mind during the investigation. His father said he always wanted to be older than he was and very anxious to get started on the road to his future. His sister, who was 11 minutes younger, said there just weren't enough hours in the day for everything Preston wanted to do. Detectives are hoping someone will have a change of heart and let them know where the shooting occurred to at least give them a starting point for the investigation. The Greensboro-Guilford County Crime Stoppers program is also offering a reward of up to $1,000 for anyone who provides anonymous information to their tip line that solves this case.

Kaitlyn Claire Arquette
Albuquerque, New Mexico

The teenage girlfriend of a notorious Vietnamese gang leader was killed in a drive-by shooting. A gunman fired two bullets into the head of Kaitlyn Claire Arquette shortly before 11 p.m. on Sunday, July 16, 1989 as she drove her red colored car along Lomas Boulevard in Albuquerque, New Mexico. Police listed the slaying as a random drive-by shooting but her parents, Donald and Lois Arquette and other relatives believe she was targeted for death. She was shot just below the left eye and in front of her ear. Unconscious when found sprawled across the front seat of her vehicle, she was pronounced dead in the hospital some 20 hours later. The 18-year-old, who had just graduated  from high school, had left a friend's apartment in Old Town and driven through the city's downtown area toward her home. At the t-intersection of John Street, a car pulled beside the woman's vehicle and a gunman began firing. The driver's window was shattered and another bullet hit the front portion of the back door panel. The car swerved into the oncoming lanes and travelled eastbound another block and a half before mounting the sidewalk on the north side of Lomas Boulevard, just east of Arno Street. An off-duty police officer, who was passing by, found Arquette slumped across the front passenger seat moaning in pain. He thought the victim had been involved in a traffic mishap but another officer who arrived moments later noticed the bullet holes and realized the young woman had been gunned down.

Arquette, who was known to everyone by the name Kait, hoped some day to become a doctor. She was an honor student and got her own apartment to learn how to live independently before heading off to college. She also had a live-in boyfriend, Dung Ngoc Nguyen, but she quickly realized he was heavily involved in nefarious activity including Asian organized crime and drug smuggling. She had planned to break up with him the night she was killed. She also made up her mind that she would tell police everything she knew about the crimes her boyfriend committed and the gangsters he associated with in New Mexico and California. Kait's mom, an author who goes by the name Lois Duncan, wrote a book in 1992 entitled "Who Killed My Daughter" which chronicles the slaying of her youngest child and poses intriguing questions regarding the initial investigation and allegations of influential people linked to underworld drug dealing. Kait initially learned of her boyfriend's involvement in insurance scams with Asian crime groups from California but later discovered his affiliation with drug trafficking. The Albuquerque Police Department listed the Arquette killing as a cold case investigation in 2002 and today considers the search for Kait's killer as a high priority.

Bethlehem Ayele
Alexandria, Virginia

She was a federal witness who should not have become a homicide victim, but after testifying against a ruthless criminal organization known as Murder Incorporated, she was shot to death while driving her car in Alexandria, Virginia. The execution-style slaying occurred around 10:15 p.m. on Wednesday, October 25, 2006 when Bethlehem Ayele stopped her vehicle at a traffic light on Commonwealth Avenue at Mount Vernon Avenue. At that precise moment a man walked up and fired a number of shots into her car, one of several that had stopped for a red light. Following the gunfire the vehicle lurched forward through the intersection and crashed into a utility pole. Police found the 34-year-old woman with a bullet wound to her head when they responded to a report of shots being fired. She was pronounced dead a short time later at Inova Alexandria Hospital.

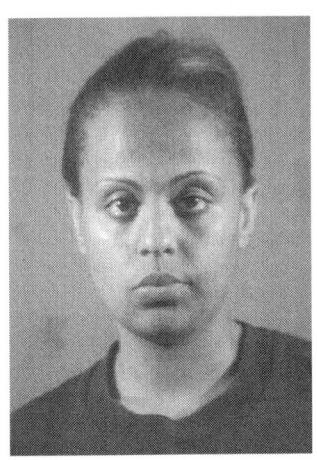

The death was a targeted hit and investigators are convinced it was in reprisal for testifying against members of a gang that controlled much of the crack cocaine and heroin distribution in the District of Columbia. The gang is believed responsible for some 31 killings between 1988 and 1999, including the slaying of several witnesses who were prepared to give evidence regarding the organization that was dubbed by authorities as Murder Incorporated and described as the most violent gang in Washington's history. At the time of her death Ayele worked part-time with a real estate firm and answering telephones at Alexandria Yellow Cab as well as helping her sister run the Ohio Restaurant at 1380 H Street in Washington. But before that, her life was very different. In April 2000 she was arrested by the U.S. Park Police who found a gun, drugs and $20,000 in her van after stopping the vehicle for a traffic infraction. She pleaded guilty several months later to conspiracy to distribute cocaine and carrying a firearm. At that time she also surrendered $200,000 in cash, two cars and a quantity of jewelry which were proceeds of crime, and agreed to cooperate with federal authorities to gather evidence against gangsters associated with Murder Incorporated. In addition, she assisted law enforcement authorities with the investigation of a double murder in Connecticut and helped set up drug stings in Florida for the Federal Bureau of Investigation as well as other investigations in Georgia. Although the District of Columbia gang most likely arranged to have Ayele killed, investigators said it is possible a contract was taken out by other gangs she targeted while in an undercover capacity.

Rather than enter the U.S. Marshal's witness protection program and live in another area under a new name, Ayele wanted her existence to be as normal as possible. She found a place to live in Alexandria and kept busy with the various jobs. At the restaurant she was known as Betty, someone the regular customers liked because of her welcoming personality and warm, friendly smile. Although the restaurant was only blocks from the crime-ridden section where Murder Incorporated had operated and in an area once considered downtrodden and unsafe, there was a rejuvenation over the past year that had transformed the neighborhood into an affordable business district for residents of the apartments on nearby 14th Street. The Alexandria Police Department's daily crime report of the incident gave no hint of the role the victim had played in putting so many hoodlums behind bars. It reads: "Homicide. Intersection of Commonwealth and Mount Vernon Avenues 10/25 10:14 p.m. Bethlehem Ayele, a 34-year-old Alexandria woman, was in her car when an unknown gunman approached her car and shot her. She was transported to Inova Alexandria Hospital here she was pronounced dead. Initial investigation leads police to believe Ayele was targeted, however a motive has not yet been determined." The local Crime Solvers program has a reward available for any information that helps identify the killer.

Katherine Baker
Kansas City, Missouri

A woman who spent the evening of Sunday, January 14, 1990 drinking at several bars in Kansas City, Missouri, was found dead five days later on a riverbank. Homicide detectives said some mushroom pickers discovered the body of Katherine Baker on Friday, April 19, 1990 on the north shore of the Missouri River, just east of the Chouteau Bridge. The killer had driven the 30-year-old victim to NE Birmingham Road in the vicinity of the Old 210 Highway and dragged her over riverfront railway tracks to the site where her body was located. The Kansas City Missouri Police have not revealed how she was killed but the case is categorized as a murder. Baker lived in Avondale but quite often after work would go drinking at Marcy's Restaurant Lounge on Vivion Road, the Depot, a bar and lounge in a Pullman railway car beside the Ameristar Casino or Helen's Jad Bar on Armor Road. She was last seen in Helen's asking patrons for a ride to another bar but left alone a few minutes later. Homicide detectives don't have a motive but believe she encountered someone at one of the bars who killed her and then dumped her body at the site less than a mile away. The Greater Kansas City Crime Stoppers is offering a reward of up to $1,000 for information that helps police make an arrest.

James Barnes

Margaret Barnes

Sylvia Holtzclaw

James and Margaret Barnes & Sylvia Holtzclaw
Greer, South Carolina

A couple was chatting with a teller when two bandits burst into the Blue Ridge Savings Bank in Greer, South Carolina and executed the victims before fleeing with between $2,000 and $3,000. Police received a panic alarm at 1:36 p.m. on Friday, May 16, 2003 but when they arrived moments later James "Eb" Barnes, 61, his wife, Margaret, 58, and bank employee, Sylvia Holtzclaw, 56, were dead. Barnes, a physics professor at the University of South Carolina at nearby Spartanburg, was shot in the chest and both women were killed with gunshots to their heads. The murder weapon, a 40-caliber automatic, was fired at close range. Barnes and his wife, known to everyone as Maggie, a receptionist and convention planner for the National Beta Club, were herded into a small office along with the teller where they were shot. Investigators said there was no sign of a struggle and described the killings as unnecessary and senseless since the victims were completely compliant. The bank situated at 330 East Frontage Road on the south side of Interstate 85, just east of the Highway 14 exit, is housed in a trailer-like building and serves as a satellite branch of the Asheville, North Carolina bank for the 25,000 residents in the area. The video tape was missing from the bank's security system but police obtained recordings from surveillance cameras at nearby businesses showing a red vehicle pulling onto Interstate 85 moments after the alarm was sounded. After reviewing the video images and interviewing a number of witnesses, detectives believe the get-away vehicle was a 1995 to 2000 Chevrolet Impala or Oldsmobile Alero.

Police were never able to determine if the security tape was stolen during the bank robbery or if someone forgot to load a new tape into the video recording device. The Greer Police Department requested assistance to probe the killings and a task force was set up involving investigators from the Greer, Greenville and Spartanburg police departments, the sheriff's departments in both Greenville and Spartanburg counties and the Federal Bureau of Investigation. A $100,000 reward has also been offered for the arrest and conviction of the killers. Some 25,000 posters were circulated across the United States to police agencies and jails in hope of finding someone who had information about the killings. Investigators have received a huge number of tips, but so far no information has come to authorities directly linking a suspect to the slayings. The victims were all solid individuals who contributed to the community and detectives continue to hope someone will come forward with information that will help solve the murders and bring some justice to relatives of three innocent people who died such violent deaths.

Kosai Barouki
Philadelphia, Pennsylvania

He had just closed his pizza and wing shop for the night in Philadelphia, Pennsylvania when he was shot and killed during a robbery attempt. Kosai Barouki was shot twice in the chest at 1:47 a.m. on Sunday, December 14, 2008 outside his Super Wings take-out restaurant on South 65th Street between Paschall Avenue and Linmore Avenue in Southwest Philadelphia. The 30-year-old man was pronounced dead a short time later at the Hospital of the University of Pennsylvania. Known as Vinny, he'd worked seven days a week for the past five years building up his business. He was making plans to get married and his girlfriend was with him when the shooting occurred. She wasn't hurt. The gunman fled in a light colored van driven by another person. The Pennsylvania Crime Commission is offering a $4,000 reward for information leading to the arrest of Barouki's killer and detectives from the Philadelphia Police Department said public help is needed to solve this crime.

Angela Barrios
Phoenix, Arizona

In the early morning hours the body of a 24-year-old woman was dumped on a quiet residential street in Phoenix, Arizona. It was at 6:45 a.m. on Monday, December 8, 2003 when police were called after the body of Angela Barrios was found on North 73rd Avenue between West Coolidge Street and West Meadowbrook Avenue. She had been stabbed and then beaten to death. Homicide detective with the Phoenix Police Department said the killing occurred during a two hour window since the victim was seen shortly after 4 a.m. getting into a light colored, possibly tan or brown Jeep Cherokee or Chevy Suburban sports utility vehicle. Investigators have not released many details about the murder of the woman, a Phoenix resident, but they are anxious to speak with anyone who saw the victim earlier in the evening or knows who she was with prior to her death. The Silent Witness program in Phoenix is offering a reward of up to $1,000 for information that leads to an arrest in the homicide.

Marilyn Barron
Paramount, California

The home where 70-year-old Marilyn Barron lived in Paramount, California was on a quiet one way street but from her porch she could hear the voices of children playing in nearby front gardens. There were cars parked on both sides of the street and usually many people doing chores or out walking. She always had a smile and a wave for neighbors and enjoyed the time anyone would stop to chat. But on Tuesday, December 9, 2003 someone came to her home on San Juan

Street between Orange Avenue and El Camino Avenue and ended her life. Los Angeles County Sheriff's Department investigators said the elderly victim was savagely beaten and then strangled. An autopsy attributed death to multiple injuries from blunt force trauma and severe compressions around her neck. The victim's body was found around 9 a.m. when neighbors didn't get an answer at her door. The investigation has turned up few leads and police are hoping a $15,000 reward will encourage people to come forward with information that will lead to the arrest and conviction of the woman's killer.

Gregory Battcock,
San Juan, Puerto Rico

The tumultuous Christmas Eve celebration in San Juan, Puerto Rico muffled the screams of an art professor as he was stabbed to death at his condominium in the city's tourist district. It was on Wednesday, December 24, 1980 when an attacker repeatedly plunged a knife into Gregory Battcock at the second floor apartment on Ashford Avenue where he was spending the Christmas holiday. The 39-year-old victim, a close friend of Andy Warhol and well known art critic, had been a professor of Art History at the William Paterson College in Wayne, New Jersey since 1970. He bled to death after being stabbed 102 times. Investigation showed the initial attack occurred in the living room, but Battcock was then forced onto the balcony where the killer appears to have knelt and plunged the knife into his prone body numerous times.

The victim lived an openly gay lifestyle and homicide detectives said the killer is likely someone he invited to his chic apartment for the evening. After graduating from Michigan State University and Hunter College, now the City University of New York, Battcock got involved in theatre costume design and became an accomplished abstract expressionist artist. He also starred in several of Warhol's films, including Batman Dracula, Horse and Iliac Passion. Through the years he was editor and a contributor for the Arts Magazine and authored a number of books focusing on new art. Investigators in Puerto Rico hope someone knows something about Battcock's slaying and will provide evidence that will allow them to make an arrest.

Diamond Baysinger,
Athens, California

Repeated appeals have failed to bring in any leads that will assist in solving the Sunday, December 12, 2004 shooting death of Diamond Baysinger. The 19-year-old victim was shot around 3:30 p.m. at 1206 West 90th Street in the Athens District, south of Los Angeles, California. Authorities have offered rewards of up to $10,000 but so far no one has come forward with information to identify his killer.

The single storey home where the shooting occurred is located near the intersection of Budlong Avenue and investigators said it's likely some people were in the vicinity and either heard the gunshots or witnessed the killing. Investigators from the Los Angeles Sheriff's Department said Baysinger didn't have a criminal record and wasn't a gang member.

Lorraine Beize
Wayne, Illinois

The strangulation death of a 21-year-old woman near Wayne, Illinois has been forgotten by almost everyone but investigators from the DuPage County Sheriff's Department. The body of Lorraine Beize was found on Tuesday, August 31, 1982 near the Chicago Central and Pacific railroad tracks running through the Pratt's Wayne Woods Forest Preserve west of the village of Wayne. The victim had been sexually assaulted and strangled. The body was found near a roadway running off Powis Road that leads to a

couple of major parking lots on either side of the railway tracks. Investigators said it's likely Beize was driven to one of the parking lots where she was raped and then killed. The preserve is a 3,462 acre site which has eight miles of trails and very popular with campers, fishing enthusiasts and horse riders. It is in a very isolated area some 30 miles west of Chicago's O'Hare airport and it could have been several days after the slaying before her body was discovered. Homicide investigators said they have not forgotten the case and are hoping someone who for one reason or another didn't come forward in the past will now contact the sheriff's department or Crime Stoppers and provide information that will lead to the arrest of the killer.

Timothy George Benton
Minneapolis, Minnesota

He walked his own way through life as a free spirit until being confronted by a killer under a Minneapolis, Minnesota railway bridge. It was just after Thanksgiving in 2002 when Timothy Benton was last seen alive. He'd celebrated the holiday at the home of friends for a few days, but left to continue his existence as a homeless wanderer. A longtime friend, Dan "Woody" Hamilton, met Benton shortly after he'd said goodbye to the people he was staying with and took him to Broadway St. and Monroe Street near the southeast entrance to Logan Park in a residential area of the city. He had no idea where Benton was planning to spend the night, but expected he'd find a comfortable and protected area since the weather had turned bitterly cold. It wasn't unusual for Benton to bunk at one of the homeless shelters on nights it dropped well below freezing, but it appears he made his way some 20 blocks to the railway tracks running under Main Street, just south of 3rd Avenue or the First Avenue bridge which both lead to Nicollet Island located in the Mississippi River. Once a booming dockyard and industrial area with railway yards and grain silos, the island was transformed into a tourist area with historic homes, a trendy inn, horse drawn carriages and the highly-respected DelaSalle High School. Despite the urbanization Benton had no difficulty finding out of the way places to spend the night, usually sleeping off the debilitating effects of the alcohol he'd consumed. On Monday, December 2, 2002 an employee of the Burlington Northern Railroad spotted Benton's body sprawled beside the tracks under the Nicollet Street bridge. He had been beaten to death.

Police assumed he was one of the hundreds of vagrants who pass through the Minneapolis-St. Paul area each year, but it turned out he was born and raised in the area and had relatives living locally. He graduated in the 1960s from Cretin High School in St. Paul and on two occasions named among the state's best young artists as well as a top scholastic athlete. Described as a good person and a free spirit, he had a wide range of interests, but booze and drugs had driven him into a downward spiral. His life became a day to day existence and each night he was forced to find a secluded spot to tuck away. Benton learned the carpentry trade but was unreliable and had difficulty holding jobs. He traveled widely in the United States and to other countries after graduating from high school, but his difficulty in keeping a steady job left him without money and he began living on the streets. He kept in touch with family and a couple of long-time friends but lost contact with others he'd grown up with or met through the years. More recently he associated with others who had fallen on bad times and spent many hours drinking and sharing stories. He would spend time with people through the day but at night he retreated to one of the various clandestine spots where he could sleep without being disturbed by police or hooligans who sometimes prey on the homeless.

It is not known if Benton was beaten by someone he knew or an individual who came across him near the railway underpass. Family members were shocked when they learned he'd been murdered and his brothers and sisters have made countless appeals hoping someone will help police solve the case. They recalled him as a happy-go-lucky guy and can't imagine why anyone would want to kill him. He was someone who would just float in and out of their lives, but never ask for any sort of help. Now his family wants help to solve his killing. His sister, Betsy Beedle, said there is someone who knows something about her brother's death and she is hoping they will talk to the police soon so the slaying can be solved. Homicide detectives from the Minneapolis Police Department have issues numerous appeals and the local Crime Stoppers program has posted a $1,000 reward but so far no one has come forward with key information that will solve Benton's murder.

Corporal Michael Beverly
Chester, Pennsylvania

The shooting death of a police officer in Chester, Pennsylvania has all the earmarks of a planned and deliberate killing, but investigators still have no idea why he was murdered. Corporal Michael Beverly was gunned down around 9:35 p.m. on Tuesday, October 16, 2001 on Ward Street between West 10th Street and Curran Street after interviewing a person regarding an earlier drug-related homicide. When the 37-year-old officer returned to his car following his meeting with the informant he was approached by an unknown assailant who shot him in the chest. After Beverly fell to the ground, the gunman fired three bullets into his head. Residents in the Highland Garden section called police about shots being fired and the first responding officers found Beverly collapsed on the street in a pool of blood outside of one of the flat roofed two-storey brick and frame city-owned homes that make up the neighborhood.

Investigators described the killing as an execution. It was determined that two people were involved but detectives have never been able to establish a motive. One man was arrested and sentenced to life in prison for his role in the slaying, but has never revealed the name of the killer. Beverly, who was married with five children, had served with the Chester Police Department for 11-years and ironically was the partner of Constable Connie Hawkins when she was fatally shot in July 1993, the only female officer in the city to die in the line of duty. A $2,000 reward has been posted by the Chester Police Association and the Citizen Crime Commission for the apprehension of the police officer's killer.

James Oren Blakeley
Edgewood, Maryland

James Oren Blakeley was seventeen when he was stabbed to death on a desolate roadway adjacent to property belonging to the Aberdeen Proving Grounds in Maryland. Where he died is a favored fishing spot for locals along the bank of the Otter Point Creek off Route 755, also known as Edgewood Road. It's a heavily travelled roadway during the day, but at night it's extremely isolated and the bush area gives privacy to lovers seeking seclusion. Police have theorized Blakeley's assailant was someone he met late Sunday, April 1, 1990 at the U.S. Adult Bookstore on Route 40, also known as the Pulaski Highway.

Blakeley left the gasoline station where he worked part-time in Conowingo, Maryland around 10 p.m. and was seen by patrons at the store around 11 p.m. That was the last time anyone recalls seeing him alive. The teenager most likely drove Route 222 along the shore of Susquehanna River after leaving work, but instead of heading to his home in Havre de Grace, he made his way to the bookstore on the north side of the roadway just east of the cut-off for Edgewood Road. Investigation has shown it was something he did on a fairly regular basis to meet acquaintances he knew from the gay community. Although no one remembers the teenager leaving, investigators are certain there are people who have additional information and probably know or could at least provide a description of his killer.

With the absence of witnesses, police have attempted to trace the teenager's final footsteps from the bookstore to the isolated spot at the Otter Point Creek. It is speculated that Blakeley agreed to drive the man he met to the wooded area along Edgewood Road for an intimate encounter. The majority of people involved in a gay lifestyle try to shield their activity and police said it's possible some of those that night in the bookstore could have driven from Baltimore, some 35 miles to the southwest or even from further afield to meet like-minded individuals. It is that same secrecy that is hampering the investigation into the slaying.

The official homicide investigation was commenced the morning of Monday, April 2, 1990 when Blakeley's partially clad body was found in a wooded area beside the creek. Forensic investigators have determined the victim was standing in front of his vehicle when the assailant plunged a knife into him. The cause of death was attributed to a stabbing, but police have not said if the victim was stabbed more than once. After killing the teen, it appears the attacker drove back to the place he met Blakeley to get his own vehicle and drive away. The bookstore was packed with people most of the evening and investigators remain hopeful someone will eventually come forward and answer their appeal for information. Police have distributed pamphlets to the gay community asking for help to solve the killing and also issued a warning saying the killer poses a danger to patrons of adultbooks stores in the area until he's apprehended.

Oleg "Al" Bohlouli
Anchorage, Alaska

Links to an international drug trafficking conspiracy led to the shooting death of a 45-year-old man in Anchorage, Alaska. Oleg "Al" Bohlouli was killed around 3 a.m. on Sunday, July 3, 2005 when an intruder broke into his home on Lucky Road. The gunman ran off after the shooting and has never been caught. Police found a large quantity of marijuana in the basement of the house located just off the Boniface Parkway and investigation later showed it was part of a massive drug distribution network. Initially detectives from the Anchorage Police Department thought the victim had personally set up the marijuana grow operation but agents from the Drug Enforcement Administration uncovered evidence revealing the house on the quiet block long street was one of several locations used by a crime group which was distributing drugs throughout Alaska. A massive amount of marijuana was grown at various locations throughout the Anchorage area, including the plants seized at the victim's home, but vast quantities of marijuana and ecstasy were also being smuggled into the state from Canada. Investigators first believed Bohlouli had awakened and tried to fight off the intruder to protect his wife and one of their four children who was at the home, but court documents released in July 2008 showed the victim was part of the international drug trafficking ring and most likely doing what he could to keep the gunman from the hydroponic crop. Several people have been arrested in the drug trafficking conspiracy but no one has been able to suggest who might be responsible for Bohlouli's murder. At his funeral, the victim was heralded as a hero for giving his life to protect the people he loved. He was born in Los Angeles on December 2, 1959 and lived there until moving to Alaska in November 2001. Bohlouli worked as a house painter and loved to fish in his spare time. Although linked to the drug trafficking network, investigators said Bohlouli is a homicide victim and they are hoping to solve the slaying. Crime Stoppers is offering a reward of up to $1,000 to the individual who calls the tip line with information that directly leads to the arrest of the killer.

Jodie Lynn Bordeaux
Powhattan, Kansas

The hopes and dreams of a 31-year-old man were shattered when gunfire killed his wife and unborn daughter at their Powhattan, Kansas home. Shawn Bordeaux and his 28-year-old wife, Jodie, were in the living room at 12:43 a.m. on Friday, November 21, 1997 when bullets began penetrating the wall of their small farmhouse on the fringe of the Kickapoo Indian reservation. The floor lamps shattered above their heads and Shawn thought a power surge had blown apart the bulbs. The popping sounds sent their two dogs scampering to the kitchen and while his wife instinctively ran toward their bedroom, Shawn went after the dogs to let them run free outside. Heading back into the living room he called out for Jodie to make sure she was okay. There was no answer. He then saw her on the floor just inside the bedroom. He ran over and noticed blood on her forehead. Still believing the bulbs had shattered, he thought she'd been cut by flying glass. He grabbed a piece of clothing to stop the bleeding and then makes his way back to the living room to call for help. While dialing 911 he sees the wall riddled with bullets and realizes there has been some sort of drive-by shooting.

Now aware that his wife has been shot, Shawn cradles her lifeless body while repeating his address over and over again to the emergency operator. Still holding the phone, he leans over and kisses his wife and then, almost instinctively, put his lips to her belly. Help was at least 15 minutes away and they wouldn't arrive in time to save the life of his unborn daughter. With his wife dead, he realized there was no way the little baby girl inside her would survive. He was kissing her goodbye along with his wife. When paramedics arrived they confirmed the baby had no chance at life. Once his wife was dead and the fetus no longer supported with oxygen it would take five minutes for life to ebb away.

The ambulance crew didn't race Jodie to the emergency departments at Hiawatha Community Hospital, nine miles away in Hiawatha, Kansas or the Sabetha Community Hospital, some 16 miles away. There was also no attempt to airlift the victim to a trauma centre 50 miles away in Topeka, Kansas. She was pronounced dead as she lay on the bedroom floor. Investigators from the Brown Country Sheriff's Department and the Kansas Bureau of Investigation worked painstakingly for almost 48 hours with the body of Jodie Lynn Bordeaux still in the home. They wanted to make sure no evidence was overlooked before the victim was taken to the morgue where an autopsy was conducted and a battery of other scientific tests by pathologists to confirm the cause of death and pinpoint any other evidence that will be valuable to convict the killer once an arrest is made. Normally the Federal Bureau of Investigation probes all homicides on Indian reservations, but the Bordeaux home was situated on land that was embroiled in a boundary dispute and the FBI didn't have jurisdiction. Through the years Bordeaux, some relatives and a number of Kickapoo tribe leaders have petitioned to have federal assistance in the investigation. Personal appeals were also made to then Attorney General Janet Reno and to Congress but without avail. The Kickapoo tribe insists the boundaries for their land was established in an 1854 treaty, but the State of Kansas is arguing that the area of the territory was redefined in an 1862 pact.

Bordeaux really doesn't care about the land battle that has raged on for years and put his house half a mile inside the disputed region. He just wants every law enforcement resource available to find the person responsible for the killing of his wife and unborn daughter. He also wants the killing listed as a double homicide. The investigation showed one or more people approached the home around 12:40 a.m. and fired numerous shots from an AK47 automatic assault rifle into the living room area. Shawn and his wife were sitting in the front room and would have been clearly visible to the assailants since the window was covered only with a sheer drape. The attackers sprayed the front of the house with bullets which shattered the glass and ripped through the siding. Investigators never revealed how many shots were fired, but did indicate that numerous shell casings were recovered. Both Shawn and his wife worked at the reservation's Golden Eagle Casino. Shawn was part of the management team which operated the casino for the Kickapoo Tribal Council and Jodie was a supervisor in the slot machine section. It's possible a disgruntled employee was behind the attack, but investigators have not been able to positively establish a link. Through the years, the Kickapoo Police Department has worked closely with the sheriff's department in hopes of finding people who might have information about the slaying, but Bordeaux is convinced there are people living on the reservation who have not fully cooperated with investigators. Shawn, who is part Lakota Indian, moved from the area unable to live in the home where he had shared so much joy and hope with Jodie. They had desperately wanted children and after having difficulty conceiving, they went to a fertility clinic.

They knew the baby was going to be a little girl and picked the name Jordan Shay Bordeaux. Shawn and his wife decided to have a quiet night together on November 21, 1997. The night before they had gone to Topeka where they had dinner at Red Lobster, his wife's favorite restaurant, and then went to Kohl's to buy a couple of outfits for the baby. They worked together in the kitchen preparing Chinese food and after dinner he rubbed his wife's back for a bit before moving to their favorite spots – Shawn in the recliner and his wife on the couch on different sides of the living room. Their two dogs were on the floor at their feet and nothing disturbed them until the shots rang out. Detectives want anyone with information that will solve the killing of

Jodie Bordeaux to contact them. They said there are likely people who have heard rumors about who may be responsible or about someone having the gun that killed the young woman. No matter how trivial the information seems, investigators want people to tell them what they know. The state government has also posted a reward of $5,000 for anyone who gives police details that leads to the arrest and conviction of the woman's killer.

Michael Botsay
Destrehan, Louisiana

A dispute with drug dealers may have led to the death of an 18-year-old youth in Destrehan, Louisiana, a town of 11,000 some 20 miles west of New Orleans. It was on Thursday, November 18, 1982 when the body of Michael Botsay was discovered in a swampy area near the Destrehan Canal.

The victim, who lived with his parents on Ranier Street in Kenner, died from a single bullet wound fired into the left side of his head. He was last seen around 5 p.m. on Tuesday, August 24 when he left home to visit his girlfriend who lived about 11 miles away in LaPlace. Botsay's car, a 1975 white Ford Mustang, was found abandoned on Highway 61 also known as the Airline Highway in the vicinity of the Destrehan Canal, midway between LaPlace and Kenner. Investigation showed the victim had spent seven months undergoing rehabilitation for narcotic addiction, but at the time of his death was still using drugs. In addition friends suggested the victim had some Quaaludes from time to time. Detectives also learned that Botsay had been in the Augie's DeLago Lounge on the Lake Pontchartrain beach the night he vanished. While there he got into an argument with a couple of men and during the dispute one pulled a gun and accused Botsay of ripping them off.

The men who confronted the victim were described as being white and between 20 to 25 years. One man was around six-feet, 150 to 160-pounds with a moustache and brown shoulder length hair. The other man was five-feet, six-inches, about 170-pounds with a stocky build, clean shaven with a brown short crew cut. When the body was found the victim was dressed in the same clothing, a t-shirt, blue cut-off jeans, blue and white Nike tennis shoes and socks that he was wearing when his parents saw him for the last time almost four months earlier. His mother, Barbara Botsay, is living in hope that someone will identify the killer. She keeps the Mother's Day card he gave her months before his death and celebrates his birthday each year to keep the memory of her son alive.

Jim Bowerman
North Miami, Florida

He was hoping to leave Florida and reunite with his former girlfriend in Los Angeles, but was murdered before it could happen. Twenty-seven-year-old Jim Bowerman had lived in North Miami enjoying a sun and sand lifestyle far different from where he'd been raised in Lansing, Michigan. He left home seven years earlier with hopes of living in California, but found things too expensive and tried Las Vegas before heading to the Atlantic coast about a year before he was killed. It was 7 p.m. on Saturday, April 12, 2008 when two uniformed police officers checked his apartment at 1550 NE 130th Street and found the rear door slightly ajar. Inside the victim was sprawled on the floor in a pool of coagulated blood. Police have not revealed how he was killed, but investigators described the death as brutal. He was a waiter at Chili's Grill and Bar at 19905 Biscayne Boulevard in Aventura, an upscale community on Miami's northern boundary. He was seen with friends at a bar Friday, April 11, but failed to show up for his 3 p.m. shift at the restaurant the following day.

Bowerman was always punctual and friends who worked with him became worried and asked police to check unit 7 in the Isa-Car Rental Apartments on the south side of NE 130th Street between Arch Creek Road and NE 16th Avenue. They discovered his body close to the front door but investigators didn't find a great deal of physical evidence that pinpointed a motive or put them on the trail of possible suspects. "We know what happened. We know how it happened. We just don't know exactly why," said Detective John Mayato. He reiterated that the death was very brutal, adding "it was a very bloody scene." Mayato also indicated that Bowerman didn't have any enemies and had no problems with anyone.

The manager of Chili's Restaurant notified Bowerman's parents, Bill Bowerman who lives in East Lansing and his ex-wife, Joanne Lose, now living in Webberville, a village just east of Lansing. Since the slaying the victim's mother and his sister, Julie Bassett, have organized a Justice for Jim campaign to help police find the killer. A $5,000 reward is available from the Miami-Dade Crime Stoppers program for information that leads to an arrest in this case and numerous appeals have been made through the media encouraging people to come forward with information.

Bowerman was born on January 11, 1981 and after graduating from East Lansing High School in 1999 he saved up and just after his 21st birthday set out for the beaches of California. His mother described him as a free spirit with pure sweetness and beauty in his blue eyes. Joanne spoke to her son six days before his body was found. She said he always kept in touch with family and friends across the United States. He told her about his plan of moving to California and starting life anew with the girlfriend he'd left out there. Everyone is devastated, his mom said. We have lost someone very precious.

There was no sign of a break-in and nothing to indicate a robbery. No one at the white single storey complex of U-shaped buildings heard anything suspicious prior to Bowerman's body being discovered. "There's got to be somebody out there that knows something," his sister said in an interview while making a public appeal for people to help find Jim's killer. "If they could bring it forward, no matter how insignificant they think the information is, it could mean everything to us."

Jerome Boyer
Philadelphia, Pennsylvania

He was an aspiring heavyweight boxer when he was murdered in Philadelphia, Pennsylvania while returning home from a fight. Just before midnight on Friday, August 3, 2007, Jerome Boyer got into an altercation with a man on Colgate Street, just west of Alcott Street in the city of brotherly love's Lawnville district. He was shot seven times in the chest. No motive has been established. At 35, Boyer was married and the father of three sons, one 18 and the others aged one and two. He worked as a welder, but constantly trained and hoped someday of earning a heavyweight boxing championship title. Darien Hardy said his step brother loved to box. His mother, Joanne Hardy described him as a good and tender hearted man and very young at heart. "I miss him a lot, I really miss him," she said. "He was my oldest." A $3,000 reward has been posted for the conviction of his killer and his mother hopes there is someone who can let investigators with the Philadelphia Police Department know who is responsible for the homicide. "I would just pray that they would just come forth and do the right thing," his mother said. "Jerome was my son, my heart truly hurts. I am praying every day that the guy that shot my son will be found."

Boyer's body was discovered in an alleyway leading to garages and the rear entrance of the apartment in the two-and-a-half-storey row home on Alcott Street where he lived. Police didn't locate any witnesses or find anyone at that hour on the one way north street between Colgate Street and Rising Sun Avenue who heard the gunshots. Boyer was born in Sharon, Pennsylvania on May 5, 1972 and developed a love for boxing as a teenager growing up in a tough Philadelphia neighborhood. With some 80 fights as an amateur, he was hoping to move to the professional ranks, but instead was arrested on criminal charges and sent to prison. He was heading home after only his second fight as a professional when gunned down. His wife, Valerie, said the gunman killed a very special person and also took a father away from their children.

Walter Dewayne Bradley
El Dorado, Arkansas

While walking in the vicinity of the train yard near Pony Street in El Dorado, Arkansas, Walter Dewayne Bradley was killed during an argument with two men. The 51-year-old victim was murdered around 8:46 p.m. on Tuesday, September 11, 2007, but the Detective Division of the El Dorado Police Department hasn't yet released the cause of death. A reward has been posted by the victim's family for information leading to the capture of the killer in this community of 20,000 people, some 20 miles north of the Louisiana border.

Michael Terrence Brady
Panama City, Florida

Mike Brady was in bed on Sunday, October 6, 1996 at his Panama City, Florida home when an intruder fired multiple shots into his head. He was taking a nap between 3 p.m. and 6 p.m. when the killing occurred. At 28, Brady had become a bit of a local celebrity and was working as a news and sports broadcaster at the local FOX television station, WPGX. Married to Cindy in 1989 and the father of a 4-year-old son, Ryan, he had served as a law enforcement specialist with the United States Air Force from 1986 to 1992 and stationed at the Bentwaters Air Force Base in England before transferring to the Tyndall Air Base in Panama City, on Florida's panhandle between Pensacola and Tallahassee.

Brady got his real estate license in 1992 and after leaving the air force was owner and president of 1st Realty of North Florida and Allied Mortgage Capital Corporation. While operating the companies he began dabbling in the media and was a phone-in talk show host at a local radio station before becoming an on-air personality with the FOX television station. Investigators have never been able to determine a motive for this slaying or come up with any possible suspects. He was born on September 25, 1968 and appears to have lived an exemplary life. It wasn't thought he had any enemies. He was a member of the Florida State Seminoles Booster Club, the Young Republican Club, the Muscular Dystrophy Association and the Bay County Association of Realtors as well as attending St. Dominic's Catholic Church. A $100,000 reward has been posted for the capture of his killer and police are anxious to have this case solved.

Rashawn Brazell
Brooklyn, New York

Three days after being reported missing on Valentines Day in New York City the dismembered remains of a 19-year-old man began turning up. Two bags were found by New York City transit workers along the tracks at the Nostrand Avenue station in Brooklyn's Bushwick area around 3 a.m. on February 17, 2005. Dissected body parts found in the bags were identified as the remains of Rashawn Brazell, a gifted student who was preparing to enroll in the medical administration program at Monroe College. The day he disappeared, Brazell had an appointment with his accountant and was going to meet his mother for lunch in Manhattan, but at 7:30 a.m. someone buzzed his apartment from the lobby and the victim went downstairs to meet the individual. Witnesses said Brazell and the man walked to the Gates

Avenue J Line subway station and rode to the Nostrand Avenue station in Bedford Stuyvesant. That was the last time he was seen alive. Homicide detectives from the New York City Police Department began a murder investigation when the two bags of remains were found along the subway tracks. The first was a black plastic garbage containing a blue recycling bag which held pieces of remains from a black male. The other turned out to be a dark colored pull-along tool bag, one of only 15 that had been made as a prototype and purchased in 2001 by the Metropolitan Transportation Authority. It contained some blood-stained drill bits and other tools that had been used to reduce the remains to tiny fragments. Initially investigators weren't able to identify the victim, but employees at the Humboldt Street recycling plant located another black plastic trash bag with a blue bag inside containing additional remains. The following day a fourth bag with human body parts was found at the same plant. Forensic experts located pieces of a couple of fingers and were able to retrieve prints which matched those in a police file when Brazell had been arrested about a year earlier on a minor marijuana charge. The victim's head was never found, but investigators utilized DNA to confirm the remains found in each of the bags came from the victim.

Experts determined the killer had used some sort of sharp instrument to trace marks on the body before utilizing an electric chain saw to dissect the victim. Each cut was precise, indicating to investigators that the killer had a knowledge of anatomy and aware of the joint areas that would allow the saw to cut through without too much resistance. Although authorities were not able to determine a cause of death, the medical examiner concluded Brazell was likely kept alive for a couple of days and tortured. There were cuts and stab wounds to his torso and evidence he may have struggled before being killed. Although the victim was gay and the murder appears to have been extremely brutal and horrific, investigators cannot conclude it was a hate crime until an arrest is made and a motive positively established.

Brazell was basically a good person who held down four jobs to pay his bills and get money for college tuition. He did a bit of web designing and some fashion modeling but was hoping to get a job at New York Presbyterian Hospital which would give him experience that would help with his college studies. He stood just over six-feet and through the compassion and understanding of his parents was comfortable with his lifestyle. Brazell also understood the adversity that many gay young people experience and was something of a mentor to friends he knew who were not accepted by their families. He had personal compassion for the homeless and families who were struggling to survive. When he was younger he would sometimes fill a grocery bag from his parents' kitchen cupboard and deliver it to someone in need. His mother, Desire, described Rashawn as the type of person who would give the last money he had in his pocket to someone if they were in need. In memory of his empathy and kindness the Rashawn Brazell Memorial Scholarship has been established to assist a New York City college bound high school student who demonstrates a commitment against racism, sexism and homophobia. To help solve Brazell's murder, New York City Crime Stoppers is offering a reward of up to $1,000 to encourage anyone with information about the killing to anonymously call the program's hotline number. In addition the New York Anti Violence Project and the organization People of Color in Crisis have offered a $15,000 reward for information that leads to the arrest and conviction of the person responsible for the death of Rashawn Brazell.

Richard Breitbarth
Whippany, New Jersey

A 48-year-old New Jersey businessman was shot and killed when he arrived at his home in Whippany. Richard Breitbarth collapsed outside 17 Baird Place, a trendy street in an upscale neighborhood running off Troy Hills Road, after being shot multiple times. His body was found on the roadway outside his home at 8:45 p.m. on Tuesday, November 12, 1996 after nearby residents heard the gunfire. He was pronounced dead at the scene. Investigators learned the victim had made a purchase at the Pathway Supermarket on Route 46 and Beverwyck Road in nearby Parsippany about 20 minutes before the shooting. They said the killer may have followed him from the store or was waiting to ambush him when he arrived home. Breitbarth was the president of Biophase Systems, Inc., a vitamin and food supplement company, but homicide detectives have been unable to clearly establish a motive or determine if any business dealings were linked to the slaying. He was a scientist and while living in Pinebrook, New Jersey in 1994 was granted patents on a number of pharmaceutical, cosmetic and hair growth formulas as well as a caffeine stimulant to prevent drowsiness. Several months prior to his death, he applied for patent under the name Richard Breithbarth for a compound which could be used in the cosmetic industry as well as being an agent to allow topical treatments for such things as acne, dermatitis, bacterial infections, burns and skin ulcerations including genital herpes and chicken pox lesions. It was probably a clerical error for the "h" being added to the name Breitbarth, but it's another puzzling part of in a complicated maze that surrounded the victim's business life.

Investigations in the wake of his killing by the Morris County Sheriff's Department, the New Jersey State Police, the United States Drug Enforcement Agency and the Internal Revenue Service led to charges against Daniel George, a friend and business associate of Breitbarth, in connection with a tax fraud scheme. George, who lived in Rockport, Massachusetts, amassed more than six million dollars which was never declared. He told authorities the money was given in various amounts as gifts to him and not as a result of the sale of products from Biophase Systems or for any work done for the company. George, a self-taught chemist who holds patents on five nutritional supplements, was convicted of tax evasion and sent to prison for thirty months after evidence revealed he had direct business dealings with Breitbarth and other health supplement companies that netting around $900,000 a year. It also came to light that there may have been exaggerated claims regarding some of the formulas developed by Breitbarth and some former partners, customers and colleagues suspected they'd been defrauded. Some people described the victim as arrogant and dishonest but he maintained a high degree of respect among his peers in the scientific community. Homicide detective have maintained an open mind and have explored numerous avenues in the hunt for his killer. They are hoping someone will give specific details about the case that will assist them in making an arrest. The Morris County Crime Stoppers program is also offering a reward of up to $1,000 to encourage anyone to call their hotline and provide information anonymously that will assist detectives to identify Breitbarth's killer.

Leon Buchanan
Jacksonville, Florida

A man who devoted five-and-a-half years of his life steering young people away from violence was gunned down in the courtyard of his apartment complex in Jacksonville, Florida. Leon Buchanan, 34, worked with Communities in Schools, a non-profit organization that mentors at-risk children in various neighborhoods across the city. Around 11 p.m. on Thursday, September 4, 2008 police were called after residents heard gunshots in the vicinity of the Les Chateaux Condominiums at 851 Bert Road in Jacksonville's Arlington district. On arrival they found Buchanan slumped against the steps leading to one of the condo units. He was critically wounded and died a short time later at a nearby hospital. The victim recently moved into the housing complex off Arlington Road, just north of the Arlington Expressway, and not many people knew him. Door to door canvassing failed to turn up any witnesses and police have not yet been able to determine a motive for the killing.

Buchanan, a native of Pennsylvania who got his bachelor of education degree after studying at Bethune-Cookman College in Daytona Beach and Edward Waters College in Jacksonville, was one of 60 fulltime advocates responsible for operating after school programs and tutoring students. Through the years he had helped youngsters at a number of schools and had just started a new assignment at Lake Forest Elementary School on Kennard Street in the area of Interstate 95 and Edgewood Avenue West. Friends described the victim as a role model and said it was shocking that someone who worked to protect children from violence would have their life ended through murder. They said he was dedicated to helping children and brought energy and passion to the job. "Not only did he lose his life," said Jon Heyman, chief executive of Community in Schools. "The kids lost a good friend." Crime Stoppers has offered a $1,000 reward for the capture of his killer and the victim's family has posted $5,000 to encourage people to come forward with information.

Calvin Bynum
Aurora, North Carolina

The 33-year-old owner of a fish market in Aurora, North Carolina was murdered while staying overnight to protect his business from burglars. Investigators from the Beaufort County Sheriff's Office learned there had been repeated break-ins at vending machines outside his store on Highway 33 and the victim, Calvin Bynum, spent the night of Sunday, August 9, 1992 in an attempt to catch the culprits. While Bynum waited inside Captain Calvin's Seafood Market someone broke in and the victim was embroiled in a violent altercation. He was struck several times with a crowbar and found dead that morning by his sister, Connie. She noticed broken glass all over the place and then saw his body sprawled on the floor. Forensic experts collected a great deal of evidence including fingerprints and possible DNA from the assailant but nothing has yet been matched to a suspect. Investigators said an air conditioning unit was taken from a window of the store but they haven't revealed if anything else was missing. In a town of some 600 people, detectives believe someone likely knows something and are surprised over the years that no one has come forward to identify the killer. They are continuing to appeal for information and once they get a name the physical evidence collected from the crime scene will link the individual directly to Bynum's murder. A reward of up to $6,000 is being offered by the Beaufort County Crime Stoppers program to anyone who comes forward and helps solve the case.

Richard James Carns
Anchorage, Alaska

A 40-year-old man was shot and killed after startling an intruder during a home invasion robbery in Anchorage, Alaska. Sometime around 6 a.m. on Tuesday, February 19, 2002 Richard James Carns confronted a man as he was fleeing from the home at 1905 Orca Place near East 19th Avenue in the city's Fairview district. The man went upstairs after breaking into the two-storey house on the dead-end street adjacent to Sitka Street Park and East Chester Park where he demanded cash and other valuables from the 65-year-old owner, Nadine Reed, and three other people who were visiting the house. Carns, who was sleeping in lower floor room, heard the commotion and came face to face with the robber as he was attempting to leave. The suspect immediately pulled a gun and fired several shots at Carns who was pronounced dead at the scene. Homicide detectives from the Anchorage Police Department described the killer as a black male in his 20s wearing dark clothing, a mask and a hood. Crime Stoppers has offered a reward of up to $1,000 and investigators are hoping someone will provide information to help them solve the murder.

Vicky Lynne Caswick
Rowland Heights, California

Thirteen months after being abducted on her way to school in Cerritos, California, the decomposed remains of the 14-year-old victim were found in the hills off the Pomona Freeway near Rowland Heights. Vicky Lynne Caswick, a Grade 9 student, vanished on Monday, April 16, 1979 while walking from her home to Cerritos High School at 12500 183rd Street, just west of Bloomfield Avenue. The Los Angeles

County Sheriff's Department has a homicide file on this case but not a lot of details have been released through the years. Detectives have appealed for anyone who saw Vicky Lynne on her way to school or with someone anytime on the day she disappeared. It appears the girl was driven, probably the same day, some 25 miles to the area where her body was discovered by a hiker in May, 1980. The location where her body was found in the vicinity of Pathfinder Road is now the site of an expanding community of executive homes that through the years spread south of the Pomona Freeway into the hilly terrain.

Sandra Luz Chacon
El Paso, Texas

Details are very sketchy but police are still trying to find the killer of a 33-year-old woman at the Tiffany apartment complex in the northeastern area of El Paso, Texas. Police were called to the two-storey unit at 9960 McCombs Street, just south of Woodrow Bean Transmountain Drive on Sunday, June 2, 1999 after building maintenance staff found the body of Sandra Luz Chacon. She was face down on the floor and had been stabbed to death. The slaying occurred on the Memorial Day weekend but homicide detectives from the El Paso Police Department were unable to find people who heard or saw anything.

The victim was the youngest child of Guadalupe Chacon who remembers her daughter as someone being so full of life. She was always fussing with her reddish-brown hair and wouldn't go out until her eye make-up was perfect. Investigators questioned family members, co-workers and some of her close friends but were not able to determine a motive for the slaying or possible suspects. Forensic evidence found at the scene, including DNA, has been used to eliminate a number of individuals who were closely connected to the victim. The El Paso Crime Stoppers program has appealed for assistance in this case several times and is offering a reward to help catch the woman's killer. The victim's family posted a $5,000 reward and through the years has put up posters across the city to encourage anyone with information to come forward.

Kelli Chapple
Orange Park, Florida

Mystery continues to surround the slayings of a 23-year-old woman and a 28-year-old man at a Jacksonville, Florida apartment complex. The shootings occurred in the early morning hours of Saturday, September 8, 2007, but the victims were not found for another 10 to 12 hours. Kelli Chapple, a bright, bubbly and ambitious college student, went out around 7:30 p.m. Friday to attend a birthday celebration with some of her girlfriends. Sometime that evening she drove to the Palisades Apartments at 5800 West University Boulevard to see David Matos, someone she had known for only a few weeks. Specific details of the homicide have not been made public, but it was while they were sharing time together an assailant entered the apartment and shot them. They died almost instantly. When the bodies were discovered, other residents in the building admitted hearing gunfire sometime around dawn, but hadn't bothered to notify police. Investigators said it's possible Matos was the intended victim and Chapple was just in the wrong place. They also described her death as senseless. Family members and friends were unable to provide much information about Matos. Chapple hadn't told any of her girlfriends she was going out with him and didn't say anything about Matos to her father and stepmother even though she lived with them.

Chapple was studying at the Florida Community College in Jacksonville and had recently changed her major to child psychology. She had taken a number of credit courses since enrolling at the school and hoped some day to work with children. Her stepmother, Judith Chapple, said she treated Kelli like one of her own children and she's been devastated by the death. When she realized Kelli didn't come home and failed to show up at her weekend job, she had a feeling something horrible had happened. After hearing news reports of a killing at a southside apartment, she went to the scene and saw Kelli's car in the parking lot. Police were unable to tell her anything at the time, but the following day homicide investigators took Kelli's father, Bernard and his wife to the morgue to identify her body. Kelli was described as a beautiful young woman who enjoyed spending time with her older sister, Leslie, who lived in New York as well as with friends and other family members. She could sing, but was too shy to perform in front of others. Judith said Kelli had a lot of friends and would sometimes stay over at a girlfriend's home if it got too late. However, she said she would always call to let them know where she was staying. She didn't contact them the night she was killed.

The apartment complex where the killing occurred is just off Interstate 95 between Barnes Road and Santa Monica Boulevard South. Homicide investigators have talked to scores of residents living in the various buildings, but no one has been able to provide any information which helps identify the killer or sheds light on what happened before Matos and Chapple were shot. The deaths have been listed as a double homicide and police said the crime scene was contained inside one apartment unit. Rewards totaling $5,400 have been posted by First Coast Crime Stoppers for the tip that identifies the killer.

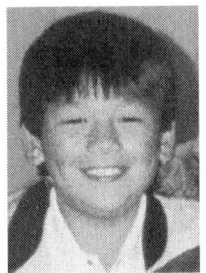

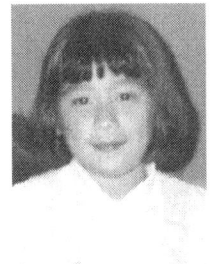

Charles Chia   Jennifer Chia

Charles & Jennifer Chia
Reno, Nevada

Eight-year-old Charles Chia and his six-year-old sister, Jennifer, got off a school bus at the Timber Hills apartment complex in Reno, Nevada at 3:20 p.m. on Wednesday, October 18, 1989. They were last seen with a playmate walking across the street toward their building on Talbot Lane. The little boy was wearing a long-sleeve white shirt, blue pullover and blue jeans. His sister had on a white dress with black dots, white socks, light green shoes and carrying a blue tote bag and a "Miss Piggy" lunch pail. That was the last time they were seen alive. Their mom, Ann Chang, who had recently divorced from her husband, had her mother living with them to look after the children while she put in the necessary hours operating a restaurant she owned. As darkness fell on the city and the children still weren't home, the grandmother called police to report them missing. Police immediately mounted a massive search in the city's southwest end where the apartment complex is located. After several hours the search was expanded across the city an all available police officers and other emergency personnel were pressed into service. The apartment was off South McCarran Street and only a short drive from the North South Freeway which links to Interstate 80, a main east west highway carrying traffic from New York City to Sacramento in California. In the initial stages of the investigation attention also focused on the ex-husband who lived in California, but police were able to establish that he was not involved.

The apparent abduction of a little boy and his sister would normally have grabbed the attention of the world media, similar to Madeleine McCann, the four-year-old British girl who vanished in May 2007 while on vacation in Portugal with her parents or the disappearance of Natalee Holloway while on Spring break in Aruba with fellow students from her Alabama high school in May 2005. But a day after the children disappeared in Reno, at 5:04 p.m. in the Pacific Time Zone, a massive earthquake rocked San Francisco killing 63 people, injuring 3,757 and damaging hundreds of buildings. The 15 second quake, measuring 6.9 on the Richter scale, was the second strongest to ever hit the United States and caused a 50-foot section of the two-tier Bay Bridge to collapse as well as bringing down portions of the Nimitz Freeway and crushing cars under tons of debris. People around the world who were watching pre game festivities for the third game of the World Series between the San Francisco Giants and the Oakland Athletics at San Francisco's Candlestick Park saw the earthquake live. Reno residents, some 200 miles away, felt the tremors, but they didn't immediately realize that the attention of the world would not be centered on the heart wrenching scenario that had their community in tears.

Although the disappearance failed to make prominence with the national media, volunteer searchers spent weeks looking for the pair. At the same time, police conducted a parallel investigation in an attempt to identify possible suspects and collect all the necessary evidence to prove guilt if anyone was ever arrested. Photographs and missing posters were distributed in a 500 mile radius, and details of the children filed with the Federal Bureau of Investigation and the National Centre for Missing and Exploited Children as well as their names added to the NCIC system, the national information computer that is available to all law enforcement agencies across the United States. It was agonizing work for detectives as they examined hundreds of reports prepared by police officers receiving information not only from residents across the city but from people living throughout Nevada and other areas of the U.S. who learned about the disappearance through the promotional effort. A few days after the abduction police also had to deal with a ransom demand when someone called Chang's restaurant, the Imperial Palace, requesting $100,000 for the safe return of the children. It turned out to be a hoax and a former employee, James Grooms was arrested on October 25 and later sentenced to 10 years in prison for the extortion attempt. Despite an exhaustive investigation police were unable to link Grooms to the abduction. He was released from prison in 1998, but remains a possible suspect.

After living in hope for a few days that she would see her children once the ransom was paid, Chang made a tearful appeal through the media on October 27 begging the person who took Charles and Jennifer to bring them back home. A publicity campaign which included billboards, buttons and fliers was launched the first week of November and mid month a television reenactment was broadcast as police continued to encourage people to come forward with any information that would help locate the children. As days turned to weeks and weeks became months, investigators continued tracking down every possible clue to find out what happened to the little boy and his sister after they left the school bus and started walking some 100 yards toward their apartment building. They were told about a balding Asian man with a pickup truck who was seen in the vicinity shortly before the children vanished, but they have never been able to locate him. During the extortion investigation detectives learned a man nicknamed "Ma" who in the past had lived with Groom and had worked at Chang's restaurant may have been connected to the disappearance, but they also were unable to ever fully identify him.

The disappearance became a homicide investigation when the skeletal remains of two little children were found in a shallow grave on July 25, 1990 off Highway 70 in California's Plumas County about 55 miles northwest of Reno. Investigators noted the Northwest Freeway which was just west of where the children lived becomes Highway 395 on the city's northern outskirts and connects with Highway 70 at Hallelujah Junction, the first major intersection on the roadway after crossing into California. Police said a highway worker discovered the remains of the children between Portola and Blairsden, California in the Feather River Canyon. The cause of death has never been revealed and police are also remaining tightlipped about the results of a specialized investigation in the summer of 1993 by forensic anthropologists and archeologists which turned up additional evidence at the grave site.

Ron Dreher, a retired Reno detective who worked with colleagues to run down thousands of leads, is convinced someone will come forward with the vital piece of information that will link the person responsible to the crime. He knows there are people who live in Reno or somewhere on the west coast who can tell police who killed Charles and Jennifer. Dreher says it's likely the killer has bragged about the crime to someone and is urging them to reveal the secret and provide police with the lead that will solve the case.

Investigators would like to find a married couple who were driving a brown van near the burial site shortly after the children vanished. The vehicle had a Miller Lite logo on the knob of the gear shift and was seen backing into a turnoff in the vicinity where the bodies were discovered. In 1989 there were sightings of the children in Northern Nevada and at Sierraville and Loyalton, California. Police said they would still like to speak with anyone who remembers seeing the children in those areas.

Mrs. Chang still lives with the hope that someday she will see the killer of her children brought to justice. She also wants to know why someone murdered Charles and Jennifer. Their deaths left a void in her life and every day she thinks about them and the future they will never have. In 1995 she offered a $20,000 reward for anyone who will come forward with information about the killer and Reno's Silent Witness program has up to $1,000 for an anonymous caller who provides the lead that solves the case.

Find My Killer

Chapter 2 – Chiang to Greene

Joyce Chiang

Joyce Chiang
Washington, DC

After dining with two friends, a 28-year-old Immigration and Naturalization Service lawyer in Washington, DC stopped at a local Starbucks to get a hot tea before walking four blocks to an apartment she shared with her brother. She didn't make it home that night and when she failed to show up for work on Monday, Joyce Chiang was reported missing. Three months later on April 1, 1999 her body was found on the bank of the Potomac River but it was another 10 days before the badly decomposed remains were officially identified as Chiang. Pathologists were unable to determine a cause of death and investigators have never definitely listed the case as a homicide, but a $50,000 reward is being offered for information leading to the arrest and conviction of a killer. Chiang, the only daughter of Taiwanese immigrants, was born in Chicago and spent her early years there before the family took her and her three brothers to California. After completing studies at the University of Chicago Laboratory School and Smith College in Northampton, Massachusetts in 1992 she went to work for California Congressman Howard Berman while attending evening classes at the Georgetown University Law Centre. She earned her law degree in 1995 and was assigned to the INS Office of General Counsel at the United States Department of Justice. Although it was Saturday, Chiang went to her office around 2 p.m. on January 9, 1999 to do some work before joining two friends at an area restaurant. After dinner her companions were planning to go to a movie, but Chiang needed to get home to call a friend in San Francisco to wish him luck on a performance he was giving that night. She asked the women she was with to drop her off at the Starbucks Coffee Shop on Connecticut Avenue near Dupont Circle. They arrived around 8:20 p.m. and last saw her heading into the coffee shop.

A missing person's report was taken by the Metropolitan DC Police but because Chiang was a United States government employee the Federal Bureau of Investigation joined the probe when her work identification was found the following day some five miles away in Anacostia Park. Her jacket, credit cards and some other belongings were later located at the nearby Anacostia Naval Station just west of the Frederick Douglas Bridge following extensive searches by FBI agents and officers from the U.S Park Police. Chiang was planning to walk from Dupont Circle to her home in the 1700 Block of Church Street but no one remembers seeing the five-foot, three-inch, 105 pound woman along the route. It is not known if she met someone at the coffee shop or encountered an individual on her way home. Investigators are still hoping to get fresh information on the case and are urging anyone to contact the nearest FBI office.

Vicki Chisholm
Fort Worth, Texas

A 22-year-old woman was robbed and sexually attacked before being killed in Forth Worth, Texas. The victim, Vicki Chisholm, was found just after noon on Thursday, April 16, 1981 near 200 South Henderson Street on a walkway that allows pedestrians to cross under the Highway 30 Interstate. She had been waiting for a bus in the 1100 block of South Henderson Street after leaving her dentist's office around 11:40 a.m. when the driver of a pick-up truck asked if she wanted a ride. Some 25 minutes later her body was discovered and an autopsy showed she had been strangled. Her killer was described as a black male. The Tarrant County Crime Stoppers program has offered a reward of up to $1,000 for anyone who can provide information that solves this slaying.

Nathaniel Brian Clark
Hollywood, Florida

REWARD $10,000

CRIME STOPPERS WILL PAY UP TO $1,000
AN ADDITIONAL REWARD OF UP TO $9,000 IS BEING OFFERED BY ANONYMOUS FRIENDS AND FAMILY. THIS REWARD EXPIRES APRIL 14, 2008.
FOR INFORMATION LEADING TO THE ARREST OF THE SUSPECT(S) RESPONSIBLE FOR THE:

HOMICIDE
OF
NATHANIEL BRIAN CLARK
THAT OCCURRED IN THE
1500 BLOCK OF S. 29 AVENUE
(NEAR FLETCHER STREET)
HOLLYWOOD, FL
THE VICTIM WAS FOUND IN HIS VEHICLE ON MARCH 12, 2007 DURING THE EVENING HOURS.
ANYONE WITH INFORMATION ABOUT THE IDENTITY OR LOCATION OF THE SUSPECT(S) IS ASKED TO CALL CRIME STOPPERS.
WE DO NOT WANT YOUR NAME, JUST YOUR INFORMATION!

CALL (954) 493-TIPS (8477) • 1 (866) 493-TIPS (TOLL FREE)
www.browardcrimestoppers.org

Police have used a sound truck and the encouragement of a $10,000 reward to get information that will solve the mysterious shooting of a man and his girlfriend in Hollywood, Florida. It was around 11:30 p.m. on Monday, March 12, 2007 when gunman pumped shots into a white Chevrolet Monte Carlo parked with its headlights on and engine running on South 29th Street, between Mayo Street and Fletcher Street on the east side of Interstate 95, just north of West Pembroke Road. Nathaniel Brian Clark, 35, died almost instantly from a gunshot wound to his chest. His 19-year-old girlfriend, Shanae LaRose, was critically injured with bullet wounds to her torso, but recovered after treatment at Memorial Regional Hospital. Clark's two-year-old daughter, Natalia, was sitting in the back seat and was not hurt. Investigators said the first emergency personnel arriving on the scene found the car door open and Clark slumped over the steering wheel. LaRose, barely alive, was collapsed in the passenger seat beside him. A detective from the Hollywood Police Department didn't indicate a motive for the slaying, but described the killing as an execution and suggested Clark, the father of five children, had been targeted for death.

The victim had stopped his car in a grassy area near one of four homes occupying the west side of the north-south street which continues southbound another block before dead-ending at the rear entrance of a white office complex which serves as headquarters for Connection for Business, an information technology and computer consulting company. It's possible people living on that street or someone from a home in the vicinity has information that will solve the killing. Members of the Broward Crime Stoppers unit have used a sound truck to patrol through the neighborhood blaring a message through loudspeakers urging anyone who can solve the killing to call the hotline. "We don't want your name, just your information." Relatives of the victim have also delivered fliers to homes in the vicinity reminding people of the reward. Family and friends have put up $9,000 and Crime Stoppers is offering up to $1,000 for the name of the killer. "It's not going to bring my son back," said the victim's mother, Juanita Clark. "It will not, but I just would like justice to be done."

Jeremy Scott Cockrell
Northport, Alabama

Seventeen-year-old Jeremy Scott Cockrell was a good student, a church-going boy, a volunteer and a friend to many people, but someone killed him on Thursday, June 22, 2006 in the bedroom of his home in Northport, Alabama. It occurred sometime between 7:30 a.m. and 10:20 a.m. and police are hoping to track down anyone who has information that leads to the killer. There is a $10,000 reward, but so far no one has come forward with the tip that will assist investigators in making an arrest. The victim lived with his mother, Ellen, at the home on Biscayne Hills Drive in the Biscayne Hills subdivision behind Northport City Hall. The victim was found by a group of his friends who arrived to pick him up for a planned day-long trip to Lake Tuscaloosa. The friends, who found his body in his bedroom, told police the door by the carport appeared to have been kicked open. Until a week before the homicide, the victim, known as Scotty to everyone, worked as a bagger and cashier at the Northport Crossing Publix Super Market. He was a junior at Tuscaloosa County High School and volunteered for four years with the United Cerebral Palsy of West Alabama and had worked the night before to help salvage items from an old cotton gin for a fundraising exhibit the organization holds each year at Halloween. He was named the group's volunteer of the year in 2006 and the annual award has now been named in his honor. Everyone called him a great kid and detectives from the Northport Police Department and the Tuscaloosa County Metro Homicide Unit are anxious to find who is responsible for his shooting death.

Chastity Antonia Marie Cogo
San Joaquin, California

A 20-year-old mother never returned to her Stockton, California home after saying goodbye to family members. Three months later on Saturday, April 20, 2002, the body of Chastity Antonia Cogo was discovered by a family who was spending the day fishing in a river at the end of West 8 Mile Road near Rio Blanco Road and the bridge leading to King Island. The site where her body was discovered is about 10 miles northwest of her home on South California Street near East Jackson Street. Cogo, who was known to her friends as Chaz, was reported missing on Sunday, January 20, 2002. Relatives said she drove off in a van that came to pick her up at her home the day she vanished. Police located the van driver and were told he dropped Chaz off later that day about a block from her house. The fishing group noticed what appeared to be a large duffle bag and spotted the body after pulling it to the shore. The victim was shot and then wrapped in a blue canvas sheet and bound with duct tape before being tossed into the water. It appears the killer attempted to submerge the victim's body in the deep waterway which is part of the Sacramento-San Joaquin Delta, but the wrapped remains floated to the surface. Homicide detectives from the San Joaquin Sheriff's Department are hoping to find anyone who saw Chaz or knows who she may have been with around the time she was reported missing by her family. Stockton Crime Stoppers has offered a reward of up to $1,000 for anyone who provides anonymous information that helps solve this case and the governor of California has authorized a $50,000 reward to anyone who can give specific details that leads to the arrest and conviction of the killer.

Stanley Cohen
Fort Worth, Texas

The 51-year-old owner of an auto parts store in Fort Worth, Texas was shot to death during a robbery. Investigation showed the victim, Stanley Cohen, was killed during some sort of violent struggle on Sunday, March 3, 2002 at the S&S Auto Parts store at 3401 Miller Avenue, just south of Richardson Street. He was pronounced dead at the scene. Homicide detectives from the Fort Worth Police Department said it appears the robbery occurred mid afternoon just after Cohen closed the business for the day. Evidence also showed the business had been ransacked before the killer fled in a company-owned truck. The vehicle was found a block away in the parking lot of the Minyard grocery store on East Berry Street, just east of Miller Avenue. Crime Stoppers is offering a reward of up to $1,000 to help solve this case and detectives are hoping anyone with information will call.

Gloria Ann Covington,
Amarillo, Texas

The partially-clad body of a 45-year-old prostitute was found in a park near a YMCA facility in Amarillo, Texas. The body of Gloria Ann Covington was spotted in the park, adjacent to the Carver Early Childhood Academy's playground on the north side of Northwest 18th Avenue just east of Lipscomb Street around 1 p.m. on Tuesday, August 5, 1997 by a nine-year-old boy who was with a group of other children. An autopsy showed the woman had been stabbed to death. Investigation showed Covington, a long-time resident of the Amarillo area, was last seen a few hours earlier in a motel area on Amarillo Boulevard West between North Madison Street and North Monroe Street, some 17 blocks from where her body was discovered. A woman, who had been with Covington and witnessed her murder, was killed a month later. The victim, Linda Gayle Jackson, 35, also a prostitute, told police she was assaulted by the man as he was pulling Covington into a light-colored pick-up truck. She described the attacker and said he appeared to be plunging a knife into Covington as he drove off with her in his vehicle. (See the segment on the Jackson homicide for details of that killing.) Ironically, the little boy who found the body, Dorien Deon Thomas, vanished 14 months later. Investigators suspect foul play in the disappearance and there's a distinct possibility the same person could be responsible for the deaths of the two women and the abduction of the boy. The man is described as a Caucasian male with red hair, blue eyes and a moustache. Investigators from the Amarillo Police Department's Special Crime Unit want anyone with information about these cases to call them or contact the Amarillo Crime Stoppers program which is offering a reward of up to $1,000 for the indictment of the killer.

Kimberly Kay Cowhick
Kansas City, Missouri

The 22-year-old victim was found dead in a wooded area in the northeastern section of Kansas City, Missouri two months after she vanished. Kimberly Kay Cowhick was last seen on Sunday, November 28, 1993 when she left a motel where she was staying with her boyfriend near Independence Avenue and Paseo Street. She told him she was going to the store, but never returned. On Friday, January 14, 1994 the victim's body was discovered in a heavy brush on North Brighton Avenue, just south of NE 72nd Avenue by workers who were clearing the area to install utility lines. The site is about 10 miles from where she was last seen. The Kansas City Missouri Police Department indicated Cowhick had been shot to death and was likely dumped in that area shortly after she went missing. A resident of Kansas City, Kansas, she was engaged in prostitution and frequented the Independence Avenue area and the vicinity of West 18th Street and Main Street in Kansas City, Missouri to solicit customers. Investigators believe she was probably murdered after being picked up by someone. The Greater Kansas City Crime Stoppers has posted a reward for information leading to an arrest and indictment in this case.

Tanya Van Cuylenborg   Jay Roland Cook

Jay Roland Cook & Tanya Van Cuylenborg
Snohomish & Skagit Counties, Washington

A young man and his girlfriend from a Victoria suburb on Vancouver Island in British Columbia were killed after being abducted on a driving trip to Seattle. It was Tuesday, November 24, 1987 when a man found the partially-clad body of 18-year-old Tanya Van Cuylenborg in a ditch near the town of Alger in Skagit County, Washington. She had been raped and died from a single gunshot wound to the back of her head. The following day the 1977 Ford van the couple had been driving was located in Bellingham, Washington at the Greyhound Bus station some 30 miles from where the young woman's body was discovered. And on Thursday, November 26, 1987 two hunters discovered the body of 20-year-old Jay Roland Cook near Monroe in Snohomish County. His body was under a bridge, some 20 miles northwest of Seattle. An autopsy showed he'd been savagely beaten and then strangled with some sort of ligature.

The pair set out on Wednesday, November 18, 1987 with money Jay's father had given him to purchase some furnace parts that he'd ordered from a company in Seattle. They drove the four miles from Oak Bay, a suburb of Victoria with some 15,000 residents to the dock area off Belleville Street where they boarded a ferry bound for Port Angeles. It was a 26 mile voyage across the Straight of Juan de Fuca and took 90 minutes to reach the U. S. shoreline. From the harbor at Port Angeles, the most direct route would have taken the couple on an 85 mile journey along Highway 101 and Highway 104 to the Hood Canal Bridge linking the Olympic Peninsula with the Kitsap Peninsula, and then to Kingston where they would have taken a ferry across to Edmonds. From there they would have connected with Interstate 5 which runs south into Seattle. The drive would have taken approximately two and a half hours.

Instead of exiting on Highway 104, Jay and Tanya continued southbound on Highway 101, a distance of 102 miles, to the community of Shelton. From there they pulled onto Route 3 and traveled to Bremerton, some 35 miles away, to take the ferry across Puget Sound to Seattle. Midway through the drive, the couple stopped in the village of Allyn and purchased ferry tickets. Later that day their vehicle was logged onto a ferry, but investigators have not been able to find anyone who remembers seeing the pair among the passengers on the vessel. Investigators can pinpoint the last time they were seen alive from the details stamped on the tickets at the time of purchase, but from that moment until Tanya's body was discovered off a rural road in Alger there is a gap of six days in the timeline police put together in an attempt to trace their final movements. There is another 48-hour gap before Jay's body was found on Thanksgiving Day under the High Bridge near Monroe.

The timeline suggest the killings occurred somewhere between the community of Allyn and the ferry dock at Bremerton in the mid afternoon of November 18, 1987, but investigators said one or both victims could have been murdered sometime the next day. Jay was likely executed first and Tanya kept alive for sexual purposes before being killed.

Although the slayings were horrific, the trauma became even more devastating through the years when the killer mailed greeting cards to the parents from various areas of the United States detailing how the murders were carried out, what had been done to the victims before their deaths. He also told them of the euphoria he experienced when taking the lives of Jay and Tanya. Police have checked with law enforcement agencies in the vicinity of where the letters were postmarked but there is no indication of similar killing in those areas. Most recently the faces of the victims were published on playing cards distributed to inmates at prisons and other holding facilities across Washington in hopes someone recalls something that will help investigators. A reward of up to $100,000 was available to anyone who can assist detective to arrest and prosecute the killer.

Deanna Cremin

Deanna Cremin
Somerville, Massachusetts

Deanna Cremin was murdered three days after celebrating her 17th birthday. The homicide occurred in the late evening hours of Wednesday, March 29, 1995 and her killer hasn't yet been brought to justice. Deanna lived with her parents, two younger brothers and an older sister in Somerville, Massachusetts, a city of some 75,000 people located two miles north of Boston in Middlesex County. It was the next morning when the high school junior's partially clad body was found a short distance from her home behind a senior's apartment complex on Jaques Street at the dead end of Fenwick Street by two girls she had once babysat. An autopsy showed Deanna had been strangled and there's some indication of a sexual attack.

Investigators aren't sure if the victim was killed where the body was found or if she had been dumped there. The boy she was dating at the time told police he walked her partway home, but left to meet up with some friends and get something to eat. He produced a receipt from a restaurant, but that hasn't cleared him of suspicion. Detectives have also focused attention on a former Somerville resident who was declared a dangerous sexual offender after being sent to prison for sexual assault and attempted murder.

Deanna's family has never given up hope the killer will be captured and have made personal appeals through the years as well as posting rewards. Billboards have been put up in the community and the popular high school junior's life chronicled in pictures on various Internet sites. Her high school friends have also kept the memory of Deanna alive in their hearts and many who still live in the Boston area attend memorial services that have been held annually since the teen's slaying.

"I want justice," Deanna's mother Katherine Cremin told Boston Globe reporter Megan Tench in a 2005 article on the anniversary of the killing. "I want it for my daughter." The idyllic middle-class life that Katherine had with her husband, Michael Cremin, was turned upside-down by the tragedy. Heartbroken she couldn't stop crying for six months. She said the murder of her daughter devastated her. "I lost my job six months after. I could not put myself together, I could not accept my daughter had been murdered," she wrote on one of the many web sites memorializing Deanna.

"I came obsessed with bringing her killer to justice. I was afraid to let my children out. I was afraid to tell them I loved them because those were the last words Deanna and I exchanged to one another the night she didn't come home. It was like a grenade went off in my family and we couldn't hold it together for quite a while." She sought comfort and escape in alcohol and tranquilizers, but her life went completely out of control. She lost custody of her sons and her marriage ended in divorce.

It is quite common that the strain from a tragedy will tear families apart.

The pain and agony from her daughter's death has never gone away, but the endless crying has stopped and she overcame her addiction with drugs and alcohol. "I am stronger from this," Katherine Cremin wrote on the web, "and as time goes on I still cry just not as often." As a mother she still worries about her children, but she is able to function much better today. "Her death almost destroyed me, and I will never be the same."

The detectives who began the murder investigation have retired, but the case has never been forgotten. With recent advances in forensics, investigators from the Somerville Police Department and the Middlesex County Sheriff's office have sent numerous items collected from the homicide scene to the crime lab for expert examination. It is hoped DNA will eventually identify Deanna's killer and bring justice to the family. The murder file contains more than 100 interviews, but investigators feel there are still people today who have information that they have never revealed that could solve the slaying.

Martha Coakley, the District Attorney for Middlesex County, is convinced there are people who witnessed the killing or have information that is vital to the investigation. She lives in hope they will tell authorities what they know. Coakley acknowledged these people would be considered heroes if they come forward and could be eligible for a reward which was doubled to $20,000 on the tenth anniversary of Deanna's death.

The timeline developed by police during the investigation of Deanna's strangulation death have the victim and her boyfriend walking on Jaques Street toward her home. They both lived on the street at the time and he would normally walk her to the door. On this night he walked her only halfway home and she continued by herself toward her house. The timeline is blank from that point until the following morning when the two girls discovered her body.

That night on March 29, 1995, Katherine Cremin was angry that her daughter didn't come home. She was also worried but put any thought that something had happened out of her mind. She convinced herself she had spent the night with friends. She was a teenager and on occasion stayed at a friend's house. Making a last minute check and finding her daughter's bed still empty she went to work knowing she would be giving Deanna quite a talking to when she saw her.

Her husband called the school and learned she wasn't in class. A short time later police were at his door to break the news that his daughter had been found dead.

Katherine Cremin got a phone call from her husband telling her to come home immediately. During the train ride home people were talking about a young girl being murdered in Somerville, but she didn't want to believe it was her daughter. When she got closer the fear inside her turned to panic as she saw police cars everywhere and the road leading to her house blocked off. She began pleading with God. "Please don't let this have anything to do with my child."

Her heart was pounding and she started to cry. She remembers being so scared and wanting to run the other way, but continued moving toward her front door. Once inside, police broke the news to her. "Her daughter, Deanna, was dead."

Katherine Cremin began crying uncontrollably and nothing anyone said could ease the pain that now completely consumed her.

Deanna was born on March 26, 1978. She had an older sister, Christine and two younger brothers, Albert and Mark. With the exception of living a couple of years in California when Deanna was a toddler, the close-knit family made Somerville, Massachusetts their home. A cousin, Stacey Wallace described Deanna as a warm and compassionate person who loved animals, particularly cats. She would rescue strays from the street and was someone who would never step on an insect. She also loved children and hoped some day to become a teacher. To ensure Deanna is never forgotten Stacey has posted memories of her cousin on the web. "She was the type of person that cared deeply for others," she said. "There was never any type of status...she saw people from what was inside." Stacey described her cousin as a very popular person with a one in a million smile that could light up a room. "Deanna had outer beauty, but she also had inner beauty," she wrote at one Internet site.

Deanna worked part-time at a local store and cared for third-graders at a nearby elementary school as well as volunteering with friends at the Somerville Cable Access Television station to help produce a puppet show for local children. She was a Red Cross volunteer and earned a bit of extra money by babysitting for families in her neighborhood. With three months left in Grade 11, she was looking forward to her senior year at Somerville High School and going off to college. "The future was wide open and full of possibilities," Stacey wrote. "That has to be one of the hardest things to imagine...what her life would be now.

Whatever road Deanna would have taken, she would have done only good in this world. Deanna had a big heart; she could do nothing but good."

She remembers her laugh, her sigh and her quiet little voice that touched so many hearts. She had her mother's green eyes. Her favorite colors were purple and green. She loved everything about life. "She made a big impact in this world, but the fact is, she should be here with us now." Each year as family members and friends celebrate births, graduations, wedding and other memorable events, Deanna isn't there to join them. Stacey said her cousin's death has left a hole in the heart of everyone who knew her. "She was a sweet, outgoing, gentle soul who in all the years I knew her growing up never once had an unkind word for anyone. She had such a glow about her that no words I write can describe just how special she was too many people. She had what one might call a pureness that not many people have. A day does not pass where she is not in my thoughts. She brought such happiness to others in her short life and she is missed more than I can put into words. It is like a constant ache that never goes away. With time it has become bearable but not less painful. It hurts to know she will never realize all her hopes and dreams. She will always be in my heart and never far from my thoughts," she wrote on the web site.

Stacey's heartfelt message includes thoughts about Deanna's Mom who she describes as the most caring, giving, selfless and honest person I have ever known. Out of anyone I have ever known in my life I respect and admire Katherine the most. She has overcome things in her life that most people could not, including myself. I couldn't and wouldn't imagine the pain she has suffered. When someone needs and ear she listens, a hand she lends, a shoulder to cry on she is there. "Never once asking for help in all these years," Stacey notes on a web site. "I couldn't for a moment host the thought of this happening to one of my children," she wrote. "It's too horrible to think it let alone live it. And that is what drives us all. We want to find justice in some form. Even more important is stopping a killer before he takes another innocent life."

Close relatives said there was an indescribable pain in Katherine Cremin's voice when she told them of the tragedy. "You could also see the agony on her face," said one family member, recalling that fateful day. "I could feel the pain in her words as she spoke."

The pain of losing a loved one in a horrible brutal manner never goes away. Life does get a bit easier as the years go by, but a vacuum or void remains. There is also no such thing as closure. A Florida police officer, whose daughter was a victim of murder, has held seminars with homicide investigators to outline the pain that families endure when the life of a son or daughter is violently ended. There is no such thing as closure. The pain never goes away. The arrest of a suspect or the finding of a body doesn't erase the nightmare and suffering that has been part of their life since tragedy struck. Those left behind find strength to carry on, but they will go through torment and anguish forever. There is no closure after a parent learns their son or daughter has been murdered.

It was that torturous grief that led Katherine Cremin into the downward spiral that eventually led to her alcohol and drug addiction. The pain was constant. As a mother she wondered if there was anything she could have done to prevent the tragic death. She is also tormented by the fact the person who killed her little girl hasn't been caught. She watched the baby she gave birth to develop into an incredible young lady and within a moment her life was snatched away.

Thoughts by a relative on another web site suggests the killer has to be "the coldest of all people" and needs to be stopped before another innocent life is taken. "Someone who can live with this crime has no heart. The chances are real of this person repeating this crime...if he has not done so already."

Although still haunted by memories of the night Deanna didn't come home, Katherine has slowly put her life back on track. She has reestablished ties with her children and found comfort from support groups and counseling sessions. Still, she has never given up hope of finding who is responsible for the murder. She agrees it is not about closure and admits she will never get over the tragedy. "This is about justice. My daughter's killer is out there somewhere."

Family members utilize billboards from time to time to remind people of the slaying and the $20,000 reward that is available to anyone who comes forward to identify the killer. They remember Deanna as a young vibrant teenager and so full of live. She loved children, she was a person who wanted to become a pre-school teacher, someone who babysat regularly and worked with Grade 3 students at an elementary school near her home. Those dreams have vanished forever and her relatives now wait until police find the evidence that will identify the person responsible for her killing. One of the latest billboard messages has Deanna speaking directly to the person who took her life. "You know what you did to me. How much longer must I wait? Please help make my time in heaven restful."

Investigators say enhancements in DNA technology have allowed forensic experts to obtain additional scientific evidence but they are not in the position of making an imminent arrest. The key to this case will be someone coming forward and identifying the killer or providing significant information that enables police to link all evidence collected so far with the individual responsible for the killing of Deanna Cremin. Until then, the case remains unsolved.

Even when an arrest is made, Deanna's mother will never be freed from the horrible memory that haunts her. Although difficult, she put into words her feeling and posted them on the Internet for the world to realize the suffering that a mother is forced to endure when a child is murdered. "I don't quite know how to start what I want to be said here, but I am going to try. I had a happy little family. I had a good job. My children by all aspects were happy, well adjusted kids growing up where their parents grew up, in Somerville, Massachusetts. Although I had the regular concerns any parent of active teenagers does, murder was not remotely in my thoughts." She said her concerns were focused on their personal and emotional health, their education and their awareness of the dangers that drugs can pose. She continued by saying their social activities and personal friendships did not raise any red flags for what happened. But, March 30, 1995 is a day she dreads to remember. "I can relive it several times a day second for second. My beautiful daughter had been strangled to death and I did not know what to do. I had no idea how to handle this and live at the same time. There is no relief to this grief. I live with it. Her dad lives with it. My daughter and my two sons live with it. I think it is our love for one another that helps us to move on in our lives. When I look at my children and I appreciate so very much, how very proud I am of them. How very much I love each one of them. How I wish I could do away with all the evil in this world so it won't come near them ever again. It is a very scary and strange feeling, because no matter what, I am always afraid something bad will happen. When things are at their best, that fear is always ever looming over. Yet, I can't let it defeat me, or anyone in my family's dreams, endeavors, and pursuits for success and happiness."

Katherine Cremin says it was about a year after her daughter died and she was seeing one of the many counselors she would consult over the years. "I was so sad and so angry. I remember this because at the time it was so profound." She said it was during one session when she was extremely upset and she had no idea how she could continue living. It was at that point her counselor looked directly at her and asked one question. "What would Deanna want you to do?" She said his words were poignant. "I don't know if anyone had said that to me before. If they had I wasn't ready to hear it. But I still had a family to raise and my children really needed me to be there for them and to be strong. And as heartbreaking as it is for me every day since March 30, 1995 – I do try to be a strong and happy mom, a good friend and neighbor. Not only would Deanna have wanted me to do that, but my three other children and countless other people needed me to be "there" for them as well as myself. Deanna was a very happy go lucky young woman. She had a whole world waiting for her to go out and enjoy it. Her life was taken by someone who remains unknown. Justice for Deanna will happen. I hope soon. No matter what, she will always be missed," she said. "That will never change. I know I am so blessed to have all the wonderful things I do in my life. I know it and I do not take it for granted. I am so aware of the power emotional tragedy can impact on my thoughts and actions. I have sought relief through so many different ways. From doing the right thing by staying healthy and sober to the total opposite, by trying to avoid confronting my heartache by taking pills or drinking too much. I learned I can't run away from this, there is no escape. I will never "get over" Deanna being murdered. No one will. Deanna gave me a lot of happiness, and she gave it freely and unconditionally. I have my memories, my pictures and videos. I have my heartbreak. But it doesn't stop there. I have a wonderful family."

She said Deanna's death came very close to destroying any happiness she could ever want. "But because of those words "What would Deanna want you to do?", I found the strength to move forward. I found that love is way more powerful than evil. I found that with time things have become less difficult. I have truly come out of the depths of despair to proceed with life. To enjoy the moments. To cherish and respect all that is good and kind. I will never say anything good came out of Deanna's death, because I would never mean it. But a lot of good came from her life here. I see it and hear it every day. A part of me will never heal, but there is a whole lot more of me that will move forward, be strong, be happy and when necessary be angry and sad. But I want to be happy and good. I want to be present and accounted for when I am needed especially by my kids. I believe I can do that today. I have a very giving nature, it is my personality. If you are in my company I want you to be able to enjoy it. Deanna would have wanted that and heck who wouldn't. None of us knows what tomorrow brings. But we all learn something new every day. Whether it be about ourselves, our families, or our neighbors. Life should be enjoyed and injustice should not be tolerated. Whoever killed my daughter will be brought to justice one day. That will happen because there are so many good people out there who have made it their mission. The things I find difficult to deal with may never change. But the way I deal with them is constantly changing. I do the best I can with what I have. I have a lot. I have the most wonderful family. I do have part of a dream. There are so many wonderful things to look forward to in life. I have a healthy outlook by all means. I have a lot of strength because I have a lot of love. For anyone who reads this and knows me, you have seen my struggles. You have seen me overcome some pretty tough situations. I almost lost everything with meaning after Deanna was murdered. And I would have if I had continued to let grief control my life. I chose to let the love inside and surrounding me be my guide. I am so grateful to have what I have. But I will not just slide back and let Deanna's murderer not be pursued. I think we can all help this quest for justice. And I am truly grateful to everyone who has put any time into helping get Justice for Deanna."

The words were spoken from the heart of a person who copes every day with void that can never be filled, but it gives insight into the suffering that murder can wreak on a mother as well as other family members and friends who are impacted when a victim's life is taken by a killer.

Billy Charles Crump, Sr.
Little River, South Carolina

A wife watched in horror as her husband was gunned down by two men at their newly purchased condo at South Carolina's Eastport Golf Club. The shooting occurred at 12:30 a.m. on Saturday, January 4, 1992 in the parking area of the couple's building on Eastport Boulevard in Little River, South Carolina, a resort community some 23 miles up the coast from Myrtle Beach and four miles from the border with North Carolina. Bill Crump, 47, had just driven home with $10,000 cash from a bingo hall he owned in North Myrtle Beach when confronted by the suspects who emerged from the darkness. "Hold it right there," one called out as Crump was climbing from his car. A moment later after approaching within 20 feet, both men opened fire, one with a shotgun and the other a revolver. Crump fell to the ground and the attackers fled. Relatives believe Crump was targeted for death in a contract killing and the gunmen were professional hit men.

Born in Charlotte, North Carolina on May 12, 1944, Crump worked his way into the car sales business and by 1987 was the general manager of Hendrick Sportswear, an automotive and NASCAR sales venture operated by Rick Hendrick. The company grew from a $600,000 business to a $20 million enterprise under Crump's guidance. When the operation was sold to Ken Barbee, Crump formed his own company, Promotional Management Inc., and signed contacts with numerous NASCAR drivers and managers to market their sports memorabilia. He also bought the bingo parlor across from the Gator Hole Golf Course in North Myrtle Beach and moved from his home in Myrtle Beach to the Little River Condo in December 1991, three weeks before he was killed.

His wife, Ann, heard the shots and saw the muzzle flashes, but she wasn't hurt. She ran to the other side of their gold-colored and now bullet-riddled BMW and saw life ebbing from her husband. The dreams they hoped to share together were fading forever. Everything her husband did was to give them and their two sons a much better life. Police efforts to solve the slaying have reached a dead end and Crump's nephew, Brian Crump, a former police officer and now a private investigator in Charlotte, North Carolina is continuing to appeal for leads to identify the individuals responsible for the killing.

Inside the car was the bag with the $10,000 in cash that Crump was carrying from the bingo hall. Also on the front seat was a 9 millimeter automatic which was always close at hand whenever he carried large sums of money. He was a cautious man and had arranged for a security guard to escort them from the bingo parlor with the nightly earnings. Friday nights were one of the most profitable and the guard walked them to their car and then followed in his vehicle for some distance to make sure no one was trailing them. His son, Billy Charles Crump Jr., is convinced someone paid to have his father killed. In media interviews after the slaying he said there was no attempt to take the money or even to get his father's wallet or the Rolex he was wearing. The gunmen were on a mission to kill.

Sonja Spruill Day
Plymouth, North Carolina

Her drug dealer boyfriend was stabbed and beaten to death in December 1993 and nine months later she was murdered in her apartment in Plymouth, North Carolina. The body of Sonja Spruill Day was found by her 11-year-old son around 3:30 p.m. on Monday, September 26, 1994 when he arrived home from school with two friends. Discovering he was locked out, the boy climbed to the second floor balcony of the home at 110G Sawmills Circle just off the Wilson Street Extension south of Pine Street. The 33-year-old victim was on the bed with stab wounds to her neck and chest. Her throat was also slashed. The victim, dressed in a shirt and shorts, was on the bed with her arms stretched out and the cord from bedroom lamps securing her hands to the posts of the headboard. A black bra was wrapped around her ankle, but not tied to any part of the bed. Day lived in a neatly-kept two-storey apartment building on the southwestern outskirts of Plymouth, a historic town of 4,100 people some 80 miles south of Norfolk, Virginia. She was a heavy crack user and resorted to prostitution from time to time to get money to buy drugs. Her boyfriend was a major cocaine dealer and it's possible both killings are in some way linked to a dispute involving drugs. There was no sign of a forced entry, but blood spatters were found in several rooms indicating Day may have been chased through the apartment after opening the door to the attacker. A reward is available through Crime Stoppers for information leading to the indictment of the killer and the North Carolina State Bureau of Investigation is hoping someone will call and provide details to allow them to solve the slaying. .

Louis DeJesus III
Anchorage, Alaska

A 21-year-old man was shot to death during a disturbance that stemmed from a ruckus earlier in the evening at the Veterans of Foreign Wars hall in Anchorage, Alaska. Louis DeJesus III was shot several times shortly before 2 a.m. on Saturday, October 12, 2002 in the parking lot after leaving the club on Oklahoma Street between Boundary Avenue and Marge Court in the city's Muldoon district. A 21-year-old woman and another person were wounded by the gunman, but recovered from their injuries. The shooting occurred when a 100 or so people came from the building and a disturbance erupted in the parking lot. DeJesus was pronounced dead at the Alaska Regional Hospital. Investigators from the Anchorage Police Department are appealing for people to come forward and identify the gunman and Crime Stoppers is offering a reward of up to $1,000 for information that leads to the arrest of the killer.

Young Soo Do
North Miami, Florida

One of the world's top Tae Kwon Do instructors, who taught defensive tactics to police, FBI and DEA agents, was shot and killed while washing cars with a friend in the rear of his martial arts studio in North Miami. The attack occurred around noon on Saturday, November 10, 2007 when a man standing about 20 feet away and holding a long brown rifle with both hands fired numerous shots. Young Soo Do, a 62-year-old ninth degree black-belt and grand master instructor died two days later in Jackson Memorial Hospital. He received massive wounds to the abdominal area and lost a great deal of blood. His friend, Leclerc Prosper, the same age, was also shot, but recovered from his injuries. He was not able to provide a great deal of information about the gunman and investigators said they are still trying to determine a motive. Do's martial arts school was at 12815 West Dixie Highway between NE 128th Street and NE 129th Street, directly across from the Goodyear Tire store. Chantel Hair Design neighbored on the north side and the offices of Excellence Income Tax were on the south side. There are no obstructions blocking the parking lot at the rear from visibility of homes on the south side of NE 128th Street, but police didn't find any witnesses.

Do was born in South Korea and served in the Korean Marine Corps as a member of the special forces Blue Dragons group during the Vietnam war. He always had a love for martial arts and taught hand to hand combat to U. S. troops while in Vietnam. From 1969 to 1971 he was the Tae Kwon Do World Champion and later the principal instructor for the Korean National Tae Kwon Do team. Do immigrated to the United States in 1975 and a year later opened a martial arts training school in North Miami. Through the years Do earned some 600 awards in recognition of his civic and business participation in the community and across the United States. He was also an honorary police chief of North Miami and the day of the shooting he was going to drive to Orlando for a meeting where he was to be elevated from vice-president to president of the Florida & Miami chapter of the Korean-American Association.

Many of the police officers working on the homicide investigation knew Do and are frustrated by the lack of leads. A reward of $57,000 has been posted for information leading to the arrest and conviction of those involved. The amount includes a separate reward of up to $1,000 from Crime Stoppers for anonymous information that helps solve the case. Do was a father figure to many who knew him, including police officers who attended his martial arts classes. The morning of the shooting, his son, Ricky, and daughter, Kathy, were giving karate lessons to a group of children. Do's daughter called 911 after hearing the gunfire and running outside. "It's my father…he's laying on the ground," she told the emergency dispatcher. She said she had no idea where the gunman was. "We just heard the shots."

Ricky, born in 1974, was leading the class through a rigorous series of exercises when the rifle fire erupted. He glanced at his sister and yelled at everyone in the gym to get down. Ricky then bolted out the rear door. His 27-year-old sister who followed him out yelled: "It's Dad…it's dad." At the same instance he saw his father, Ricky spotted a thin black man with a moustache and wearing what appeared to be a white tank top running north toward NE 129th Street. He started to chase him but ran back to his father when he realized how badly he was hurt. He cradled his Dad's head in his lap. Do begged his son in Korean to call his mother and also told him that he loved him.

Do treasured his black 2006 Cadillac STS, the fourth luxury car he'd owned since moving to the United States. He got the vehicle serviced at Rapid Oil Change around 9 a.m. and then drove the short distance to his martial arts studio where he glanced at the newspaper and chatted with Ricky and Kathy before they started the 11 a.m. karate class. He also called Prosper who agreed to come at noon to help wash his vehicle. They met in the rear parking lot and Prosper used a pressure washer from his yellow van to spray dirt from the black Cadillac while Do cleaned the interior of the vehicle. Prosper was directing a stream of water in the area of the left front tire when gunfire erupted.

As Do fell to the ground after being shot several times in the stomach, the gunman directed fire at Prosper hitting him in both legs. No words were spoken and the attacker escaped by sprinting through an adjacent alleyway and sped off in a car from the parking lot of the Farm Stores drive-through market, north of the martial arts school on West Dixie Highway at NE 129th Street. Prosper didn't look directly at the assailant and never saw his face, but was able to tell police he was a black male, between 20 and 25 years, 5-feet, 9-inches to 6-feet tall, with a medium build and short hair. He was dressed in a white shirt and dark baggy pants. At the hospital Do told his son the man had a moustache. Investigators said there was another black male in the getaway vehicle described as a dark colored 2004 or 2005 C-class Mercedes-Benz with tinted windows. A security camera recorded images of the car, but they were fuzzy and investigators were unable to read the license number.

Forensic investigators from the department's Crime Scene Unit located five shell casings at the scene. Do was shot three times in the abdomen and Prosper struck once in each leg. Both were airlifted to hospital and Do underwent four surgeries. He was hooked up to a ventilator, but doctors told the family there wasn't much hope for his survival. Around 5 p.m. Monday, some five hours after being removed from the life support system, Do succumb to his injuries. Apart from Ricky and Kathy, he is survived by his wife Soon Shin and another daughter, Stella. The family attempted to run martial arts classes at the school, but the memories were too painful and a few months later moved the academy to 2626 NE 188th Street, a quiet roadway off the West Dixie Highway in the vicinity of Miami Gardens Drive and Biscayne Boulevard.

Some 2,000 people, including North Miami Mayor Kevin Burns and Police Chief Clint Shannon, attended the funeral service and in the tradition of many Asian cultures, the cortège transported Do's body past the important places in his life, including the parking lot where he died to collect any spirit that may have been left behind. Sergeant Scott Croye, a homicide detective with the North Miami Police Department, is determined to solve Do's killing and is distressed at the lack of information. Croye wants anyone who knows anything about the shooting to contact police or the Miami-Dade Crime Stoppers unit.

Nancy Dunning

Nancy Dunning
Alexandria, Virginia

It was a targeted slaying but investigators haven't been able to find any reason why someone would want to kill the sheriff's wife in Alexandria, Virginia. Nancy Dunning was fatally shot after being confronted by an individual on Friday, December 5, 2003 when she made a brief stop at her home to check the mail before meeting her husband, James, and son, Christopher, for lunch at the Atlantis Restaurant in the Bradlee Shopping Center. Upon entering the two storey brick house on West Mount Ida Avenue in the Del Ray area of Alexandria, it appears the 56-year-old victim noticed the intruder and attempted to run outside. She was shot several times in the back. There was no sign of a forced entry and nothing was taken from the home. Police said it looks as though Dunning was targeted by the killer but investigations so far have failed to determine any possible motive. She was a real estate agent who had lived in the area almost 30 years and was very well known. Her husband, who had served as the sheriff in Alexandria since 1986, was also a well known individual and in recent years some extremely high profile prisoners had been detained at the holding facility, including Zacarias Moussaoui, a self-confessed al-Qaeda operative considered the 20th hijacker, who was sentenced to life in prison for conspiracy in the September 11, 2001 terrorist attacks in the New York City, the District of Columbia and Pennsylvania.

When his wife didn't show up at the restaurant specializing in both Greek and Italian cuisine, James Dunning and his son went to the family home on the winding street between Commonwealth Avenue and Russell Road. They found the victim dead just inside the front door. Known as the Queen of Del Ray because of her active involvement in the community, she had left the house sometime after 9 a.m. to buy several Christmas gifts at a nearby Target store for an underprivileged high school senior the family was helping as part of a local charitable project. Through the years, she participated in numerous events and activities to assist people in need and to improve the community where they had lived since moving to Alexandria in 1970. She was raised and went to school in Fairfield, Connecticut and still had many friends and family in that area, including her sister, Christine Niedermeier, who served as a state representative for eight years and later made an unsuccessful bid for the United States Senate. Family members are convinced someone was paid to kill her but police are keeping an open mind and exploring all possibilities, including the likelihood a previous relationship or event could be a factor that led to the death. Investigators also believe someone close to the victim has information that would help solve the killing but for one reason or another have not felt comfortable enough to reveal the details. A $100,000 reward fund was established by friends and relatives who have also distributed leaflets, taken out newspaper ads and put up billboards in hopes of getting tips to assist police find Dunning's killer.

Susan "Susie" Gilbert Dwyer
Sparr, Florida

She lived a life of crack addiction and prostitution before being found dead in underbrush along a rural roadway near Sparr, Florida. It was on Wednesday, July 17, 1996 when the remains of Susie Dwyer were discovered among some small trees on NE 47th Avenue near County Road 329 just north of Sparr, a tiny village of a few hundred people in Central Florida. The 27-year-old victim was last seen Saturday, June, 29, 1996 at the Hell Lovers Motorcycle Club at 517 SW 2nd Street, between SW 5th Street and SW 6th Street in Gainesville, the city where she was born and lived most of her life. Her father, Gus Gilbert, said drugs led his daughter into the dangerous life of prostitution, but she didn't deserve to die the way she did. He's hoping someone will come forward and identify the killer to get justice for Susan. Investigators were told the victim left the biker clubhouse in the early morning hours after telling members she had an appointment. It is assumed the young woman with long brown hair and blue eyes was going to meet a client, but homicide detectives were unable to locate the person to get more details about the final moments of her life. There was also indication the victim had been at a biker bar at 6315 SE 13th Street a short time before she vanished, but police couldn't confirm the information. She was slightly built and stood only five-feet, three-inches. She also used a variety of names at time, including Susie Gilbert and Susan Grovin. Her body was badly decomposed when found some 29 miles south of Gainesville and dental records were required to positively identify the remains. Police said they also weren't able to determine the exact cause of death but have no doubt the victim was murdered. Crime Stoppers has authorized a reward for anyone who helps solve the case and investigators from the Marion County Sheriff's Office are hoping someone will give them the name of the killer.

Anthony Lee Dye, Sr.
Commerce, Georgia

A sniper firing at long range killed the owner of a barbecue restaurant in Commerce, Georgia. Anthony Lee Dye, Sr., had just locked the door of the Spring House Barbecue at 11:25 p.m. on Wednesday, June 5, 1996 when he was struck in the head with a rifle shot. The 32-year-old victim was found outside the restaurant in the predominantly white community of 5,200 people some 70 miles northeast of Atlanta, after people in the area reported hearing gunfire. He died almost instantly. Investigators from the Banks County Sheriff's Department and the Georgia Bureau of Investigation have described the slaying as an assassination, but have not formally established a motive. Dye was a well-known entrepreneur who owned five restaurants in the area and hoped to have a chain of barbecue outlets serving Atlanta and neighboring communities. Some of his six brothers and sisters had been helping him manage the restaurants located throughout Barrow, Clarke and Banks counties, but all have closed since Dye was killed.

Police looked at a number of people, including individuals who were associated with Dye and his family, but all were ruled out as suspects. A number of possible motives were considered but investigators are not prepared to be specific. Relatives have suggested the slaying could be racially motivated and confirmed Dye had received a number of threats after opening the restaurant on Highway 441 just south of Interstate 85 in the vicinity of Industrial Park Boulevard and the sprawling outlet mall. Detectives indicated the victim was targeted by someone firing a high-powered rifle from a considerable distance. They have questioned numerous people but were never able to focus on a specific suspect. Dye had divorced from his wife and was living with their two children, a boy and a girl, about 20 miles to the south in Athens. Because of the threats he hadn't been at the restaurant on Commerce on a regular basis, but went that night to check how things were going. A relative, who heard one of the threatening phone calls that the victim had received, said it was from someone purporting to be from the Ku Klux Klan with a message that they didn't want blacks running restaurants in the county. After graduating from Clarke Central High School he joined the United States Air Force but didn't reenlist after his first tour of duty. Dye returned to Athens and ran a nightclub in the community before opening his first restaurant. Friends said he was a hardworking individual who put his heart and soul into making the Spring House the best barbecue restaurant in the south. Rewards totaling $8,500 are available to encourage people to come forward with information and assist investigators to solve this crime.

Lois Maxine Ensey
Fort Smith, Arkansas

Married six years and the mother of two children, the 23-year-old victim had just started working at the convenience store in Fort Smith, Arkansas when she was murdered. A customer called police to J's Nite Owl Grocery around 7 p.m. on Thursday, July 19, 1979 after finding the store open but the clerk was missing. Investigation showed the cash register was open and all the bills had been taken. Lois Maxine Ensey was last seen around 6:45 p.m. by two young girls who went to the store to buy some gum. There was no sign of a struggle and police were not exactly sure what had occurred but issued a description of the four-foot, 11-inch, 130 pound woman with brown hair and blue eyes.

They got the answer nine days later when the victim's body was found just off Treece Road, a rural cutoff from Highway 71, some 11 miles south of Fort Smith in an area known as Rye Hill. She had been shot with a .38 caliber revolver and forensic tests showed she was killed shortly after being abducted. She was dressed in the blue jeans, red and blue shirt and tennis shoes that she had worn to work. Her glasses were found near the body and her wallet was in her pocket. Homicide detectives from the Sebastian County Sheriff's Department are urging anyone who knows who is responsible for the killing of Lois to contact their office immediately. Her husband died from a heart attack in 2005 without knowing who took his wife's life, but their children, who are now young adults, are hoping someone will have courage to come forward with the information. The Fort Smith Crime Stoppers program will pay a reward of up to $1,000 for anyone who calls the tip line anonymously with information that solves this case.

Elbrous Evdoev
Pine Brook, New Jersey

The Crime Stoppers program in Morris County, New Jersey is still hoping to get information that will solve the gangland slaying of Elbrous Evdoev, a Russian-born mobster operating in the New York City area. The fully dressed body of the 32-year-old gangster was found at 4:41 p.m. on Saturday, March 6, 1993 frozen solid in a snow bank at the far end of the parking lot at the G. I. Auto Parts, Inc. auto salvage yard on Old Bloomfield Avenue in Pine Brook, New Jersey, a 25 mile ride along Interstate 280 from New York City's Holland Tunnel. The victim, who also went by the names Oslan and Ostep, had been shot three times in the head.

Evdoev was last seen around 8:20 p.m. on February 15, 1993 outside his residence at 3710 Laurel Avenue in the Sea Gate area of Brooklyn. Born in Odessa, Russia, the victim ran a strip club known as VIP International on East 7th Street near Avenue U in Brooklyn and through affiliation with a Russian Organized Crime group was actively involved in extortion, black market racketeering, prostitution, rape, false marriage schemes and other criminal activity. Almost a year earlier Evdoev survived two separate shooting incidents in New York City. On June 5, 1992 he was shot in the jaw and back and on July 4, 1992 received bullet wounds to the shoulder and hand. He didn't indicate if he knew who the gunmen, but did tell police Monya Elson had put out a contract on him. Elson was a gangster who at the time was running counterfeiting and drug trafficking operations from Brighton Beach in Brooklyn, the base of the Red Mafia in the United States. He was also the partner of Semion Mogilevich, the group's leader, described as the most dangerous mobster in the world.

At the time Evdoev was killed, various mobsters from Russian crime syndicates and some New York City based Mafia families were waging a territorial war that left numerous people dead. Several other people were killed to prevent them from testifying against mob bosses and other lives were taken in retaliation following disputes over profits stemming from scams and other criminal enterprises. Arrests were made in several of the deaths, but a number, especially those committed by hitmen, remain unsolved, including the killing of Evdoev.

Stephen W. Edenfield
Tampa, Florida

Police have the fingerprint of the killer, but they haven't yet been able to identify the individual. It was around 1 a.m. on Saturday, February 1, 1997 when 41-year-old Stephen W. Edenfield was attacked and stabbed to death in his apartment on the second floor at 5820 North Church Avenue in Tampa, Florida. The condominium complex known as the Tampa Racquet Club is a block west of the North Dale Mabry Highway and some three blocks north of West Hillsborough Avenue. It's an upscale gated community with a collection of two and four storey apartment buildings, a gym, tennis courts, an Olympic size swimming pool, a club house bar and many other amenities for year round residents and seasonal guests. The murder was in apartment 208 and a reward of up to $1,000 is being offered by Crime Stoppers of Tampa Bay for information that identifies the killer.

Edenfield, a service representative for 18 years at General Telephone Enterprises, was openly gay and would sometimes invite friends to his apartment. Around midnight he stopped his vehicle at the gates of the complex and indicated to a security guard that the man following in a dark colored vehicle would be visiting for a couple of hours but not staying overnight. The guard waved the vehicle through and didn't copy down the license number. Several hours earlier the victim went for dinner at his sister's apartment in another building on the complex to celebrate their mother's release from hospital after recovering from a stroke. He left around 9:30 p.m. and was expected to return the following morning, but failed to show up. At the time his mother, brother, Jim Edenfield and sister, Debra Allen, all lived in separate condo units in the complex which is also quite close to Tampa International Airport. Police said the victim had helped care for his mother since moving into the Tampa Racquet Club five years earlier.

Investigators were not able to establish where Edenfield was in the two-and-a-half hour period between 9:30 p.m. and midnight, but have pinpointed the stabbing to 1 a.m. when a neighbor reported hearing the sounds of a struggle. Evidence suggests the victim, who was just over six feet and weighing some 250 pounds, fought a life-or-death battle with his attacker. Piecing together what happened in the final moments in the apartment, police believe the assailant grabbed a small statue and struck Edenfield over the head. Seconds later he armed himself with a large butcher knife from the kitchen and began stabbing the victim. Homicide detectives with the Tampa Police Department said it appeared the attacker became furious over something and plunged the knife into Edenfield over and over. Half an hour after neighbors heard the commotion, a man was spotted driving the dark colored car from the parking lot.

When Edenfield didn't arrive at his mother's apartment at a scheduled time the next morning and the phone appeared to be off the hook, his brother thought he had overslept. He went to awaken him and when he didn't get a response to his loud knocking, Jim found the door unlocked. Inside the television was blaring and he saw a statue that normally sat on a side table lying on the floor. After calling his brother's name several times, he made his way to the bedroom where he saw Edenfield on the bed. Still thinking his brother was asleep, he pulled back the blanket and saw nothing but blood. His brother's face and hands were a crimson color. The bed sheets and Edenfield's clothing were also soaked with blood.

The statue on the floor was the one that had been used to club the victim. Police also found the kitchen knife and located some dried blood in a stairwell near the apartment unit that didn't come from the victim. Forensic experts said it could have come from the attacker who was likely cut and scratched in the encounter with Edenfield. They also determined that no sexual activity took place immediately prior to the killing and the victim hadn't consumed alcohol or taken drugs in the time leading up to his death. Investigators said they are not revealing every piece of evidence that was found at the murder scene, but they did confirm coming up with a fingerprint that cannot be linked to any of Edenfield's family or known friends who visited the apartment from time to time. Police said there's a strong possibility, like the blood in the stairwell, the fingerprint from the apartment belong to the killer.

Detective Lisa Haber of the Hillsborough County Sheriff's Office, who coordinates the Tampa Bay Crime Stoppers program, said they have highlighted this case on the anniversary of the killing in hopes of bringing in fresh leads. "This case is still unsolved and there is a family waiting for information," she said. Relatives learned of Edenfield's lifestyle when he publicly announced he was gay some 20 years before his death, but he kept his social life quite secret and never introduced his family to his close friends or any of the men he brought home. Because those closest to him were unable to provide police with the names of places he frequented or a list of his friends, investigators said it has made solving the case much more difficult. Even piecing together the two-and-a-half hour time span after leaving his sister's apartment and arriving at the gatehouse of the complex has been virtually impossible. In the years since the killing no one has come forward with information about Edenfield's whereabouts during that period. With renewed emphasis on the case police want gay groups to encourage any of their members to come forward if they know anything about the killing and are encouraging gay publications to highlight and promote the homicide appeal.

Miranda Fenner
Laurel, Montana

The town of Laurel with its 6,200 residents seems one of the most tranquil communities in Montana and a place far removed from the violence that plagues big cities in America. Sitting just fifteen minutes west of Billings, it's the gateway to Yellowstone National Park and adjacent to the Pryor Mountains where bighorn sheep, mule deer and wild horses roam freely. More than a hundred years ago it was part of the Wild West, a place where Calamity Jane and various other outlaws made their home and also the scene of some savage battles between local Indians and the United States Cavalry. Through the 20h century Laurel developed into a quaint town surrounded by farms ploughed in the lowlands at the base of mountains and also served as a railway stop. It's on the north side of Interstate 90 and the highway exit at Route 310 links directly to the community's business center. It was in Laurel's downtown in the 400 block of West Main Street on Sunday, November 15, 1998 when 18-year-old Miranda Fenner was attacked by an unknown assailant while working as a clerk at the Movie Store. She was repeatedly stabbed and her throat slashed.

Despite its close proximity to Billings, Laurel is an out of the way community where time seems to have stood still. People know their neighbors and the town's restaurants, grocery stores and gas stations have become meeting places to exchange friendly chat. Almost everyone in the town also knew Miranda and her family who moved to the community in 1990. They were shocked by the horror of the death six weeks before Christmas, a time when residents illuminated their homes and businesses to transform the community into a City of Lights to celebrate the holiday season and attract visitors.

It was around 8 p.m. when Miranda was forced to the rear of the store where she was working alone on the night shift. The attacker stabbed her multiple times in the neck before slashing her throat. Bleeding profusely, the victim, who graduated from Laurel High School six months earlier, dragged herself to the front and made it partway outside before collapsing. A passing motorist spotted Miranda slumped in the doorway and called police. She was airlifted to St. Vincent Hospital in Billings but was pronounced dead by an emergency room physician an hour after she arrived. Evidence indicates that Miranda was murdered during a robbery. All other possible motives have been eliminated. There was no suggestion anyone had stalked her prior to the killing and she definitely wasn't involved with drugs. It appears the killer went into the shop and took Miranda's life either because she would be able to identify him or he was attempting to coerce her into handing over more money.

Miranda's killing was brutal, senseless and completely unnecessary. The town was outraged. One woman told a KULR-TV interviewer that she hoped the authorities would catch and do away with the man responsible. Another Laurel resident said it's impossible to imagine how anyone could do something so brutal to another human being.

There was also an immediate fear of the killer being someone who lived in the town and preparing to take the life of another teenage girl.

Laurel had set up a Crime Stoppers program in 1991, but through the years and an absence of crime, volunteer board members lost interest. At the time Miranda was killed, David (Sandy) Stevenson, the president of Laurel's Chamber of Commerce, had total control of Crime Stoppers. He began a fundraising campaign from the jewelry store he operated and soon had collected some $25,000 for a reward fund to find the girl's killer. Bright yellow reward posters were printed up and volunteers circulated them across Montana and to other states in hopes someone would have information to solve the slaying. A few months later Stevenson left town and authorities discovered he'd absconded with the money. A warrant was issued charging him with felony theft.

When notified by Larry Tanglen, a reporter with the town's newspaper, the Laurel Outlook, Alan Pratt, who was president of Crime Stoppers International at the time, express outrage that someone could hijack a local Crime Stoppers program and steal cash donated for rewards. He was also disappointed that a person who had gained respect in the community could take advantage of a horrible murder and victimize residents who were doing everything they could to find Miranda's killer. Pratt, who lives in Hawaii and several other representatives from Crime Stoppers groups in different areas of the United States traveled to Laurel to help residents rebuild a Crime Stoppers organization and make sure a tipline was in place to receive calls from anyone wanting to provide information to investigators anonymously. With Pratt were Captain Vic Piersol of Seattle-King Crime Stoppers, Richard Carter of Arlington, Texas, executive director of Crime Stoppers International and Police Chief Ric Paul from Gillette, Wyoming. They met with Laurel's police chief Rick Musson and then attended a town meeting to encourage people in the community to trust Crime Stoppers despite the deception that had been perpetrated by a businessman they had supported through the years. Resident vowed to champion Crime Stoppers in memory of Miranda and to demonstrate that they were not prepared in any way to accept violence in their community.

Unfortunately there have been no tips on the Crime Stoppers line that have put investigators on the trail of the girl's killer but police continue to appeal for assistance. They are also hopeful an arrest will be made. Tips do come in from time to time and everything is followed up by detectives. Through the years the girl's parents, Mike and Sherry, have done whatever they can to help investigators crack the case, including making personal appears. Her mother said it's emotional and draining, but she's confident there are people who have information that will help the police get Miranda's killer.

Police have interviewed more than 700 people since the slaying and submitted scores of samples to the crime lab. Investigators admit being frustrated at times but have not lost focus of their goal to solve the killing. They have recently asked the lab to re-examine evidence from the crime scene in hopes new technology can provide fresh clues. The case remains a top priority investigation with the Laurel Police Department and the Yellowstone County Sheriff's Department.

Miranda was a typical teenager who lived at home with her parents. She had just graduated from high school and was full of dreams for her future. Her killing shocked the community. The video store where she worked closed down a few months after the slaying, but most resident remember the night horror visited their small town and continue to look for justice.

Gregory Fitz
Cleveland, Ohio

A 37-year-old man became the random victim of a killing in Cleveland, Ohio after being in the wrong place at the wrong time. Gregory Fitz was driving a car with three passengers in the 2200 block of West 38th Street near Siam Court on Saturday, April 14, 2007 when a group of men stepped in front of his vehicle. One suspect brandished a revolver and demanded money. Words were exchanged after Fitz handed over $10 and made an attempt to drive off on the brick and asphalt covered two lane roadway just north of where it comes to a t-intersection with Siam Avenue.. The gunman opened fire and the driver was struck in the torso. He managed to drive the car a short distance from the suspects and then one of the passengers got behind the wheel and took the victim to the Metro-Health Medical Center less than two miles away. Fitz underwent emergency treatment but was pronounced dead at 6:20 a.m. Homicide detectives from the Cleveland Police Department are hoping to hear from anyone who has any information about those responsible for the slaying or can provide the names of people who were in the vicinity and may have witnessed the murder. Crime Stoppers of Cuyahogo County in Cleveland has offered a reward of up to $2,000 to anyone who can provide anonymous information that will help police identify the gunman. Additional reward money has also been made available to encourage witnesses to come forward and provide details that will allow police to arrest and convict the killer.

Carole J. Fleming
Beloit, Kansas

A 51-year-old woman was shot to death at her home in Beloit, a community of 4,000 people in the north central area of Kansas. Officers from the Beloit Police Department were called to the home early on Friday, August 15, 2003 and found the body of Carol Fleming. An autopsy showed she died from a gunshot wound to the head. Investigators have released few details on the murder other than saying they collected a great deal of physical evidence and forensic results obtained by experts at the Kansas Bureau of Investigation laboratory in Great Bend will be useful in linking the person responsible to the crime once a suspect is identified. The victim grew up in Ionia, Kansas and was a long-time resident of the Jewell County and Mitchell County area. Since the death of her husband following a heart attack, she had been operating a family-owned business in Beloit. The state government has offered a $5,000 reward for anyone who comes forward with information that will allow police to make an arrest.

Gregory Vincent Foldenauer
Jonesboro, Georgia

Robbery is believed the motive for the shooting death of a man outside his Jonesboro, Georgia home. It was about 2:30 a.m. on Wednesday, June 27, 2007 when Gregory Vincent Foldenauer was shot in the driveway of his executive home at 8685 Woodside Lane, a secluded tree-shrouded dead-end street running north from Park Villa Way near the Pointe South Parkway. The 52-

year-old Bank of America employee was just getting home from work when he was confronted by an attacker as he stepped from his vehicle. He was shot in the abdomen and was dead on the driveway when emergency crews arrived at his home. He had been employed at the bank for 33 years and a $10,000 reward has been posted to help capture the killer. Investigators from the Clayton County Police are also appealing for any information that will assist their investigation into the murder.

Omari Ateef Ford
San Francisco, California

A 23-year-old man, described as a role model for students, was shot to death outside a home in San Francisco, California. Omari Ford, was gunned down by an unknown assailant following some sort of confrontation around 2:10 a.m. on Saturday, October 30, 2004 in the vicinity of San Jose Avenue and Broad Street. Detectives said there were quite a few people who were with the victim or heading to a nearby home to attend a party, but none of those individuals have provided information that would help solve the homicide. Ford, who lived in Daly City and known to friends by the nickname Omillian, was not associated with gangs and didn't use drugs. He was class valedictorian when he graduated in 1999 and had worked as a teacher's aide at Visitacion Valley Elementary School but was laid off because of cutbacks. Homicide investigators from the San Francisco Police Department determined there had been some sort of argument with a man who left but returned a short time later and shot Ford. A statement released by police described the slaying as an outrageous act and said the gunman displayed a viciousness and wanton disregard for the safety of others. The Office of the Mayor in San Francisco has authorized a reward of $100,000 for anyone providing information that leads to the arrest and conviction of the killer. Police are urging anyone with information to call the homicide detail or the police department's anonymous tip line.

Mary Virginia Garcia
Crook County, Wyoming

It began as a driving adventure with three friends, but ended with the death of a young woman on a lonely stretch of highway in northeastern Wyoming. It was on Wednesday, June 26, 1996 when the body of

Mary Virginia Garcia was found in a culvert under Highway 212 a short distance south of the Montana border. She had died after being shot three times in the head. The 19-year-old, who preferred her maiden name of Webb, was born in December 1976 in Arkansas but moved with her family while in her mid teens to Wenatchee, Washington. It is a quaint community of some 27,000 people north of Interstate 90 in the eastern foothills of the Cascade Range. It's also known as the Apple Capital of the World and the buckle of the power belt because of the numerous water-driven electrical generating plants that have been built in the vicinity. She met and married Ismael Garcia soon after graduating from high school and was living in a basement apartment at 525 South Mission Street, just south of Spokane Street and some three blocks from the Columbia River. To help build a good life together, she got a job at the Mill Bay Casino, almost 50 miles north of Wenatchee in the Lake Chelan resort area.

Webb got a break in the summer and made plans to travel to Conway, Arkansas with two friends. She was going to visit grandparents Ben and Leona Roach and some other relatives as well as seeing some of the friends she made while living there. The trio left sometime Wednesday on June 5 and travelled eastward from Wenatchee to Spokane and drove a total 710 miles through Idaho and into Montana where their car broke down in Billings. Her two friends decided to abandon the trip and head home, but Webb was eager to see her grandparents and set out to hitchhike the remaining 1,500 miles distance from Billings to Conway. There was a great deal of east-west traffic, especially with cross country trucks, and she didn't expect to have any difficulty getting individual rides that would take her hundreds of miles to Sioux Falls, South Dakota and then southward through Omaha, Nebraska, into Missouri and finally to Arkansas. She most likely got a ride from a long distance trucker either in Billings or somewhere along the eastbound Interstate 90 before the weigh station at Crow Agency. There is an entrance for Highway 212 just south of Crow Agency and that roadway is a favorite route for transport drivers since it saves them from dipping down into Wyoming and encountering heavy truck traffic flowing onto Interstate 90 from the extremely busy north-south Interstate 25 route.

Investigators cannot be sure Webb's killer was a truck driver since she could have also been picked up at any point by a motorist traveling through Montana or someone living anywhere in that region. Crook County Sheriff's deputies and detectives from the Wyoming Division of

Criminal Investigation located no evidence that has assisted them in developing a suspect. They are also not exactly sure how long she had been in the culvert. Her father, Thomas Webb who lives in Wenatchee and her mother, Mary Fuerte, a resident of Chelan Falls, some 40 miles north of Wenatchee, told authorities she had vanished on June 13 when she didn't arrive at her grandparents home at the anticipated time. It was another 13 days before her body was discovered. Crook County is a sparsely populated area in the northeastern Quadrant of Wyoming and Highway 212 runs a distance of 38 miles through the state from the Montana border to South Dakota on the east. Traffic at times is quite light in that area and the killer would have ample opportunity to drag the young woman's body into the culvert without anyone seeing. There is a possibility, however that someone may have seen a vehicle pulled over to the side of the road sometime during the latter half of June in 1996 and investigators are still hopeful someone will remember something to assist them track down the killer.

Terry Giles   Joseph Poulin   Linda Plummer

Terry Giles, Joseph Poulin & Linda Plummer
Portsmouth, New Hampshire

Three people died when a deliberately set blaze roared through a six-unit apartment building in Portsmouth, New Hampshire. Firefighters found the bodies of Terry Giles and Joseph Poulin in top floor units some 14 hours after being called to the fire at 3:25 a.m. on October 11, 1986 at 314 Islington Street, between Cabot Street and Rockingham Street. Linda Plummer, who received burns to 85 percent of her body, jumped from a third floor window to escape the flames, but died five months later at the Massachusetts General Hospital in Boston. Investigators determined an arsonist was responsible for setting the fire and those killed were listed as victims of a triple homicide. The Portsmouth Crimeline program is offering a reward of up to $20,000 for information leading to the arrest of the person responsible and detectives from the Portsmouth Police Department are asking anyone with information about the blaze to report what they know. All three victims shared the same unit on the third floor of the complex. Investigation showed 29-year-old Giles and 26-year-old Poulin had been overcome by smoke. One victim was found on a kitchen floor and the other in a bedroom. Plummer, who was 39 at the time, battled her way through the flames to a rear window in an attempt to escape the inferno. She landed on a cement area at the back of the building and was first taken to Portsmouth Regional Hospital where she was stabilized before being transferred to the Boston facility. She died March 30, 1987. Everyone else who lived in the building escaped without injury. Detectives said some of the former tenants may be aware of something but do not realize that the information is valuable. They are now appealing to those individuals and any others who could now be living anywhere in the United States or even another country to contact them so investigators can evaluate the information and determine if it can help identify who is responsible for the three deaths.

Kathleen Ann Goebeler
Lyndon, Illinois

A 29-year-old woman who danced at strip clubs in Pittsburgh, Atlantic City and the West Virginia area was found dead some 600 miles away beside an abandoned railway track alongside a highway running between Chicago and Moline, Illinois. The skeletal remains of Kathleen A. Goebeler were discovered on Tuesday, May 20, 1986 on the south side of Interstate 88, about two and a half miles east of the Crosby Road exit and just north of Lyndon, Illinois, a community of about 500 people. When the body was found the Interstate was known as Illinois Route 5, a four lane highway running west from Chicago. There was also an unpaved road running northbound from Moline Road, east of Lyndon, leading to the area of the railway tracks. The killer went to great lengths to conceal the victim's body. He climbed over a barbed wire fence and then put the body in a densely wooded area well off the roadway. It was while the owner of the abandoned railway line was inspecting the track just north of the village of Lyndon that he found the victim's decomposing body. There was no clothing, identification or jewelry but her right ear was pierced and she had given birth to at least one child. Her wisdom teeth and molars were missing and identification experts were able to get fingerprint impressions from the victim's left hand. The physical description and other pertinent details were checked against data on the National Crime Information Center computer but nothing matched. Investigators asked Canadian authorities to check missing person files in that country, but again the results were negative. Arrangements were made for a reconstruction expert in New Jersey to fashion facial features from the skull and the image produced was sent around the world via the Internet. These initial efforts were not successful, but Investigator Jerome Costliow made repeated checks of police networks to put a name to the young woman who had been buried as a Jane Doe at Oak Knoll Memorial Park in Sterling, some 20 miles east of where her remains were found. Without a name, only the words "One of God's Children" were on the bronze marker at her grave.

Late in 2003, investigators on the case arranged with the Federal Bureau of Investigation to have the victim's prints processed through the Integrated Automatic Fingerprint Identification System, an FBI data bank that holds records dating back to the 1920s on some 46 million people. On January 2, 2004 the Illinois State Police were notified that their 1986 murder victim was Kathleen Goebeler from McKees Rocks, Pennsylvania. Her fingerprints were on file following her arrest for burglary and criminal mischief. Further investigation showed Goebeler had been officially reported missing in January 1987, but the police officer who took the report didn't submit the details to the national missing persons data bank because the individual was an adult and there was nothing to indicate she was in danger. After identifying the murder victim, investigators were able to determine she was last seen sometime between April 11 and April 18, 1986 in the vicinity of her residence in McKees Rocks, a suburb of Pittsburgh. They also notified her mother, Patricia May of Stowe, Pennsylvania, who had lived in hope that her daughter would some day be found alive. After being told of her death she wondered why someone would want to kill the girl she knew as Kathy and hoped police would be able to find her killer. Police learned the victim had married Rodney Goebeler in 1974, but they divorced three years later. A year after their marriage, she gave birth to a daughter. Further investigation showed the victim got into drugs and earned money as an exotic dancer but she would always stay in touch with her mother and her two brothers. It was after Goebeler, who also used her maiden name, Kathleen Ann Johnson, failed to call on her birthday and at Christmas that her mother filed a missing persons report.

The victim would often hitch-hike and police speculate she may have been picked up by her killer in McKees Rocks, a community of 7,000 and only five miles from her mother's home in Stowe, Pennsylvania. The area is close to Interstate 79, the first link in a network of superhighways leading to Chicago and numerous cities in the United States northwest region. Police have never revealed how Goebeler died and they have never established any sort of motive. Investigators have developed a great deal of information since identifying the victim in 2004 and hope anyone else who can shed light on the death of Kathleen Goebeler will come forward and tell what they know. May told investigators she last saw her daughter around April 12, 1986, two weeks after her husband died. He had been in failing health and Kathy was with her Mom and other family members at the bedside when he passed away.

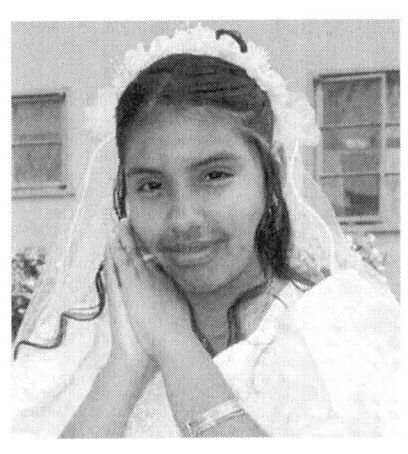

Veronica Gonzales
Bell, California

She was an innocent victim who died in her mother's arms. Thirteen-year-old Veronica Gonzales was staying at a girlfriend's apartment in Bell, California when a commotion erupted in the courtyard. It was 11:32 p.m. on Friday, April 30, 2004 when she opened the door to a second floor balcony walkway at 7024 Chanslor Avenue. That exact moment gunfire erupted and the victim was struck by a stray bullet. Investigators with the Los Angeles County Sheriff's Department said the shots were fired after two men jumped out of a car and chased a group of teenagers into the courtyard between two small apartment units. No one else appears to have been hurt and police were never able to determine what touched off the violent encounter at the complex near the Long Beach Freeway and Florence Avenue. Authorities have offered a $25,000 for information that leads to the arrest and conviction of her killer. The girl was taken to a nearby hospital but doctors were unable to saver her life. She died cradled in her mother's arms.

Jared Graybeal
Goldsboro, North Carolina

Sixteen-year-old Jared Graybeal of Goldsboro, North Carolina was found dead on April 4, 1996 in a farm field just off Highway 70 between

Kinston and La Grange in Lenoir County. The East Wayne High School student had been stabbed in the chest and neck. A knife believed to be the murder weapon was found along a roadway a half mile away. The victim was last seen in a white car at the Café Edelweiss on North Berkeley Boulevard near New Hope Road in Kinston. There's a $7,000 reward for the identity of the killer. John and Linda Graybeal are convinced their son was taken forcibly from the restaurant but they don't have any concrete evidence and are appealing for people to come forward and help investigators from the Goldsboro Police Department, the Wayne County Sheriff's Office and the State Bureau of Investigation find who is responsible. People can also call the Lenoir Country Crime Stoppers or the Wayne County Crime Stoppers program if they do not want to contact investigators directly.

Tamara Greene
Detroit, Michigan

Following persistent rumors she'd attended a wild party in the mansion of the Detroit, Michigan mayor, a 27-year-old stripper was murdered in drive-by shooting. Tamara Greene, an exotic dancer who went by the stage name Strawberry, was executed while dropping her boyfriend off on Roselawn Street near West Outer Drive around 3:40 a.m. on Wednesday, April 30, 2003. Greene died instantly after being shot 18 times but her boyfriend recovered from a bullet wound to his neck. He had just stepped from the car and was out of the direct line of fire when the gunman pulled the trigger on the .40-caliber Glock automatic. Greene's murder was one of a number of events igniting a scandal which led to felony charges against Detroit mayor Kwame Malik Kilpatrick and his removal from office. Under a plea agreement Kilpatrick was sentenced to 120 days for obstruction of justice but the other charges, including perjury and misconduct by an elected official, were dropped. He was never charged in connection with the Greene murder and there is still no direct evidence that confirms that strippers had performed at the city-owned Manoogian Mansion, the official residence of the mayor. What brought the mayor into the murder investigation were complaints that Kilpatrick had fired Deputy Police Chief Gary Brown for conducting unauthorized investigations into the alleged party and the transfer of Lieutenant Alvin

Bowman from head of Detroit's homicide squad after he launched a probe into the stripper's murder.

Officially Tamara Greene is Detroit's 113th murder of 2003. There are no suspects and the homicide is categorized as a drive-by shooting. The killing of Greene, who danced at various strip clubs and sometimes performed sexual acts, initially didn't get a great deal of attention from police but when rumors surfaced that she'd been assaulted by the mayor's wife, Carlita, during a party at the Manoogian Mansion, homicide detectives were ordered to take a closer look at the slaying. Investigation showed the victim stopped her green 1997 Buick Skylark at the curb to let out her 32-year-old boyfriend. At that moment a white-colored Chevrolet Blazer came around the corner and a man began firing shots at Greene. Five years after the woman's slaying, Police Chief Ella Bully-Cummings made a public appeal through the local Crime Stoppers program for help to solve the homicide. "If you know anything about this case – I would ask that the public provide us with that information," the chief said. The victim's pastor revealed that six months before her death, Greene confided in him that someone was trying to kill her. A week before the murder, someone also attempted to kill Greene's boyfriend and there's still some confusion as to who the intended target was the night she was gunned down. Homicide detectives from the Detroit Police Department are hoping someone will come forward with information to help clear up a mystery that embroiled a number of prominent individuals in a scandal and law suits.

Greene's family members, including a son, Jonathon, who was eight at the time of the killing, are still hoping police will solve the slaying, but some relatives don't believe anyone will be arrested. They described Tamara as an ambition, bright and beautiful person. At the time of the murder she was making plans to open a lingerie store to supply apparel to dancers. She was attempting to change her life and get away from the city's seedy side. Crime Stoppers of Southeast Michigan have offered a reward of up to $1,000 to anyone providing information about the slaying and some police officers have set up a separate reward fund which they hope will total $5,000 to encourage people to come forward.

Find My Killer

Chapter 3 – Hagerman to Jowers

Amber Renee Hagerman
Arlington, Texas

The murder of this nine-year-old girl launched the Amber Alert system, but her killing in Arlington, Texas hasn't been solved. The chain of events that led to the death of Amber Renee Hagerman began shortly after 3 p.m. on Saturday, January 13, 1996 when a man dragged her into his black pick-up truck around the corner from her grandparents' home. Four days later the little Grade 3 student was found dead in a drainage ditch. Her throat had been slashed. Amber and her brother had gone for a ride on their bicycles while visiting their grandparents. They left the home on Highland Drive to cycle around the block, but instead of turning left onto Ruth Street, they made a right hand turn and headed toward Browning Drive and an abandoned Winn Dixie store near East Abram Street where they could race down the loading ramp. Her brother left after only a few minutes but Amber remained to ride her bike around the vacant parking lot. The grandparents sent him back to get his sister when he arrived at their home without her, but a short time later he came back telling them she wasn't there. The grandfather, Jimmie Whitson, immediately drove to the parking lot. There was no sign of Amber, but her pink bicycle was on the ground. A police officer pulled into the lot in response to a 911 caller who saw a man pulling a screaming girl into the front seat of a full-size pick-up truck. It was now obvious that Amber, the girl with blue eyes and brown hair, had been abducted and the Arlington Police Department mobilized to find the victim.

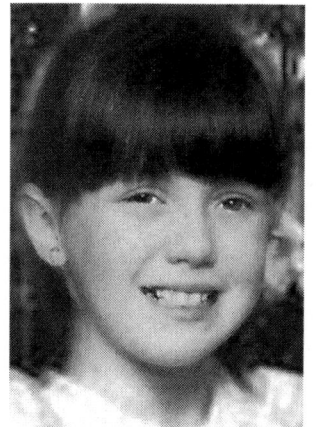

Jimmie Kevil, the eyewitness who called 911, told police the man stopped his vehicle and then sprinted across the parking lot toward the girl. The abductor yanked her from the bike and dragged the terrified and struggling child back to his truck. She was screaming while flailing her arms and kicking with her legs. Kevil, a 78-year-old retired machinist, was in his backyard when he heard the commotion and felt totally helpless as the man drove off. It was clear something was wrong but all he could do was call the police. The only description obtained by investigators suggests the man is either white or Hispanic with a skinny build and possibly in his mid 20s. Amber's mother, Donna, who was 28 at the time and had just separated from her husband, Richard Hagerman, made many appeals and wrote two open letters to the killer, but so far no one has been charged in the slaying. Not wanting their daughter's death to be in vain, the parents worked with local police and media outlets to establish an emergency alert system that had been suggested by Bruce Seybert which would advise the public whenever a child goes missing. The system was implemented across Texas by Governor Rick Perry and in 2003 a law was enacted to operate the Amber Alert program nationwide. Police are continuing to investigate possible suspects and want to hear from anyone who has information they have never revealed about the abduction and murder, or details from anyone who has direct knowledge of who is responsible for the killing of Amber.

Cynthia Haisley
Rochester, Minnesota

She was homeless and living under a bridge in Rochester, Minnesota when someone killed her. It was on Saturday, October 3, 1998 when the body of Cynthia Haisley was found under the bridge crossing Cascade Creek at the entrance to a wilderness park off 16th Street in the affluent northwest section of the city. The 43-year-old victim and mother of two children had spiralled into a life of despair and was surviving outdoors with a couple of derelicts after moving to the city from Kansas several months earlier. She received facial injuries and several skull fractures and investigators surmise she was battered with a rock taken from the waterway's bank. A couple out for a Saturday morning stroll spotted her body sprawled beside the bridge but detectives said an overnight rain had washed away a lot of the evidence. A native of Missouri, her two daughters, Nicole and Nina, were being looked after by her parents who lived in her home town. Police said the transients were using cardboard to insulate them from the cold and wet ground and a few blankets to fight off the chill of the autumn nights. The place was also strewn with wine and alcohol bottles as well as food wrappings and scavenged items they had used to keep themselves alive.

It was a very sad existence, but Haisley would sometimes head over to the Dorothy Day Hospitality Centre, a community funded shelter for the underprivileged on SW 1st Street in the core of the city. Sometimes she would spend time at the Salvation Army hostel on NE 1st Avenue. She could get meals there, shower and get some clothing as the weather began turning cooler. Unfortunately detectives from the Rochester Police Department have been unable to put together a proper timeline in the days leading up to the time Haisley was killed and those who she was living with couldn't provide reliable information because they were highly intoxicated at the time of her death. A $20,000 reward was posted for information that helps solve the slaying, but so far no one has come forward with details that would allow police to identify the killer. Her mother, Donna Mae Creek, died at the age of 74 in November 2008. She was hoping to live long enough to see her daughter's killed arrested. Haisley's daughters and other family members continue to make pilgrimages on a regular basis to the spot where the body was found and lay flowers in Cynthia's memory.

Sara Lynne Halsey
Las Vegas, Nevada

While struggling to prevent a woman from stealing her purse, a 20-year-old university student was shot and killed in Las Vegas, Nevada. Sara Lynne Halsey was standing with a friend in the parking lot of the Shark Club, a former nightclub at 75 East Harmon Avenue around 10:45 p.m. on Friday, May 21, 1993 when a car stopped beside her and the female passenger asked if she had a light for her cigarette. As Sara flicked her lighter, the woman grabbed her purse and tried to pull it from her shoulder. The victim struggled to fend off the would-be thief but was shot once point-blank in the chest as the car drove off. Sara, a student at the University of Nevada in Las Vegas, died a short time later at the hospital.

There were several people in the vehicle, described as a dark 1980s model Pontiac TransAm or Chevy Camaro, and police don't know if the person who fired the gun was a male or female. The passenger had a dark complexion with a soft voice and wearing a dark blue or black baseball cap with a white X on the front. Detectives from the Las Vegas Metro homicide squad said the car was last seen heading westbound on Harmon Avenue towards Las Vegas Boulevard and the north-south 15 Interstate. Sara always had a smile on her face and a bright future ahead of her. Her stepfather, Bill Cavagnaro, who was a lieutenant with the Metro Police Department at the time of her slaying, is convinced the case will be solved. He said someone knows something and they just have to give the information to detectives. Crime Stoppers of Nevada is also offering a reward of up to $1,000 to anyone who anonymously calls their tip line and provides details that solve the case.

Sharon Kay Hammack
Grand Rapids, Michigan

Hours after being reported missing, the body of a 30-year-old prostitute was found in a ditch along a rural roadway south of Grand Rapids, Michigan. A truck driver discovered the body of Sharon Kay Hammack on Thursday, October 3, 1996 on 76th Street SE near Kraft Avenue in the vicinity of the Broadmoor Country Club. The victim, clad only in a bra and wearing a pearl necklace, was wrapped in a blanket. Other items she was wearing at the time of her disappearance were never found. Hammack was last seen about 15 miles away on Banner Street near South Division Avenue and evidence indicated she had been strangled. Homicide detectives from the Kent County Sheriff's Department have not determined a motive, but Hammack is one of 11 women from the Grand Rapid area who were killed in a two year span from 1994. Ten of the victims were involved in the sex trade. Investigators said they hope to talk to anyone who saw Hammack in the hours before she was killed or anyone who might know who was with the victim just prior to the murder.

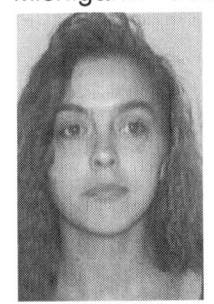

Tenisha Hardy
San Francisco, California

A 15-year-old girl died after being shot while walking along a street with a friend in San Francisco, California. Tenisha Hardy was struck by one of at least two bullets fired on Friday, April 27, 1990 by someone standing with a group of men on Webster Street near Fulton Street.

Investigators didn't specify the exact address where the killing occurred, but Webster between McAllister Street and Grove Street, is a wide roadway with a centre boulevard and multi-dwelling homes and small apartment buildings on both sides. Homicide investigators from the San Francisco Police Department canvassed the neighborhood, but were unable to find people who had information that would help identify the person who killed Tenisha. The victim's mother, Debra Franklin, has become an anti-violence advocate and has attended numerous news conferences and other events through the years where police have appealed for assistance to find perpetrators responsible for various killings. The City of San Francisco approved a $250,000 reward for information leading to the arrest and conviction of Tenisha's killer. Detectives are hoping there is someone who has information and will come forward and tell them who committed the murder.

James Kevin Hargroves
Fort Worth, Texas

A cab driver who was a counselor and minister to the homeless in Fort Worth, Texas was beaten to death in a loft apartment at a warehouse building where he lived with two other people. It was on Friday, September 3, 1993 when James Vincent Hargroves was found unconscious in the unit on the west side of South Jennings Avenue between West Oleander Street and West Magnolia Avenue. Homicide detectives from the Fort Worth Police Department said the 46-year-old man was killed during an apparent robbery. Hargroves was a volunteer for the Fort Worth Area Habitat for Humanity and handed out meals at a nearby soup kitchen as well as serving as board chairman of the Loaves and Fishes food bank organization. There was no sign of a forced entry at the residence and police have not indicated if anyone else was at home when the attack occurred. Hargroves had Bibles in his taxi which he handed out to prostitutes and other street people and it's likely he invited someone back to his home that he met while driving his taxi. Friends said he was always trying to help someone.

Twila Harris
Kansas City, Missouri

Police found a woman stabbed to death after responding to calls for help in the courtyard at a small three storey apartment building in Kansas City, Missouri. They followed a trail of blood and discovered a door ajar in a ground floor apartment unit at 3744 Warwick Boulevard, just north of East 38th Street. The 26-year-old victim, Twila Harris, was on her back and bleeding profusely from stab wounds to her upper body. Shortly before 5 a.m. on Tuesday, October 18, 1994, the victim was pronounced dead at the scene. Neighbors called police after hearing screams coming from the courtyard of the building. They also reported seeing a man running westward along East 38th Street toward Walnut Street. Kansas City Missouri Police have not released a lot of background information on the victim and have not been able to establish a motive for the slaying. A reward is available from Crime Stoppers to anyone who can identify her killer.

Lacy Milton Hatchell
Fort Worth, Texas

The 31-year-old victim attempted to crawl to his Fort Worth, Texas home after being beaten and shot, but he didn't make it. The body of Lacy Milton Hatchell was found by a newspaper carrier in the early morning hours of Friday, December 28, 1984 on the sidewalk only doors from his home at 4743 Poppy Drive East. At the time of his death he was married and had a six-year-old son. It appears the victim was confronted by an attacker when he arrived home after putting in extra hours to take inventory at the pharmacy where he worked. Investigators said Hatchell had just got out of his car a block from his home when the attack occurred. He was savagely beaten and shot through the neck. Gunfire also hit the victim's vehicle and investigators could not ascertain if he was shot while still in the car or just as he was getting out. After being wounded, Hatchell attempted to make his way to his home but didn't have the strength to keep going. He died from a loss of blood and blunt force trauma. Born in Fayetteville, North Carolina on March 3, 1953, Hatchell had plans to leave that morning to take his family to his parent's home for a New Year's get together. Homicide detectives from the Fort Worth Police Department have followed numerous leads through the years but nothing so far has proved fruitful. Investigators are still hoping someone will call with the name of the killer and give them a motive for the slaying. The local Crime Stoppers program has also offered a reward of up to $1,000 for information regarding Hatchell's murder.

Diana Hernandez
Las Vegas, Nevada

She was alone for only a few minutes, but in that time frame a seven-year-old girl vanished from the Las Vegas, Nevada apartment complex where her family lived. Diana Hernandez had just returned to the Sandpiper Village apartments at 3955 Algonquin Drive after visiting a nearby Toys R Us store with her mother. It was about 4 p.m. on Saturday, April 2, 1994, a day before Easter, when Diana headed to her parent's apartment unit while her mother, Maria Hernandez, stopped to talk to someone in the office. That was the last time the little girl was seen alive. The next day her body was found in a garbage dumpster at the northeast corner of the apartment complex. Investigation showed she'd been sexually assaulted and then suffocated. Volunteers were asked to assist officers from the Las Vegas Metropolitan Police Department to search for the missing girl and two months later some of those involved in the hunt officially organized the Nevada Child Seekers Volunteer Search Force. The organization formed in memory of Diana Hernandez, December 11, 1989 – April 3, 1994, remains available today to comb areas whenever someone in the community goes missing. The abduction and slaying of little Diana remains an active file with the Las Vegas police and investigators continue to appeal to the public for information that will lead to an arrest. The local Crime Stoppers program is also offering a reward of up to $1,000 for anyone who calls the tip line and provides information that is instrumental in solving the case.

Evelyn Hernandez & Alex Hernandez
San Francisco, California

A week before she was to give birth, a 24-year-old woman vanished along with her five-year-old son in San Francisco, California. Evelyn Hernandez, who came to the United States from El Salvador at the age of fourteen, spoke by telephone to her sister about 9 p.m. on Wednesday, May 1, 2002 from her apartment at 224 Lowell Street, between Brunswick Street and Byron Court. Earlier in the day she deposited a cheque and made a small cash withdrawal from the automatic teller machine at her bank branch a couple of miles from her apartment. She walked from the bank to a nearby Ross Dress for Less store where she purchased a wallet and then picked up her son, Alex, from Buena Vista Elementary School. Detectives with the San Francisco Police Department have found no one who remembers seeing the woman or her son after May 1. A couple of days after she vanished the wallet that Hernandez bought, was found in a gutter along Linden Avenue near Canal Street. Inside was the $40 she'd taken from the ATM cash dispenser and a government subsidy cheque. The unborn baby's father, Herman Albert Aguilera, officially reported Hernandez missing on May 7, 2002 after being unable to reach Evelyn for several days. Exactly 12 weeks after she disappeared, her badly decomposed torso and legs were found washed up on the shoreline adjacent to The Embarcadero, a waterfront roadway, just north of the San Francisco-Oakland Bay Bridge. On the torso was a maternity blouse. There was no sign of Alex or the full term fetus, a boy she hoped to christen, Fernando.

Aguilera, 36 at the time, was a mechanic with United Airlines and also married. He last saw Evelyn on April 30 when they spent part of the day together. He bought a bed for Alex at a local Ikea store and went to the San Francisco General Hospital to pick up Hernandez who had just undergone final tests before the delivery of their baby. It wasn't until Evelyn got pregnant that Aguilera admitted he was married and with the pending birth, she realized he had no plans to ever leave his wife. He was paying for her apartment and helping with other expenses but she no longer wanted him as her lover. Hernandez did agree to let him visit his soon to be born son but made it very clear their romance had ended. On their final day together, Aguilera drove Evelyn home from the hospital and assembled the bed he'd purchased before driving over to pick up Alex at school. He left the apartment shortly after dropping the boy off and that was the last time he was with Evelyn. The next day, she took a bus to the bank and browsed in several nearby stores before buying the wallet. She went home after collecting her son from his school and at 6 p.m. was seen by a neighbor taking letters that had been delivered to the mailbox of her apartment. Included in the envelopes dropped off by the mailman that day was the government cheque that was found in her wallet. At 9 p.m., with Alex asleep, Evelyn chatted with her sister, who lived 17 miles away in Richmond, about a baby shower she was hosting. Evelyn assured her she'd have no trouble getting there. She also didn't express any fear or indicate anything was wrong during their conversation.

Police would like to find anyone who saw Hernandez anytime after she was last heard from on May 1, 2002. They would like to know is she was under any duress or who she was with. Initially investigators believed she had left the apartment to get away from Aguilera but when she didn't arrive at San Francisco General Hospital around the time of her due date, everyone became increasingly concerned and detectives from the missing persons bureau intensified their search fearing Evelyn, her son, Alex, and the unborn child were victims of foul play. Inside the apartment police located passports for the woman and her son. She was a legal immigrant and had worked as a vocational nurse as well as having jobs through the years at Costco and the Clift Hotel on Geary Street, one of the most elegant places to stay in the city. Evelyn had numerous friends but her disappearance and the eventual discovery of her body didn't ignite the media frenzy or the international headlines that erupted when Laci Peterson vanished from her home in nearby Modesto on Christmas Eve 2002. Twenty-seven year old Peterson was pregnant and scheduled to deliver her first child in February, but her body was found April 14, 2003 on the Bay's eastern shoreline near Richmond. A day earlier her fetus was found about a mile away on the same shore. Her husband, Scott Peterson, was convicted in the murders of Laci and their unborn son, Conner, and sentenced to death.

Evelyn was born on February 23, 1978 and lived in San Francisco's Crocker-Amazon district. She was nineteen when she had Alex. The boy's biological father was in the United States Navy and has never seen his son. She came to the United States with her mother in 1992, but most of her relatives were living in El Salvador when she vanished. Her sister and some of her friends circulated flyers throughout the neighborhood, but couldn't encourage the media to immediately publicize the disappearance. It wasn't until a month later when police held a news conference that the case was mentioned locally on radio and television stations and the San Francisco Chronicle carried an article about a young pregnant woman and her five-year-old son who had mysteriously vanished. All personal belongings of Evelyn and her son were still in the apartment. There was no sign she had rushed out after going into labor. It just appeared as though the two of them failed to exist after leaving the apartment. The wallet was found beside a canal, close to the limousine company where Aguilera had a second job working as a chauffeur. The canal, which flows into the San Francisco Bay, was searched by police divers and both sides scoured by police dogs but there was no sign of the young woman or her son. Her decomposed body washed up on the shoreline beside the Embarcadero adjacent to Folsom Street. It wasn't until September that DNA tests confirmed the remains were those of Evelyn Hernandez but police had already surmised they were and began an investigation into what they referred to as a triple homicide. To date no other parts from Hernandez have been found and they have never located the four-feet, 45 pound Alex or his unborn brother.

Aguilera told authorities he had called Evelyn several times on the evening of May 1 without getting an answer but assumed she just didn't want to talk with him. He drove to within two blocks of her apartment that night, but turned around and went home when he came to the realization their relationship had ended. Aguilera also called the hospital a couple of times to see if she had given birth but after learning she hadn't shown up and her friends had not seen her, he alerted police that she was missing. The mayor's office has authorized a reward totaling $100,000 for information that leads to the arrest and conviction of the person or persons responsible for the death of Hernandez, her unborn fetus and Alex, her five-year-old son. Investigators said they are hoping someone will come forward and provide information that will put them on a path that will resolve the case and bring whoever is responsible to justice.

Helen Hill
New Orleans, Louisiana

Five months after returning to New Orleans following the devastation of Hurricane Katrina, a doctor was wounded and his wife shot dead when an intruder burst into their home. Awakened shortly before 5:30 a.m. on Thursday, January 4, 2007 by a commotion in the backyard at 2444 North Rampart Street, 36-year-old Helen Hill came face to face with a man when she opened the kitchen door. She screamed to her husband, Dr. Paul Gailiunas, who was sleeping in a rear bedroom to call 911. She then yelled at the assailant to leave her baby alone. Gailiunas grabbed their two-year-old toddler who had been sleeping in the same room and made his way toward the living room. At that moment there was a gunshot and Gailiunas, still clutching the baby, saw a gunman standing over his wife. Hoping to get their baby out of harms way, the 35-year-old medical doctor ran to a rear bathroom. With the intruder right behind him and no opportunity to lock the door, Dr. Gailiunas crouched in a fetal position to shield the baby as four shots were fired. Bullets struck his hand, cheek and left forearm, but the baby escaped injury. He rolled to the floor and lay motionless while covering their child with his body. There were no more shots, instead the gunman fled from the house, probably believing he'd also killed the young father and left no one who could identify him. Gailiunas carried the baby to the bedroom and called for help on his cellular phone. He then went back to the entrance to the living room where he saw his wife with a bullet wound to the neck. She had died almost instantly. When police arrived moments later Dr. Gailiunas was cradling the uninjured baby while kneeling over the body of his wife.

Homicide detectives learned the man who killed Hill had tried to force his way into a bed and breakfast operated by a couple four doors away. The 60-yar-old wife was awakened just after 5 a.m. by someone banging at the door. When she answered a black man carrying a gun tried to push past her but she managed to shut the door while calling to her husband. The gunman bolted and cut through the backyard of the home where Gailiunas and his wife lived. Hill opened the back door after hearing the noise and was confronted by the gunman. Her killing was one of five homicides in New Orleans in less than 24 hours and caused outrage among locals who came back to help rebuilt the city, but instead were encountering rampant crime and senseless violence, most fueled by the drug trade.

Dr. Gailiunas and his wife met while they were attending Harvard and had been married 10 years. They moved to New Orleans in 2001 and Gailiunas opened a neighborhood clinic with a partner to provide medical services to low income and poverty-stricken residents in the city. Hill was a filmmaker who had received numerous awards for her work. At the time of her murder she was using a $35,000 grant from the Rockefeller Foundation's Program for Media Artists to produce "The Florestine Collection" an animated feature telling the story of 100 hand-sewn dresses that were rescued from the garbage in New Orleans. Gailiunas and Hill started out as friends in university and two people with very similar interests eventually falling in love. They both knew education was the key to their future together and after graduating from Harvard, Paul Gailiunas pursued his medical degree at Dalhousie University in his hometown of Halifax while Helen Hill traveled to California to attend the California Institute of the Arts in Valencia, near Santa Clarita, some 30 miles north of Los Angeles. After earning her master of fine arts in experimental animation in 1995, Hill joined Gailiunas in Halifax. They were married two years later and Hill became a Canadian citizen with the thought they would spend their lives together in the Maritimes. However, a deep desire to live in New Orleans, developed during a 1992 vacation, drew them to that city. They became part of the social fabric and made many friends in the artistic community. Their son was born in New Orleans on October 17, 2004. Less than a year later they were forced to flee as a Category 5 hurricane with sustained winds of 175 miles an hour churned its way through the Gulf of Mexico on a path that would wreak havoc on the city they now called home.

Before the storm struck, the couple boarded up their home and found sanctuary with Hill's family in Columbia, South Carolina. But they weren't prepared for the devastation that New Orleans endured. They lost most of their possessions when levees broke and their home was flooded with five foot deep water. Not able to immediately return, Hill and her husband spent a year in South Carolina. Once back in New Orleans, Dr. Gailiunas began working at a medical clinic operated by a religious charity a few blocks from his home which provided health care to the poor. Apart from her work in filmmaking, Hill was also an activist for animal rights as well as an anti-smoking and anti-tobacco campaigner. Although Dr. Gailiunas was uncomfortable with the lawlessness that seemed to plague the city, both became entrenched in activities that gave them purpose and they had a common goal of wanting to help rebuild a city that had lost so much.

Born May 9, 1970 in Columbia, South Carolina, Hill attended Dreher High School where she developed her love for animation. Her brother, Jacob, said both his sister and her husband were people who were determined to make a difference. He described Helen as the best person he knew and someone who was sweet, compassionate and selfless. Rewards totaling $15,000 are being made available through the local Crime Stoppers program for information that leads to the arrest and indictment of the killer. Homicide detectives from the New Orleans Police Department said they want anyone who knows who is responsible or is aware of someone who has bragged about the killing to contact them or Crime Stoppers. Both Jacob Hill and Paul Gailiunas have made public pleas asking people to call Crime Stoppers. Dr. Gailiunas also wrote an open letter to the community three weeks after the slaying to let the community know how much everyone had lost with Helen's murder.

"My lovely wife," he wrote, "my lovely wife, and the most interesting, original, beautiful, funny person I have ever known. A stranger invaded our home and attacked us and in the space of a few moments, her life ended violently. Helen Hill was a true creative genius who chose to express herself through the medium of independent filmmaking and experimental animation. She made short, intense, personal, bright, colorful films. She was the best, most loving wife anyone could imagine. And she devoted the last two years to raising our little son, Francis, with the greatest of love, care and creativity. Even before this terrible tragedy, I lived in fear of violence and unpredictability that has become a daily fact of life. But Helen loved New Orleans with a great passion. Helen believed deeply, at the core of her being, in the equality and dignity of all people. She took part in Eracism meetings, the progressive Gillespie Community Breakfasts and political rallies to help bring back New Orleans in the most fair and inclusive way. Together, we brought free meals to the poor and homeless people with the local Food Not Bombs Group. We welcomed our neighbors into our home, African-American, Honduran and white, the neighborhood kids and the elderly. Helen deeply desired to share our love and good fortune with others. I am writing to you, all the citizens of New Orleans, to ask you two things. First, please, if you have any knowledge of the person who killed my wife, please come forward and speak. Please be brave and tell the police or Crime Stoppers what you know. Help bring this villain to justice for filling my wife's final moments with terror and for taking her away from her baby and her family and friends. He must not be allowed to hurt more people and destroy more lives. Please be brave and speak. Second, please do everything you can to heal your desperately broken city. Helen herself was an innocent victim. But her murder, like too many others, is a symptom of a sickness, a terrible sickness caused by grinding poverty, hopelessness, bad parenting, a lack of respect for human life, pre and post hurricane neglect and persistent racism against African-American people. I am begging you to reach out to your neighbors, across the border of race and class, and help them when they need you. Don't stand by while people hurt each other. There has been an outcry against violence in New Orleans since Helen's death. Please do not stop until things improve."

Arlene Hoffman
Laguna Niguel, California

She was business savvy and politically connected but her life wasn't always easy. Since the early years of her marriage she and her husband struggled through legal battles and bankruptcy as they worked to establish their own business. It was like a roller-coaster ride. Arlene Hoffman devoted the early years of her marriage doing secretarial chores and office duties for her husband as well as holding down other jobs to bring in cash, but after a few years was able to seek out her own career as an executive assistant or secretary to the president at some major Southern California firms.

On Friday, December 30, 1994, the day she was beginning a new position as personal secretary for Jim Silva, the newly-elected Orange County supervisor, the 57-year-old woman was found dead in her fashionable condominium in Laguna Niguel, California. She'd been hit in the chest with a hunting arrow fired at very close range.

She was starting her new job on the last working day of what had been a very difficult year. She'd left her job to look after her husband as he battled cancer until his death in May and then spent time grieving and putting perspective in her life. Working in a key position in the top county office was the challenge she needed to ride the roller-coaster to the pinnacle and put her in the backroom of California's political scene.

When millionaire industrialist and philanthropist Norton Simon retired in 1969 as chairman of Hunt Foods, Hoffman also left the company to assist him in an unsuccessful Republican primary battle for a U.S. senate seat. She went to work as an office manager and secretary for Conrad G. Tuohey, a prominent California lawyer and assisted him with his 1972 bid to run for a seat in Congress. He was defeated in a landslide victory by Republican Del M. Clawson. Hoffman wasn't wealthy, but was left with enough money to live comfortably and was able to remain in the home that she had shared with her husband on a quiet crescent off Bear Brand Road in the Camino del Avion and Golden Lantern area of Laguna Niguel, a city of some 60,000 in the San Joaquin Hills near California's Laguna Beach.

When Hoffman failed to show up for a staff meeting on what would have been her first day at work, the county supervisor became concerned and called police when he was unable to contact her by telephone. Sheriff's deputies heard a dog barking and spotted a woman on her back in a pool of blood on the marble floor in the foyer of the condominium. She had bled to death and a pathologist determined the victim had been shot in the chest with a hunting arrow or similar type weapon. The killer had retrieved the arrow from the victim before fleeing. Investigator said nothing was stolen from the home and there was also no sign of a break-in. It's possible the woman had either answered the door to the killer or was shot when retreating into her home after being confronted by someone while taking her pet poodle for a walk. Investigators have never been able to come up with a motive for the slaying or identify a possible suspect.

Friends from New Jersey where she grew up and people who knew her in California said Hoffman was a kind, strong and gentle woman. They didn't know anyone who would want to harm her. She had testified against an eminent doctor and top campaign contributor who was indicted for embezzling money from government run medical insurance programs. The doctor, who served almost three years in prison, died several years ago. Police ruled out any connection with that case and Hoffman's death as well as not finding any links with anyone associated with businesses her husband ran through the years. Her son, Charles, posted a $25,000 reward and Crime Stoppers is also offering money to anyone who can provide information that leads to an arrest.

Jackie Hogue
Bishop Hills, Texas

The body of Jackie Hogue was found in her ranch style home on Thursday, February 24, 1994 by deputies from the Potter County Sheriff's Department who went to check on her well being.

Investigation showed the victim had been murdered, but police have not determined a motive or identified possible suspects.

Bishop Hills, some eight miles northwest of Amarillo, Texas, has a population of about 200 people living in homes scattered on streets nestled in the foothills off Tascosa Road, Hogue worked in the medical field and left behind children who now as young adults are hoping their mother's killer will be found. The Amarillo Crime Stoppers program continues to offer a reward for information that leads to the arrest of the person responsible.

Karina Holmer

Karina Holmer
Boston, Massachusetts

She was an outgoing young woman with a flair for adventure who used a $1,500 lottery win to set out and see the world. Karina Holmer left her village in Sweden and travelled to Dover, Massachusetts, a suburb 20 miles southwest of Boston, where she got a job as a nanny. Her dream of world travel ended sometime after 3:30 a.m. on Saturday, June 22, 1996 when she was seen dancing with down-and-outers in an alleyway running beside the Club Zanzibar, a nightspot on Boylston Street across from the Boston Common in the city's theatre district. Holmer had been partying with friends but after passing out inside the bar she went outside for some fresh air. Bouncers wouldn't let her return and she ended up in the laneway, known as Boylston Place, adjacent to the nine-storey building housing the club. That was the last time that anyone has indicated seeing the 20-year-old blonde woman alive. Karina ended up somewhere in Boston where she was tortured, most likely sexually assaulted and then strangled. The ghoulish killer washed all traces of evidence from his victim's naked body and then cut her in half at the waist. The upper torso was stuffed into an industrial-size black garbage bag which was found shortly after sunrise on Sunday, June 23, 1996 in a refuse container a few blocks from the Zanzibar.

As a young girl and teenager, Karina grew up in Skillingaryd, a village of some 3,800 residents in the southern part of Sweden, about 150 miles from Stockholm. She was described as a nice and beautiful girl. She always wanted to travel and the opportunity came when she scratched a lottery ticket and won 10,000 Krona, which equaled about $1,500 in U.S. currency. It wasn't enough money to completely pay for her travel, so Karina applied for a nanny job and was hired in March 1996 by commercial photographer Frank Rapp and his artist wife, Susan Nichter, to look after their two children. Holmer lived with the family through the week, but on weekends had use of an apartment Rapp used as a studio on A Street, in the vicinity of the Massachusetts Turnpike and the SE Expressway, just east of the entertainment area. Being away from home for the first time, she enjoyed the freedom and loved to party with friends. The night Holmer vanished she had gone with three friends to the Zanzibar, one of a number of clubs along Boylston Street, between Charles Street South and Tremont Street. She danced and through the night had way too much to drink. When she left to get some air, people described her as being wasted.

Investigators found one individual who recalled seeing her walking from the area with an older man. Police tracked down a number of people who were at the trendy bar but were never able to link them with the disappearance and slaying of the young au pair. It was a man searching garbage containers for pop cans and bottles that he could return for cash who discovered the victim's remains. The piece of body located in the dumpster weighed 48 pounds. Forensic tests showed Holmer had been strangled with a rope or cord and not as a result of the killer putting his hands around her neck. There was no bruising on the body indicating any sort of beating and no evidence that she was able to fight back. There was a high level of alcohol in her blood stream and the pathologist thought she might have been in an incapacitated state before being killed. This is a case that has haunted detectives not only because of the brutality, but the fact someone took the life of an innocent young woman as she tried to fulfill her dream of travelling the world.

John Young Ki Hong
Norristown, Pennsylvania

For more than a dozen years John Young Ki Hong operated Young's Grocery Store at 199 West Spruce Street in Norristown, Pennsylvania. That changed in the afternoon of New Year's Eve in 2001 when the 59-year-old convenience store owner was stabbed to death during a robbery. A $10,000 reward has been posted by the Citizen's Crime Commission for information leading to the arrest and conviction of Hong's killer. It was sometime between 1:30 p.m. and 2 p.m. on Monday, December 31 when an attacker lunged across the counter and stabbed the victim numerous times. Hong fell to the floor and died within minutes from severe blood loss. The attacker grabbed the cash register and fled. A few minutes later a customer discovered Hong in a pool of blood. She ran across the street and called 911 for help, but an ambulance crew arrived too late to save the man's life. He was pronounced dead at the scene.

Hong had been working alone in the store to make sure people had the opportunity to pick-up any last minute items they may require to celebrate the arrival of the New Year. Many of his regular customers had dropped in, some just to wish him well and encouraging him not to stay open too late. He was planning to close the store a bit early and be home with his wife who over the years had shared the work of running the neighborhood store in the city of 31,000, about 16 miles northwest of Philadelphia. Hong's daughter ran to the store as word of the stabbing spread like wildfire through the neighborhood. She screamed in anguish and collapsed into the arms of a police officer when she realized her father was dead.

Gordon Glantz, the managing editor of the Norristown Times Herald, has written articles about the slaying urging people to come forward. He described Hong as a man with a soft spot for neighborhood kids who couldn't afford to buy candy and also someone who had no tolerance for thieves. It's likely the store owner was attacked after attempting to spurn the bandits demand to hand over the cash. Through the years police have focused on Lark Ramsey, described as "one of baddest, most violent and dangerous thugs" in the community. Since 1985 when he turned 18, Ramsey has been in and out of jail for drugs, assault, robbery, weapons and escape attempts. He is currently serving an 18 to 40 year sentence for bank robbery and sexually assaulting a 15-year-old girl. Additional charges have been filed against him after a nursing assistant was choked during a rape attempt inside the state prison.

Investigators said Ramsey is a strong suspect but they are trying to determine if others took part in the robbery where Hong died. It's possible a couple of people were inside the store on the north side of West Spruce Street between Cherry Street and Maple Alley. They also don't know if someone was waiting in a car, but since the cash register was carted away, it's most likely the attacker fled in a vehicle. Detectives are convinced there are people who have information that will answer the question as to who was responsible for the killing of Hong. Seven years after the killing in July 2008, Montgomery County District Attorney Risa Vetri Ferman said she knows "without a doubt that there are people who know the murderer and some of his associates." She said people know what happened, how it happened and why it happened. "We would ask those people who have refused to speak with us in the past or who have not cooperated with us in the past to come forward and help us. It would be an important step for the community in Norristown to seek closure in this murder case."

Vahid Hosseini, San Jose, California

The police report lists the crime type as homicide, section 187 of the penal code. It was at 4:25 p.m. on Friday, May 23, 2008 when a gunman targeted a businessman in the parking lot of the Bank of the West at 1010 South 1st Street, between Edwards Avenue and Goodyear Street in San Jose, California. The 47-year-old victim, Vahid Hosseini, a popular local shopkeeper and president of the largest mosque in the area, was critically wounded when shot in the head. He lingered in hospital for 11 days before succumbing to the injury. Hosseini had operated the Willow Market at 215 Willow Street in the predominantly Hispanic neighborhood for more than 25 years. His store sat on the north side of the street between Vine Street and South Almaden Avenue. Friends had urged him to move his business a few blocks away to a safer and more upscale spot, but Hosseini scoffed at their concern. He had no fear of the gangbangers, drug dealers and other hoodlums who's renamed the area Ghetto Glen after claiming local streets as their territory.

As he did every Friday, Hosseini drove his Lexus three blocks to the t-intersection where Willow Street met South 1st Street and pulled into the bank's parking lot. He made his usual $50,000 withdrawal and was carrying the cash from the bank in a canvass tote bag when accosted by a gunman. After grabbing the bag the attacker, wearing a black-hooded sweatshirt, fired a single shot into the victim's head and then ran toward a gray or silver-colored sports utility vehicle occupied by two other people. The gunman and the occupants of the vehicle were Hispanic males described as being in their 20s and 30s.

On June 3 when Hosseini died, his 43-year-old wife, LeeAnn, was with him. He also has two daughters, Cassandra and Alexandra, who were 25 and 20 at the time of his death. Although she tried to run the store, the murder of her husband devastated her life. Her weight dropped drastically and she needed counseling to cope. Her husband was a kind man. The money he was withdrawing from the bank was to cash pay cheques for his Latino customers, many who didn't have the proper documentation to open bank accounts. His employees, some with him for more than 10 years, adored him and he was loyal to his family, his friends and the other people who ran businesses in the neighborhood. Hosseini had worked to combat crime, graffiti and loitering that had become rampant in the area of town where his market was located and he was considered a good friend of law enforcement. He was also passionate about his mosque and for 10 years served in various capacities, including president, on the board of directors of the Shia Association of the Bay Area.

No one could believe that a bandit could target and execute the owner of the Willow Market. They could see him being the victim of a robbery because of his regular habit of picking up a large amount of cash every Friday, but they couldn't understand why someone would deliberately kill him. The murder was described by police as callous. After grabbing the tote bag, the bandit pressed his gun to the back of the victim's head and pulled the trigger. The bank is situated between a Wash N' Dry store to the north and a wheel alignment and tire business on the other side. Cars are able to enter the parking lot from both South 1st Street and South 2nd Street. The bandits were probably stopped on one of those streets keeping watch to determine which of the bank's two parking lots Hosseini would use. When he entered the bank they pulled the SUV into the same lot and one suspect positioned himself near the bank wall where he could ambush the victim as he walked towards his vehicle. Investigators said the robbery was carried out with lightning speed with the sports utility vehicle racing away seconds after Hosseini slumped to the pavement. There were no security cameras in the parking lot and investigators said they could only get a general description of the assailants from witnesses who saw their vehicle speeding away.

Rewards totaling $40,000 have been posted by the bank, the Shia association and various donors for information leading to the arrest of the killer. San Jose Crime Stoppers has also offered $1,000 for anyone anonymously providing a tip that helps identify the gunman.

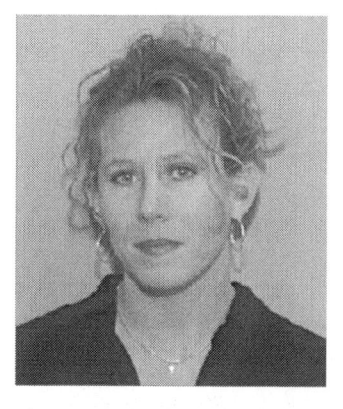

Melissa Lynn Howard
Crestview, Florida

A divorced mother of three was stabbed to death in her Crestview, Florida home shortly after being awarded custody of her young son. The body of Melissa Lynn Howard was found by three friends who forced their way into her Tiffot Court home around 11 p.m. on Friday, January 6, 2006. The 33-year-old victim had been repeatedly stabbed in the neck during a vicious altercation. There was also blunt force trauma to her head, but investigators said that injury could have resulted when she fell to the floor. Howard, a surgical nurse at the North Okaloosa Regional Medical Center, was murdered sometime through the evening. Howard's oldest daughter summoned help from her boyfriend and two other people to get into the house after coming home and finding the door locked. The victim had been alone through the evening but police said there was no sign that anyone had broken into the small brick house at 222 Tiffot Court, a dead-end street running south from Kyle Lane in this Florida panhandle community of 22,000 people, some 50 miles east of Pensacola. Police canvassed residents in the quiet neighborhood where the killing occurred, but no one noticed anything out of the ordinary through the evening. Evidence collected by forensic investigators from the Florida Department of Law Enforcement has indicated only one person was involved in the slaying and a knife was likely used to kill the victim, but no weapon was found during a comprehensive search of the home and adjoining property. Furniture was shifted out of position and some items knocked to the floor indicating a substantial struggle had taken place. The victim also had defensive wounds on her hands indicating she had attempted to ward off the attack.

Howard, who had worked at the hospital for five years, would have been alone through the evening until around 11 p.m. when her daughters were expected to arrive home after being out with friends on Friday night. Although she had gained custody of her son, Taylor, a grade 5 student, he was spending the night with her ex-husband, Brian Dean Howard, at his home almost five miles away on Beacons Bend Road. He had fought a three year custody battle to have the boy permanently live with him. During the time frame when Melissa Lynn was murdered, Howard indicated he spent some time at a restaurant with his son and then went home. He was at home when police arrived shortly after the killing to advise him of the murder. Investigative reports note there was a large pool of blood beside the victim, indicating she probably bled to death after the attack. Investigators from the Crestview Police Department are appealing for anyone with information on the murder to contact them and the Emerald Coast Crime Stoppers program in Okaloosa County is offering a reward of up to $1,000 for anyone who anonymously calls the tip line and provides information that solves the homicide.

George Calvin Hurst
Lexington, Kentucky

A 73-year-old man who had just won some money in a lottery was shot to death outside his Lexington, Kentucky home. Police received a call at 6 a.m. Sunday, October 21, 2001 and found George Calvin Hurst face down on the sidewalk at 424 Gunn Street. He had been shot and was pronounced dead a short time later. Police were told that a man and woman, both described as being black, drove off in a gold colored Saturn about an hour before the victim was found. The woman was wearing a white sweater and had some sort of covering on her head and the man was dressed in a brown and white jacket. Detectives from the Lexington Division of Police have very little information regarding this killing and are appealing for anyone to come forward and provide any details they may have to help identify the killers. The local Bluegrass Crime Stoppers program is also offering a reward of up to $1,000 for information that assists in solving the case.

Byron K. Hutchins & Keith Andre Hutchins
Fort Wayne, Indiana

Four days after a domestic dispute at a home in the Pontiac Place district of Fort Wayne, Indiana, police were recalled to the house for a double slaying. Around 11:30 a.m. on Monday, April 5, 2004 a neighbor found the bodies of Byron K. Hutchins, 37, and Keith A. Hutchins, 36, at 3110 Abbott Street. Both men had been shot in the head. The home, situated on the west side of the well groomed and tree-lined street between Eckart Street and Drexel Street, was occupied by Keith Hutchins, his wife, Patricia and her daughters, Kerria and Angelia Williams. The two men were cousins. Homicide investigators were unable to determine a motive for the killings and have not found anyone who heard a commotion or saw anything suspicious. Authorities have not indicated if anyone else was at the house when the shootings occurred. The neighbor who called police said he found the front door ajar and spotted a body on the floor after going inside to make sure everything was okay. The man immediately ran home to call police. The second victim was discovered by police, but investigators have not indicated exactly where each body was situated in the house. Police interviewed people in the area and learned two men left the residence a short time before the neighbor found the bodies. Keith, who was born November 20, 1967 in Fort Wayne, had served with the U. S. Army until 1991 when he received an honorable discharge. Byron, who graduated from Snider High School in 1983, is survived by his wife, Pamela, a son, Byron and a daughter, Bria. Family members of both men were unable to suggest any reason for the killings and Crime Stoppers has offered a $1,000 reward to encourage anyone to anonymously call if they know who is responsible.

Reginald Infante
Fairfield, California

There are descriptions from a couple of witnesses but virtually no physical evidence to help police in Fairfield, California solve the drive-by shooting of a 14-year-old boy. Reginald Infante was walking with two friends around 9:55 p.m. on Friday, June 12, 1998 on Tanglewood Drive near Bay Tree Drive when five shots were fired. They had watched a softball game at Laurel Creek Park and were heading to the Solano Bistro on Claybank Road. The three were walking eastbound along the residential street in the upper middle class neighborhood when a car drove up from behind and a passenger stuck his head from the window and yelled at the trio asking if they had a problem. The dark blue or black Honda Prelude then made a u-turn and as the vehicle drew alongside a volley of shots rang out in rapid succession. Reginald was struck in the back but the other boys, aged 15 and 16, were not hurt. Neighbors, who heard the gunfire, assisted the boy until emergency crews arrived. He was rushed to the NorthBay Medical Centre where he was pronounced dead at 7:15 p.m. Saturday, June 13 after being taken off life support. Homicide detectives from the Fairfield Police Department described it as a random shooting. They also indicated the boys were not affiliated with any gangs and hadn't been involved in any sort of a dispute with anyone prior to the shooting.

Investigators have not been able to determine a motive for the slaying or identify specific suspects. The shots were fired from a .22 caliber weapon by a passenger in the vehicle who was described as a white male, 17 to 18 years old with close cropped spiked blond hair shaved at the sides. He was possibly wearing a blue and yellow Michigan State University jersey. Witnesses were unable to describe the driver, but said the car appeared to be a four-door 1992 Honda Prelude with dark tinted windows, low to the ground with chrome trim or skirting all around the vehicle.

Reginald, known as Reggie to family and friends, lived with his parents in Suisun City, a community of 26,000 about three and a half miles to the south of Fairfield. He had just graduated from Grade 8 at Grange Middle School the day before being shot and his mother and father, Reden and Cecilia Infante, have held rallies and vigils to keep public attention focused on the murder. They also put up a personal reward and hope the hunt for their son's killer will continue until an arrest is made. Reginald loved playing basketball and was active in the local chapter of the DeMonlay organization that helps people 12 to 21 prepare to be future leaders and with the Reach Youth Ministry, a Catholic sponsored program that organizes retreats for young people. He also enjoyed karaoke singing. The killing wasted the life of a young teenager who hoped some day to make a difference in the lives of others. William R. Gresham, Fairfield's interim Police Chief, described the killing as a cowardly act and in September 2002 the then California governor, Gray Davis, authorized a $50,000 reward for the arrest and conviction of those responsible for the boy's killing.

Arlene Ivey
Thomaston, Georgia

A 78-year-old woman was strangled by attackers who ransacked her trailer home in a rural area in Upson County south of Thomaston, Georgia. The body of the victim, Arlene Ivey, was found around 10 a.m. on Thursday, September 15, 2005 in Potato Creek at Hannah's Mill Road, a thickly forested area north of Thomaston, a town of some 9,600 resident. Detectives from the Upson County Sheriff's Department later discovered the victim's home on Wonnum Road, a private drive servicing a trailer community between Highway 80 and Allen Road, in the hamlet of Salem, had been partially ransacked. Evidence indicates the woman was overpowered and killed before being driven some 16 miles from her home in south Upson County and dumped in the creek. A $1,000 reward was posted for information leading to the identification, arrest and conviction of the killer or killers.

Ronald & Christine Jabalee

Ronald & Christine Jabalee
New Baltimore, Michigan

A message written in blood may identify the killer of a New Baltimore, Michigan couple. The bodies of Ronald and Christine Jabalee, both 58, were found in the garage of their home around 7 a.m. on Saturday, October 7, 2006 after they failed to show up for work at their family-owned meat store. The murder occurred some 12 hours earlier and an autopsy showed the victims were savagely beaten and then stabbed numerous times. Ron worked weekdays at a major food distribution company in Detroit while his wife and their three children, Nikki, Ryan and Ron, ran the family business, RJ's Meats, in the vicinity of the Fisher and Chrysler Freeway interchange near the Eastern Market in Detroit. On Saturdays the couple would make an early drive from their home, some 35 miles to the north, to help serve customers on what was usually the store's busiest day. When they failed to arrive Ryan called his girlfriend who lived in the New Baltimore area and asked her to check on his parents. Police were called a short time later after she saw blood flowing down the driveway from the garage.

Investigation showed the couple had dinner together and Ronald went to the garage while his wife sat in the den watching television. It appears the killer came up the driveway and had a casual conversation with Ronald. Investigators said it's possible he may have even known the individual. At some point Christine came out, possibly after hearing voices. There was then an argument which escalated into a violent struggle where both Ronald and his wife were severely beaten. Two knives were missing from a butcher block in the kitchen of the home at 53355 Washington Street and detectives from the New Baltimore Police Department theorize the killer went into the house and retrieved them before stabbing the couple to death. While on the floor and bleeding profusely, one of the victims, possibly Christine Jabalee, scrawled a message on the garage floor with blood. Unfortunately the killer spotted the writing and washed most of it away before leaving. The letters – S S E U I C – were found under the car but police so far have been unable to decipher what the couple was trying to say.

Investigators don't even know if the couple tried to leave a message for their children or were indicating who was responsible for the murder. The time of death is estimated during a two hour period from 6 p.m. to 8 p.m. Ronald usually called his son on Friday night to find out how sales had gone, but that evening he didn't call. When the couple failed to arrive at the store early the next morning, the children realized something was wrong but they could never have imagined anyone would kill their parents.

Investigators were told the couple didn't have an enemy in the world and were well respected and liked by everyone in their community of 11,000 residents as well as in the food industry where Jabalee had worked all his adult life. It appears, however, that the killer had devised an elaborate plan to get access to the home on the roadway directly across from Andrew Circle in the northwest section of New Baltimore. Police said the attacker was carrying a gasoline can and may have pretended his car was out of fuel. If Jabalee didn't know him, the killer probably indicated he lived in the community and may have engaged in some small talk before Jabalee's wife came into the garage. Police have ruled out robbery as a motive since Jabalee's wallet was still in his pocket and Christine was wearing some valuable jewelry. It also doesn't appear that the home was ransacked. The victims received blunt trauma injuries and it's likely the killer brought some type of club with him or found something in the garage which he used to attack both victims who were beaten about the head and body. Investigators stressed that it wasn't a random type of incident, but the victims seem to have been targeted for some reason. Investigators have wondered if the slayings could be somehow connected to Jabalee's brother, Roger, who was sent to prison for a minimum of seven years after being implicated in a drug trafficking operation involving members of outlaw motorcycle gangs. The Detroit-based Crime Stoppers' 1-800-SpeakUp program is offering a $160,000 reward for information leading to the arrest of those responsible for the murders of Ronald and Christine Jabalee. The money came from contributors who wanted Crime Stoppers to put up more than the $1,000 they traditionally offer to anonymous callers. Initially they had pledges totaling $200,000, but the total has dwindled since there were time limits on some of the money that had been offered. Investigators said they hope someone will come forward soon and provide the critical pieces of information that are still needed to identify the person responsible for the murders of the Jabalee couple. They have described the killings as senseless and said help is needed to give justice to the two victims and their family.

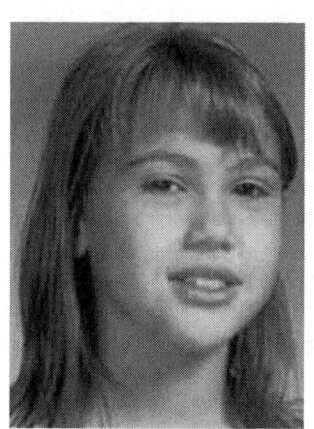

Adreanna Anita Jackson
Lakewood, Washington

The fourth-grader left her family's apartment in Lakewood, Washington not sure if school would be closed because of an overnight snow storm. Tillicum Elementary School was closed but 10-year-old Adreanna Anita Jackson didn't arrive home and there was no sign of her until skeletal remains were found on Tuesday, April 4, 2006 in an overgrown lot some two miles from her home in the area of Portland Avenue and Wadsworth Street Southwest. Her father, Jon Federicci told authorities he walked her partway to school and it wasn't until late in the afternoon he and his wife, Yvette Gervais, realized their young daughter was missing. She was last seen around 7:45 a.m. on Friday, December 2, 2005 and no one remembered seeing the girl anywhere along the seven-block walk from the apartment to the school on Maple Street. Rewards of up to $60,000 have been offered for information leading to the arrest and conviction of whoever is responsible for the Adreanna's death, but so far police haven't found any evidence to assist them in identifying possible suspects. A number of law enforcement agencies working on the case, including members of the Federal Bureau of Investigation, have expressed frustration because pathologists were not able to provide a cause of death or establish positively that the girl was a homicide victim. During the four months since the disappearance all that remained were the skull and a piece of her spinal column. Identification was confirmed through dental records.

Prior to the disappearance of Adreanna, a number of other young girls have gone missing in the Tacoma area through the years and some were murdered.

- Michella Welch, 12, of Tacoma vanished March 26, 1986 while playing with her younger sisters at Puget Park. She was found dead a few hours later.
- Denise L. Sallee, 17, of Pierce County was found partially buried March 29, 1986 in Parkland. She disappeared from a bowling alley at a Tacoma shopping mall on January 24, 1986.
- The body of Shan M. Morehouse, 15, of Auburn was located March 14, 1986 in some woods at Seward Park in Seattle. She died from blows to the head.
- Thirteen-year-old Jennifer Marie Bastian didn't come home after going for a bicycle ride on August 4, 1986. Her body was found 24 days later 20 yards off a pathway in Point Defiance Park.
- The remains of Rose Marie Kurran, 16, of Lynnwood were found in a plastic bag on August 31, 1987 near the Sea-Tac Airport. She frequently hitchhiked and was last seen on the Pacific Highway.

- The body of Debbie Gonzales, 14, of Auburn was found in a wooded area beside the Auburn-Black Diamond Highway, west of Black Diamond on September 26, 1987. An autopsy failed to determine the cause of death.
- A day after she disappeared from the Ponders Corner near her home in Tacoma, Shannon L. Pease, 15, was found April 4, 1988 in a Lakewood area field.
- The body of Kimberly DeLange, 15 of Sumner was found August 20, 1988 off Highway 410, east of Enumclaw. She was last seen at the Puyallup Shopping Center.
- Kerry Anne Walker, 15, of Renton, a freshman at Renton High School, was found dead December 22, 1989 north of Tukwila. Her mother last saw Kerry Anne asleep at their home two days earlier when she left for work.
- The body of Michelle Koski, 17 of Seattle was found August 25, 1990 near the intersection of Highway 522 and Echo Lake Road in Monroe. She had been strangled.
- The body of Anna Lee Chebetnoy, 14, of Puyallup, Washington was discovered on September 17, 1991 just off Highway 410, east of Enumclaw in around the same location where the remains of Kimberly DeLange were found two years earlier.
- Sarah Habakangas, 17, was found strangled November 5, 1991 off Interstate 90, east of North Bend. She had moved to Tacoma six months earlier from Virginia.
- Three-year-old Lenoria Jones of Tacoma disappeared July 20, 1995 while with her aunt at a Target store on South 23rd Street. There has been no trace of her since that time.
- And two-year-old Teekah Lewis vanished while with her mother at a Tacoma bowling alley on January 23, 1999. She also hasn't been found.

All of these homicide and missing person cases remain unsolved.

Linda Gayle Jackson
Amarillo, Texas

Her killing in Amarillo, Texas was brutal and may be linked to the murder of another woman in the city a month earlier. Police were called to what was thought to be a traffic accident around 7:15 a.m. on September 11, 1997 but found the body of Linda Gayle Jackson on North Wilson Street, between Knight Street and La Mesa Avenue, an isolated stretch of unpaved roadway in the city's east end. Investigators said the killer beat the 35-year-old victim unconscious and then dumped her body from his vehicle and drove over her. Jackson, a known prostitute, was pronounced dead at the scene. A month before her death the woman had witnessed the killing of another prostitute, Gloria Ann Covington, and provided a description of the killer to police. Members of the Amarillo Police Department Special Crimes Unit haven't found specific evidence to tie the cases together, but it's possible the same individual murdered both women. Jackson, the mother of two daughters, was born in Amarillo, graduated from high school and attended Amarillo College for a couple of years. She had worked for a while at a local computer company. Through the years detectives have undertaken a number of initiatives to encourage people to come forward with information, including putting up a 30 foot billboard appealing for help. Police said they are continuing their efforts to find anyone who can help solve the Jackson's slaying. The Amarillo Crime Stoppers has also offered a reward of up to $1,000 for anyone who will call the tip line anonymously and provide details that will lead to the arrest of the killer.

Patricia Gail Jackson-Lee
Fort Worth, Texas

Homicide investigators are still trying to determine why someone wanted to kill a 27-year-old woman found with her hands tied behind her back in Fort Worth, Texas. The body of Patricia Gail Jackson-Lee was discovered on Sunday, September 3, 1995 in a vacant field in the 500 block of Precinct Line Road. An autopsy showed she had been strangled with a piece of clothing. The Tarrant County Crime Stoppers program in Forth Worth is offering a reward of up to $1,000 for information that helps solve this case and detectives from the Fort Worth Police Department are hoping someone will come forward soon with information.

Gary Jenkins
Sharon Hill, Pennsylvania

The body of a 47-year-old man was found in his apartment after he failed to show up for work following a weeklong vacation. It was on Monday, May 7, 2007 when police went to the home of Gary Jenkins on Reese Street in Sharon Hill, Pennsylvania and found his body wrapped in a comforter in a second floor hallway. He had been savagely beaten and stabbed multiple times.

Described as a dedicated employee who had worked himself up from an entry level position to a department head at CAPP/USA in Clifton Heights, co-workers were very concerned about his well-being when he didn't return after a brief holiday. When management personnel made repeated calls to his home number and mobile telephone without getting an answer, the Sharon Hill Police Department was notified and a car dispatched to check his two-storey, semi-detached home located between Calcon Hook Road and Coates Street.

Police found the body at 12:25 p.m. but they didn't reveal when the slaying occurred. Although the back sliding door was unlocked investigators have said they believe the victim likely knew his killer and had let the individual into the house. Coworkers said Jenkins was a quiet person who kept to himself but was always willing to help at work. It was totally out of character when he didn't show up after his vacation and that's why everyone got immediately concerned. The company where he worked, a major manufacturer of environmental controls, has posted a $2,500 reward and police hope someone will come forward who saw something suspicious on the street where Jenkins lived or can help trace his movements through the week he was on vacation.

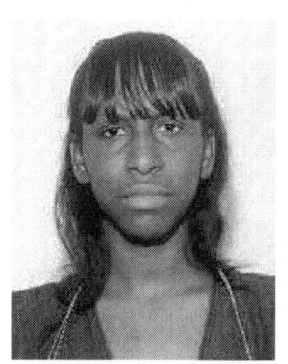

Alisha "Lisa" Johnson
Marshall, Virginia

A week after a 19-year-old woman vanished in Alexandria, Virginia, a portion of her leg was found some 50 miles away in Fauquier County. The victim, Alisha "Lisa" Johnson was last seen around 2 p.m. on Sunday, July 28, 1996 when she left a friend's apartment to purchase some hair gel at the former McCrory Five and Dime store on Mount Vernon Avenue. She was never seen alive again. Alisha, a single mother of two who was known as "Lisa" to family and friends, went to a Washington DC club the previous evening to listen to go-go music and spent the night at her girlfriend's apartment on Four

Mile Road. She came home to get a change of clothing around 3 a.m. and wasn't expected to return until sometime after dinner on Sunday. After not hearing from her for a couple of days, family members reported Alisha missing to the Alexandria Police Department. Although her leg was found on the lawn of a home in Marshall and subsequent searches by police dogs turned up another leg several days later in a wooded area half a mile away, the severed limbs were not linked to the disappearance of Johnson until four years later. Unfortunately the anthropologist who examined the legs concluded they were from a white female between 20 and 30 years old. Johnson was black and computerized searches failed to match up the body parts with her missing person report. Deputies from the Fauquier County Sheriff's Department undertook numerous searches over a wide area where the legs had been discovered but didn't locate any other remains from the victim. It was only through a computerized DNA check that investigators got definitive information the legs came from Johnson. Officers from the Fauquier County Sheriff's Department have teamed up with the Alexandria Police Department and have tracked down numerous leads in the past few years but still haven't determined a motive or come up with a possible suspect.

Until told Alisha was dead, family members distributed missing person flyers and held annual vigils in the neighborhood where she vanished. Her mother and sisters always held hope she would be found alive and were devastated to learn she was a victim of murder. The vigils are now memorial services and family members have used them to issue appeals for justice. They want the killer found not only so he can be punished for the crime but to have the opportunity to find out where her other remains are so they can give Alisha a proper burial. The family has been plagued with tragedy since Alisha vanished. Her sister, 27-year-old Sonya Johnson, was murdered in 2002 by a man she was living with and Sonya's two-year-old daughter, Sade, was killed in 1998 by a caregiver who immersed her in a bathtub filled with scalding water. Alisha's life was also filled with turmoil. She was a mother at a young age and in the past made some bad choices when picking friends. She liked to party and still had a teenage wild streak which got her into trouble with the police a couple of times. However, friends said she was trying to turn things around when she disappeared. She was spending more time with her children, a daughter, who was four at the time and a one-year-old son. They said Lisa realized there was a much better future ahead and had just started setting some goals when her life was taken away.

Lativia Johnson
Grand Rapids, Michigan

The eight-year-old was just reaching for milk in the refrigerator after helping her family decorate for Christmas when a shotgun blast came through the window of the family's Grand Rapids, Michigan home. Lativia Johnson was killed instantly when struck in the head on Thursday, December 16, 1993 at the two storey house located at 1150 Ionia Avenue SW, just north of Hall Street. Grand Rapids Police have made numerous appeals through the years, but have never been able to determine who fired the shot that killed the little girl. Investigators have no motive and very little evidence. They are relying on someone to come forward and help them solve the mystery of this shooting.

Nick Johnson
Sprague, West Virginia

A retired miner was found dead in his Sprague, West Virginia home following a brutal attack. Cold case squad investigators from the West Virginia State Police said evidence indicated Nick Johnson was overpowered and assaulted on Thursday, June 8, 1978 probably after answering the door to someone. The victim lived alone in this community, just north of Beckley and until retiring spent most of his life working in coal mines throughout the area. He enjoyed frequenting Barney's Bar in Beckley to swap stories with friends and probably opened the door of his home thinking someone had dropped by to see him. West Virginia State Police investigators said they want to hear from anyone who may have information that will help solve Johnson's killing.

Annete Jones
Kalamazoo, Michigan

The 23-year-old victim was bound and gagged before being strangled in Kalamazoo, Michigan. The body of Annete Jones was found on Wednesday, November 13, 1991 at her home at 123 West Dutton

Street, a three-storey walk-up, near South Burdick Street. No other details of the homicide are available.

Walter Allen Jones
Hope Mills, North Carolina

A retired Army Staff Sergeant and former high school ROTC drill instructor was killed while trying to prevent burglars from entering his Hope Mills, North Carolina home. Walter Allen Jones was shot around 1:39 a.m. on Thursday, July 24, 2003 after encountering one or more intruders at the rear door of his residence on Country Downs Drive, just off Thrower Road, some seven miles southeast of the town center in the Gray's Creek area. The 54-year-old victim went to the rear door after hearing some sort of noise. His wife, Chun, who has muscular dystrophy and unable to walk, was in bed but pressed a panic alarm after hearing the gunfire.

When deputies from the Cumberland County Sheriff's Department arrived at the house they found Jones collapsed on the back porch. He was pronounced dead at the scene. Investigation showed the burglars had been trying to enter the home through a side window or other locations and made their way to the rear of the house when they heard Jones at the back door. The victim sold men's clothing at flea markets and Sheriff's office detectives said it's possible the burglars knew he sometimes kept money at home. In fact, there was a break-in at the house two weeks before the killing where some $2,000 in cash was stolen. Investigators want anyone with information to contact their office or the Fayetteville/Cumberland County Crime Stoppers program which is offering a reward of up to $1,000 for anonymous tips on the case. A reward is also available from the Carole Sund/Carrington Memorial Reward Foundation in California.

Joseph "Todd" Jowers
Tuscaloosa, Alabama

The life of Joseph "Todd" Jowers ended on Sunday, October 13, 1996 in the parking lot of a Tuscaloosa, Alabama nightclub. The 32-year-old victim had just walked a friend to her car and was heading toward his vehicle when someone fired a single gunshot into his head. The shooting occurred between 2 a.m. and 2:15 a.m. and robbed a family of their oldest child and only son. Since that fateful night the victim's parents, Walter and Norma Jean Jowers, have mourned their loss while living in hope that their son's killer will be found. They recall with joy the day, May 25, 1964, when Todd was born, but describe his murder as the most tragic and terrible day of their lives. They have also shared their feelings on a web site set up in his memory and described what they have gone through since police came to their door in 1996. Despite the pain, they remain driven by the dream that someone will come forward with information to solve the slaying.

A poem written by his father a year after the killing gives a glimpse into who Todd was and the heartache the family has experienced because of a gunman's senseless act.

With a smile on his face.
With a song in his heart.
Remember him this way,
for we know he is in a better place.

With every new day, we meet more friends
he held dear;
And comfort comes in knowing,
he's gone on,
On to past loved ones;
they draw him near.

We shall all reflect of missed good-byes
and ponder of our love for him.
Did we love him enough?
Did he really know?

Our fear of death is of the moment itself;
not our destination or the
great love awaiting;
When God calls us home,
we shall see him again
and rejoice as we go!

He has left us in such a tragic way;
Our hearts and minds are filled
with great anger and deep sorrow untold.

We try with God's help
as each day goes by;
night comes like a friend
and once again in our dreams.

Our Child we do hold.
Our hearts have been tested from
other loved ones gone on;
tho I think nothing can be worse
as the loss of our Child.

Memories, tears, laughter,
good friends and loved ones,
Helps fill your heart and mind;
But nothing fills your arms,
that's what aches the most.

Just to hold your Child;
Please God, Once more,
for just a little while!

His mother has also attempted to put their anguish into perspective and give understanding to those who may lose a child through illness, accident or even the tragedy of a homicide. "I have really learned a lot about grief in reading and through the experience of grieving. In grief you go through many stages. You should not try to busy yourself to the point that you do not grieve properly. You're asking "What is the proper way to grieve?" There is no proper way; it is a physical and emotional track you will follow. Grief is the hardest work you will ever do! It drains you of physical, emotional and spiritual stamina. Unless you pace yourself and direct your energies toward your grief recovery, you will experience physical illness, emotional despair, relational detachments as well as possibly bitterness.

"You must allow time to grieve. Allow time to let your body and mind recover. Lean into the pain; face the grief head on because the grief will be waiting long after the pace has slowed. Grieve with Hope, Not Despair!! Matthew 5:4, Psalm 23, Psalm 30:5 My faith in God has given me Hope, not Despair!!! God and my faith have been my shelter in a storm beyond all storms!! There is a hole inside of me that never gets filled, this is grief!! There is a place in my heart that always yearns for Todd, this is grief! There has been so much time since I hugged my son or was able to say "I Love you"! But there is Hope!!! I think of the things we will never do together. But there is the love we shared, the memories I will forever cherish!! There is HOPE!!!," her message reads. "If someone you know has lost a child, remember to be there in silence and give them love. Some of the hardest days I had were the not talking about Todd people who think if they say nothing, all will be better. But this is not true. Talk about my child to keep his memory alive!!! The more I talk and think of Todd, the closer I am to him!! Someday when all the earth has passed and my life here is over, I will again see my Sweet Loving Son!!!"

The killer saw Todd as a lifeless form on the parking lot of the nightclub but his family knew him as a young man who loved life and all those around him. He got enjoyment from singing country music and some older rock and roll tunes. Although he didn't have children of his own, he loved spoiling his nieces and nephews. He found pleasure being outdoors and satisfaction from carpentry, a trade he learned from his father. He was also known to his family and friends as a wonderful outgoing and friendly man who was liked by all. The memorial site lists his favorite foods as catfish, hushpuppies and Reese peanut butter cups, and his favorite drink as Mountain Dew. It recalls how he played Santa on Christmas Eve for his sisters' children and the special bond he always had with his parents.

"Todd was a loving, kind and giving person," says a remembrance from his mom. She said he never met a stranger until the night he was killed. There seems no motive for the slaying. His mom said it was just an unknown assailant who shot him point blank in the back of the head. She said detectives have been very cordial and informative but there have never been any real answers pinpointing to who is responsible for killing her son. She recalls the police officer telling them about the murder. "My first reaction was disbelief. They had the wrong identity." She called her sister who lived in Tuscaloosa and asked her to view the person at the morgue they said was her son. After what seemed like an agonizing length of time, her sister called back and confirmed it was Todd. Her son had been living and working in the west-central Alabama city of some 85,000 people and she hadn't seen him for nine months. He loved country music and enjoyed singing those songs. His mother imagines him now singing with angels. She also says she has grief, but it's tempered with the hope that someday she will see the killer caught and punished for the horrible act perpetrated against her son. The Tuscaloosa County Crime Stoppers program is offering a reward of up to $1,000 to anyone who calls in anonymously with a tip that helps solve this case.

Find My Killer

Chapter 4 – Karp to Magliulo

Carolyn Sanders Karp
Amarillo, Texas

The owner of a tavern was found dead after a fire broke out in her trailer in the northeastern section of Amarillo, Texas. Firefighters were called at 4:45 a.m. on Saturday, July 11, 1992 to battle a blaze in a trailer parked beside the Sneak Joint Lounge at 10321 East Amarillo Boulevard west of West Parsley Road. The body of Carolyn Sanders Karp was discovered after the flames were extinguished and an autopsy showed she'd been murdered. The killing occurred two days before Karp's 56th birthday and could have been linked to a robbery, but investigators from the Amarillo Police Department special crimes unit have not officially established a motive. Her mother, Lois Rhea Sanders, died at the age of 92 in March 2005 without ever finding out who killed Carolyn. Crime Stoppers has offered a standard reward for any information leading to the arrest of the killer.

Navid Kazemi
Bethesda, Maryland

A 19-year-old university student who was to testify at a grand jury about a shooting that blinded a man in Bethesda, Maryland was shot to death at his home. The body of Navid Kazemi was found in a pool of blood in the foyer when his mother, Pari, arrived home from work around 6 p.m. on Saturday, November 28, 1992. There was no sign of a forced entry or a struggle and police didn't find the murder weapon. Investigation showed the victim, a philosophy and pre-med student at the University of Maryland, had been shot in the head at close range and in execution style. Homicide detectives from the Montgomery County Police said the killing occurred sometimes between 3:30 p.m. and 5:30 p.m. at the home on Rockhurst Road just south of Stoneham Road. Navid, born on November 11, 1973, was brought with his four siblings to the United States in 1979 from Iran by his parents who were looking for a better life for their family. He was five-feet, four-inches, 150 pounds with dark brown eyes and dark brown hair. He was also a devotee of the martial arts and relatives said the killer must have taken him by surprise. Almost three months earlier, on Sunday, September 13, 1992, Navid was driving around with two friends firing paint pellets at street signs. At some point during the evening an individual approached their vehicle asking for directions and one of the occupants with Navid fired a pellet into the man's face. The 34-year-old man was blinded as a result of the attack. Navid admitted his involvement to police and named those who were with him in the car. He was scheduled to testify against them at an upcoming grand jury hearing. Investigators questioned the friends but found nothing to link them with Navid's homicide. The Montgomery Crime Stoppers program is offering a reward of up to $5,000 for any information leading to the arrest of the killer.

David & Carol Ann Keeffe

David & Carol Keeffe
Athens Township, Pennsylvania

David Burke Keeffe, a prominent lawyer, and his wife Carol Ann, shared an idyllic existence at their tree shrouded home in Athens Township across the Susquehanna River from Sayre, a community of some 5,800 people nestled in Pennsylvania's Endless Mountain region at the New York state line. But that tranquility was shattered on the evening of Friday, November 17, 2006 when the couple was executed after driving home in separate vehicles. Sixty-year-old Carol arrived home first and was shot inside the garage after opening the door of her car. David, 56, who had spent the day at his office in the family-owned DeSisti and Keeffe law firm, was shot to death when he arrived a bit later. The couple had been looking forward to a relatively relaxing evening before setting off the next morning on a trip to their vacation home in Cape Cod.

After leaving the office of the firm he ran with his father-in-law on North Keystone Avenue in Sayre, Keeffe stopped at Mangialardo's Restaurant on South Thomas Avenue for some take-out food. The receipt showed he was there around 5:30 p.m. He most likely drove south on Keystone and turned left onto Lockhard Street, past the Robert Packer Hospital and made a right hand turn at the t-intersection with Lehigh Avenue. He would have made a left turn at the next block and then right onto Thomas where he stopped at the restaurant before heading eastbound on Lockhart Street and across the bridge toward Route 1043 northbound. He would have travelled past several fashionable homes on the east side of the roadway, also known as Riverside Drive, before making a right hand turn onto Sayre Hill Road. In three quarters of a mile he would have reached a section of Moore Road that led to the tree-lined drive shrouding the private estate where Keeffe and his wife had their house. Adjoining homes were occupied by Carol's parents, Michael and Ann DeSisti and the other by her sister and her brother-in-law.

The property was extremely secluded and the killers would have to be very familiar with the terrain. They would also have to know the routine of the family and it's possible those responsible for the murders stalked the victims to determine the best time to lay in wait for them.

It was the couple's daughter, Melissa, who called the Athens Township Police Department on Sunday, November 19 when she was unable to reach her parents. Officers went into the house and found the bodies of David and Carol in the garage. Both had been hit multiple times with shotgun blasts to their heads. The five-member police force headed by Chief Larry Hurley sealed off the crime scene and requested help from the Pennsylvania State Police to handle the investigation. While forensic experts collected evidence from the home and adjacent property, police officers from Athens Township and state troopers began interviewing various neighbors as well as residents living along Moore Road and the network of streets leading away from the secluded estate where the couple had lived since 1975 when Keeffe graduated from the Suffolk University Law School in Boston, Massachusetts. Keeffe was born January 5, 1950 in Cambridge, Massachusetts. The couple married on July 10, 1971 after meeting while they attended Syracuse University in New York. Carol, born August 16, 1946, taught senior high school English in Syracuse and later in Melrose, Massachusetts while her husband earned his law degree. He joined her father's firm after graduating and became a top civil and criminal defense lawyer who argued cases before federal and state court judges in Pennsylvania and New York. Keeffe was involved in a lot of civil litigation and personal injury cases and was also certified to represent people charged with murder.

Apart from talking to neighbors, police set up roadblocks on Riverside Drive near the East Lockhart Street bridge a day after the bodies were found to question motorists and determine if they had been in the vicinity on Friday evening around the time Keeffe was driving home. People were specifically asked if they had been in the area between 2 p.m. and 7 p.m. on Friday or if they knew others who could have been in the area. The interviews and other investigations have given authorities a snapshot of the moments leading to the killing, but so far they have been unable to identify anyone as a possible suspect. Police were anxious to find people who saw the victims as they were driving home. They also wanted to know if any residents had noticed anything unusual or suspicious during the five hour period covering the final moments leading up to the deaths of the Keeffe couple and what investigators believe was the time window when the killer or killers may have made their escape. Since the estate is behind locked gates, police have speculated those responsible may have parked their vehicle on one of the nearby side roads and walked through the heavily treed property to reach the isolated home.

The gunman who killed Carol stood behind her and then fired multiple shots into her head. When her husband pulled into the garage moments later, David stood face to face with his killer. He also received "multiple gunshot wounds to the head" according to a pathologist's report. There was no evidence that anything was stolen. Although the homicide has all the earmarks of a deliberate and planned killing, investigators have been unable to determine a motive. Police have delved into the backgrounds of clients and others who Keeffe associated with through the years but haven't discovered anyone who may have held a grudge as a result of a litigation gone sour or someone who thought they were wrongly convicted. Authorities have admitted one or both of the victims was targeted for death and there isn't a killer running around randomly seeking people to murder. The investigation has been painstaking and systematic as police follow leads and track evidence collected from the crime scene. But despite the exhaustive probe investigators are still making public appeals for the tidbit of information that will turn out to be the key that puts together all the pieces in the jigsaw puzzle and solves the mystery behind the double slaying.

The couple loved their life in the rural area. Nothing ever happened there. It was a safe community. They were secure. Keeffe and his wife had time to enjoy small town America and thought there was no other place to raise their children Melissa, now a lawyer who joined the family firm in 2002, and David, who lived in New York City when the killings occurred. Following the marriage of their daughter to Mathew D. Jones, who is also with the law firm, the couple spent a great deal of time looking after their grandchildren Caroline and Parker. Articles in the media suggest Keeffe didn't have an enemy in the world and was one of the nicest people you could ever meet. Staff writer Nancy Coleman of the Daily Review, a newspaper in Towanda, Pennsylvania which serves the tri county area of Bradford and Sullivan counties in the Keystone state and Tioga County in New York, spoke to many Sayre residents and others in the area who knew Keeffe and his wife. She chronicled how people felt about the victims a few days after the killings. "There was no finer lawyer who ever appeared in front of me," Bradford County Judge John Mott told the newspaper. "He represented the best of what the legal profession had to offer. David was forceful and zealous, yet professional and dignified. I considered him a personal friend. He was just a great person as well as a great lawyer." Judge Mott said Keeffe would represent people who couldn't afford a lawyer if he believed in their case.

Sally McQuay's house is next to the Keeffe and DeSisti law office. Keeffe was her lawyer and someone she considered a friend. When Coleman interviewed her, McQuay picked up a photograph on display in the living room of a smiling girl dressed in pink. It's the granddaughter of the murdered couple. She described Keeffe as a very nice man. She said he was always well dressed. He was also someone who loved golf and taking walks. "What a waste of a person who tried to help people," Coleman quoted her as saying. Rick Jennings, an attorney with Richard A. Wilson and Associates in Wyalusing, a village of some 500 people 30 miles south of Sayre, described Keeffe as one of the best lawyers in the region. "A guy who loved his work." He said he also cared about people. The Bradford County Bar Association said Keeffe has practiced in the area since 1975 and developed the respect and admiration of his colleagues and judges. "He was an excellent trial attorney in both the civil and criminal fields and was always willing to assist other attorneys in dealing with difficult legal issues."

Coleman's article said Carol attended Epiphany School and Athens High School before being accepted at Syracuse University. Judge Mott described her as a "lovely lady" and attorney Maureen Beirne of Athens said she was a "very friendly and outgoing" person. She was an education major in college and when her children grew up was a typical grandmother. Former Sayre School District Superintendent Tom Salpino said Carol was happy, upbeat and sophisticated. He described her husband as someone who was very family-oriented and a typical grandpa. Salpino said Keeffe enjoyed golf but also a person who would relax, watch the birds, the clouds, breathe and think.

Ten days after the killings, Melissa, 31 at the time, spoke to television station WNEP in Moosic, Pennsylvania about her parents. "They were wonderful people, not only my parents and my children's grandparents, but they were friends of ours," she said. "I don't know many people who can say they were good friends with their parents." Melissa had lived near her parents for the past four years after she and her husband agreed to become the third generation of lawyers at the family law practice her grandfather founded in 1946. It would also give them the opportunity to bring their children up in the small town environment where she was raised and the added stability of having her parents living nearby. She described her Dad as "hard working" and someone who would work for free if a person couldn't afford to pay legal fees or if he strongly believed in the cause. "He grew up Boston Irish-Catholic and had a great heart," she said. Melissa also loved her Mom and described her as a person who knew the right thing to do in every situation. "She always sent the perfect gift, wrote the perfect card and did the perfect thing," she told the television station during a news interview.

Melissa described her parents to another interviewer as "the most wonderful, caring and generous people you ever wanted to meet." She said they both touched the lives of people, her mother as a teacher and father who took his job very seriously and believed it was important that everyone have equal access to the justice system. They were also wonderful grandparents and Melissa said her children and the children her brother hoped to have will now miss out on happy experiences.

All members of the family put their grieving on hold while concentrating efforts on assisting investigators to find who was responsible for the killings. Police formed a task force which began operating from an area on the upper floor of the Athens police department. The investigative team, comprised of officers from Athens, the Pennsylvania State Police and the Bradford County District Attorney's Office, began compiling names of people who knew the couple. They also reviewed court cases where Keeffe had represented clients, especially criminal and civil proceedings where rulings had not been favorable. Relatives were asked if they were aware of any threats that had been directed toward the couple and to think back to any situation that could have spurred someone to murder. Investigators were not surprised to discover that the couple had many friends among area residents and were considered by most in the community to be great people and part of a really nice family. Keeffe was the president of the Bradford County Bar Association and had served on the Board of Governors of the Pennsylvania Trial Lawyer's Association for 10 years until the mid 1990s. He was also associated with the Northeastern Pennsylvania Trial Lawyer's Association, a director from 1981 to 1995 with the Commonwealth Bank and Trust Company in Williamsport, Pennsylvania and an ardent supporter of many local charities.

Rewards for information in the double homicide total $118,000. The Bradford County Bar Association has posted $68,000 and the family put up $50,000. A separate reward is available from the Pennsylvania Crime Stoppers program for anyone who anonymously provides information that leads to an arrest in this case.

Eric Keller
Vacaville, California

A secret side to a man's life may have led to his death in a farm field on the outskirts of Vacaville, California, midway between San Francisco and Sacramento. Eric Keller, a 41-year-old international marketing manager for a high tech graphics company that provided computer equipment to Hollywood and others in the animation industry, was beaten to death when confronted by attackers on Saturday, January 9, 1999. He had been driving the 230 mile route on Interstate 80 from his San Jose home to spend the day at the Alpine Meadow Ski Resort in Tahoe, California. The victim was found two days later at the end of a dirt road about a half mile off the highway near the Lagoon Valley Road interchange. He had been savagely beaten about the head and upper body and died as a result of blunt force trauma. A day earlier a California Highway Patrol officer found the victim's 1998 dark blue Saab on Riviera Road which runs beside Interstate 80, just east of the interchange. There was no sign of Keller in the vicinity.

The victim was naked from the waist down when his body was located. He had severe injuries to the front and back of his head as well as fractured ribs and a punctured lung. In contrast his pants, briefs, socks and shoes were neatly folded on a nearby haystack. Keller had called his wife, Karen, who remained in a New Jersey home the couple owned before the victim took the high paying Silicone Valley job, to let her know he would be away for the entire day. She sounded the alarm when he failed to call to let her know that he was back and almost the same time as she was filing the missing person's report, the Highway Patrol officer found his car. The body was located after a massive search of the area involving police dogs and officers on horses. In New Jersey he'd worked with Siemens but left in 1997 when offered a position with KLA-Tencor as president of marketing. When the company was forced to downsize a few months later, Keller was hired by Silicon Graphics and at the end of 1998 was named director of the global service sales team.

The focus of the investigation into the death of Keller changed six weeks after his body was found when police learned of his dark secret. An initial search of his home had turned up an assortment of sex toys but it wasn't until they received some tips and spoke to business associates on the east coast that they were able to confirm Keller was bi-sexual and the beating death could be some type of gay hate crime. Police have also confirmed the victim had a quantity of the illicit drug ecstasy shortly before his death, indicating the possibility he was about to have a consensual encounter with someone. An investigator familiar with the gay community said the drug is most common with the rave culture, but has been used by same-sex lovers to increase intensity during intimacy. Apart from being confronted by attackers, police said it's also thought Keller and someone he was with could have encountered assailants who saw them in the farm field. If someone was there they are hoping that person will now come forward.

The victim was last seen in the Campbell area of San Jose the day before his death buying some items at a local store. He called his wife that same night to tell her about his trip to the Lake Tahoe region. He was an active sports type who often went hiking or skiing. The missing report described him as a white male, five-feet, ten-inches, 140 pounds with brown eyes, brown hair and a moustache. Keller's wife and most of his friends and business associates didn't know his secret and described him as hard working, a good husband and great individual. When Karen stayed behind in New Jersey, she had a good position as a lawyer and was also responsible for the care of elderly parents. At least once a month she would fly to California or Keller would return to New Jersey. They met in Lancaster, Pennsylvania where Karen was born and moved to New Jersey after Keller graduated with his MBA from the University of Pennsylvania's Wharton Business School. They didn't have any children and were next planning to get together in January to celebrate Keller's upcoming birthday. The case is still an active investigation and detectives are hoping someone will come forward with information.

John Kennedy
Winter Haven, Florida

An overnight attendant was stabbed to death during a robbery at a Winter Haven, Florida hotel that was being used as a halfway house for substance abusers. John Kennedy was cleaning toilets in a lobby bathroom on Saturday, April 19, 1977 when he heard someone trying to steal money from a cash drawer. The 74-year-old man made his way to the reception area where he was repeatedly stabbed while trying to overpower the culprit. His lifeless body was found at 5:27 a.m. when the owner arrived at the hotel now known as the Haven Condominiums at 235 6th Street Northwest just north of the Pope Avenue and Avenue B intersection. Kennedy, who had worked at the six storey hotel for 14 months, was described as a conscientious worker and someone who didn't have an enemy in the world. Detectives from the Winter Haven Police Department are hoping someone who knows the killer will come forward with the information. A reward of up to $1,000 is also available from the Heartland Crime Stoppers program.

Jahaira Keys
Carson, California

Gang rivalry led to the shooting death of a teenage girl outside a nightclub in Carson, California, a suburb of Los Angeles. It was 12:42

a.m. on Thursday, May 3, 2007 when Jahaira Keys was shot in the head after some gang members became embroiled in a fight in the parking lot of Bistro 880, a restaurant and lounge on East Dominguez Street at Bonita Street, across from the IKEA store. During the disturbance a heavy set black woman, who investigators believe is associated with one of the gangs, got out of a car that stopped on the roadway and began firing shots randomly towards those standing outside the nightclub. A bullet struck Jahaira in the head. She died instantly. It was the first time the 17-year-old Grade 11 student had been at the club which had been booked by some gang members for a private party. There were a number of fights inside the club when rival gang members showed up displaying colors, but security guards forced everyone outside. Jahaira was one of numerous people milling around the parking lot watching various people fighting when the shots rang out. The gunman was described as between 17 to 20 years, around five-feet, eight-inches with a heavy build and wearing blue jeans and an orange t-shirt. The car was a white Nissan with tinted windows.

Friends described Jahaira as a happy, cheerful person who was always smiling and her mother, Bertha, said she feels lost in this world without her. When the city unveiled a billboard looking for information to solve her daughter's slaying and the deaths of three other young people she said "all I want is for the killing to stop." A $10,000 reward is available for anyone who helps police find the girl's killer.

Kaysone Khounpanya
Hurst, Texas

A 49-year-old Laotian woman who aspired to become a famous singer was stabbed and then fatally shot in her Hurst, Texas apartment. Kaysone Khounpanya was found dead on Tuesday, January 11, 2000 in her Booth Calloway Road apartment when a friend called police after becoming concerned when he hadn't seen her for a week. Investigation showed an attacker had confronted the victim in her apartment and tied her up after stabbing her in the neck. When Khounpanya, who was face down on the bedroom floor, struggled and attempted to free her hands which were tied behind her, the assailant put a pillow against her head and fired a single shot from a handgun. An autopsy showed it was the gunshot wound that killed her. The victim was well known by Asian residents in the Dallas and Fort Worth area and often sang at weddings and other events. She came to the United States from Laos in 1976 and got her citizenship twenty years later. Detectives with the Hurst Police Department haven't been able to determine a motive for the murder, but robbery is a possibility since the residence was ransacked. She was a grandmother and friends described her as "a sweet woman" who was loved by everyone. They said she never raised her voice in anger and couldn't think of anyone who would have killed her. Born on June 2, 1950, she loved music and hoped someday to become an Asian singing star. Divorced with three grown children she lived with relatives and friends in Massachusetts until 1997 when she met a keyboard player who convinced her to move with him to Fort Worth which had a 3,000-member Laotian community. She regularly performed at Laotian functions throughout the area, but got a factory job to supplement her income after breaking up with her boyfriend about a year after moving to Texas. Khounpanya was living alone when she was killed. Investigators said they don't know exactly when the victim died, but are hoping people who knew the victim will come forward with information to help them pinpoint the time. They are also asking that anyone who can identify the killer to give the name to police so the case can be solved. A reward is also available to anyone calling anonymously with a tip to Crime Stoppers that leads to the arrest and indictment of the killer.

Jamie Kidder
San Bernardino, California

Someone on a mission to kill savagely beat a five-year-old boy and his mother in a San Bernardino, California apartment. The attacker had broken into the apartment and was waiting for Nancy Louise Kidder and her young son, Jamie, shortly before noon on Tuesday, September 24, 1996 when she brought him back from his morning kindergarten class. The stereo was turned up to silence the screams as the boy was battered with some sort of blunt object before the intruder launched a murderous attack on the 29-year-old mother. Jamie died but his mom survived after spending months in hospital recovering from life-threatening injuries.

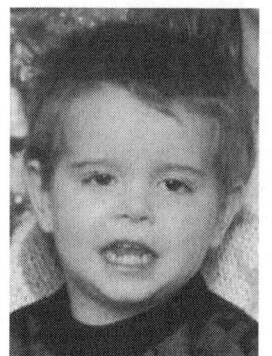

The victims were found in the apartment in the 3600 block of North E Street later in the afternoon when her eight-year-old son came home from his Grade 3 class at Marshall Elementary School. His mother was unconscious in a pool of blood on the kitchen floor and Jamie's lifeless body on the floor in an adjoining room. There was no sign of a robbery and investigators from the San Bernardino Police Department could only conclude it was a deliberate attack designed to kill both victims. Nancy Kidder was in a coma for almost two weeks and to this day has no memory of what occurred in the apartment. She remembers picking up her son from school and police talking to her several weeks later in the hospital. She also has permanent injuries from the attack including muscle and nerve damage, vision problems as well as anxiety and depression. Forensic investigators recovered blood and hair samples from the crime scene that weren't associated to the victims along with some fingerprints, but checks through the years have not matched them to any suspects.

Jamie was a bright, inquisitive boy who was enjoying his first month at school. When he was born his mother was addicted to methamphetamines but there were no signs the drug had affected him. Nancy, a single mother, had struggled to fight the addiction and had been drug free since Jamie's birth. Because of her former drug habit she obviously had associated with some individuals who police believed were capable of this type of brutality, but all investigations in that area have so far led to dead ends. Detectives were also unable to come up with any possible motive for the attack and cannot even fathom why anyone would want to harm a five-year-old child. Nancy is now married and living in another community but continues to keep in touch with investigators and hopes they will eventually track down her son's killer.

Jone Knapton
East Moline, Illinois

A computer programmer who was in the process of getting a divorce from her husband failed to return to her East Moline, Illinois home after going out for dinner with friends. Jone Knapton, the 47-year-old mother of a teenage daughter, was in a good frame of mind during the July 3, 2003 meal and it was totally out of character when she vanished. She was officially reported missing three days later. It was on Friday, July 10, 2003 when her torso was found floating in the Green River, 18 miles east of her home community, near Geneseo, Illinois in rural Henry County. Police searched the river and the banks for several days, but didn't find any other parts of the body. It was another three weeks before forensic experts formally identified the remains as the missing woman and a murder investigation began into her death. Jone had planned to spend the July 4th Independence Day weekend holiday at home working on a major computer project, but when a friend visited the house on July 5 there was no sign of her. A family member checked the home the next day and alerted police after finding her computer, purse and cell phone missing. There was no sign of a struggle or foul play but they had never known Jone to be away without letting someone know. A homicide task force was established involving members of the Illinois State Police, the East Moline Police Department and the Henry Country Sheriff's Department. Through the years they have interviewed hundreds of people but have not publicly announced a motive or identified anyone as a possible suspect. The woman's insurance company filed suit to determine if her husband, Larry Knapton, or the couple's daughter, Nichole, should get the money from the victim's life insurance policy. They claimed Knapton was responsible for his wife's death even though police have never linked him in any fashion to the slaying. The court ruled the money from the $100,000 policy should go to the husband who is also entitled to his wife's pension and retirement savings. Detectives from the task force are continuing to appeal for information and a $35,000 reward is available for anyone who can assist police to apprehend and convict the killer. The Quad City Crime Stoppers program has offered a $1,000 reward for anyone wishing to provide anonymous information that will crack the case.

Teofilo Knight
Tacoma, Washington

As a bouncer he was an imposing figure at six-feet, 250 pounds, but no match for a cowardly gunman who hid in the shadows and killed the victim in the parking lot of his Tacoma, Washington apartment. It was just past 4 a.m. on Sunday, December 2, 2007 when Teofilo "Teo" Knight was shot after returning home from work as a member of the security staff at Champions Sports Bar in Lakewood, a medium size city seven miles southwest of Tacoma. Investigators said the 28-year-old victim parked his vehicle at the apartment building on South 58th Street, near Orchard Street, when someone fired several shots from a secluded area. Knight, a Native American, succumb to his injuries at the Madigan Army Medical Center at Fort Lewis three days later. Although a number of people heard the gunfire, police didn't find anyone who saw the killer or witnessed the shooting. Investigators also don't have a motive for the slaying. Police have looked at a number of incidents at the bar, but haven't found anything that could be responsible for the victim's murder. Crime Stoppers of Tacoma and Pierce County is offering the standard $1,000 for help in solving this killing.

Jan Marie Knott
Deerfield Beach, Florida

Jan Marie Knott usually left the door unlocked when she took the family dog for a walk in the quiet Deerfield Beach, Florida neighborhood where she lived with her husband. Police believe the 47-year-old woman followed that routine when she was alone around 11 p.m. on Friday, October 2, 1998. Some 90 minutes later her husband, William, came home and found her in a pool of blood in the hallway of their home at 1104 SE 14th Court. She had been stabbed multiple times with a knife pulled from a wooden butcher block on a kitchen counter. It was a middle class neighborhood and their fashionable home was located mid block on the south side of the street between SE 10th Terrace and SE 12th Avenue. Police described the killing as brutal and senseless and through the years they have been unable to determine a motive or identify the killer.

The victim was well liked by her neighbors and friends. Her job was selling cosmetics for Mary Kay and homicide detectives were never able to find anyone who would want to harm her. Investigators have theorized someone, possibly a burglar, entered the home while Knott was walking the dog and was trapped inside when she returned. They have also considered the possibility that someone confronted the victim when she arrived home and pulled her into the house where she was attacked. Police said the dog was inside but its leash was found on the driveway. Since nothing was stolen investigators could not confirm she was killed in a break-in and there was no sign of a struggle outside.

Police went door to door looking for anyone who may have seen anything and distributed posters urging people to call Crime Stoppers if they want to provide information anonymously. There is a $1,000 reward for naming Knott's killer.

Her daughter and only child, Michelle Zubrowski, who was 26 at the time of the slaying, told a television interviewer that her mom was her friend. "A lot of people thought we were sisters. We were very close." She couldn't believe someone had killed her mother when she was told of the stabbing and lives with the hope the murder will be solved. She wants to know why the person killed her and tell him he robbed his mother of the joy of being a grandmother. Michelle had spoken to her mother just before 11 p.m. and investigators believe it was shortly after she left the house to take the dog for a walk.

Earlier in the day the victim's mother spoke by phone to Knott several times and later told investigators her daughter sounded anxious during the conversations. She asked if anything was bothering her but her daughter assured her that things were okay. Police found the knife but investigators won't reveal if forensic experts from the Broward Sheriff's Office uncovered any other evidence that can be used to link a suspect to the woman's death. Through the years police have interviewed hundreds of individuals but are still hoping to find that one person who holds the key that will solve the case.

Rickey Dale Krater
Tulsa, Oklahoma

An hour after being reported missing, Rickey Dale Krater was found shot to death in a Tulsa, Oklahoma alleyway. No details of the slaying have been made public and police have never discussed a possible motive. The 37-year-old victim had been wounded in an earlier shooting incident and took frequent walks to help him recovery from the injuries. Krater was on one of these walks on Monday, January 8, 1996 when he was shot to death in the alleyway behind a building at 812 East 6th Street between South Kenosha Avenue and South Lansing Avenue. It was 9:30 p.m. when police received a phone call saying he was missing. His body was found at 10:30 p.m. Homicide detectives are hoping in the years since the murder someone may have heard a person bragging about the killing or there is someone out there who knows who killed Krater and doesn't want to live with the secret anymore.

Benjamin Jonas LaComb
Jacksonville, Florida

It was almost 4 a.m. when a car brought two men with gunshot wounds to the emergency bay at the Baptist Medical Centre in Jacksonville, Florida. Benjamin Jonas LaComb, 27, died from his injuries, but the other victim, a 42-year-old Jacksonville man, survived. The shooting incident occurred around 3:45 a.m. on Saturday, November 1, 2008 on Sunshine Street, in a working class neighborhood of the city, between Maplewood Street and Fleming Street. It took around seven minutes for the driver to reach the hospital which was less than three miles away. Homicide investigators have not determined a motive and don't know what LaComb was doing on the street directly adjacent to the city's Hollybrook Park. The victim had been addicted to drugs but friends said he appeared to be putting his life back together. He was working at his father's tire business and was in regular contact with his mother who moved to Ohio several years following the couple's 1983 divorce.

Crime Stoppers has posted a $1,000 reward for information that leads to the arrest of LaComb's killer and friends are trying to raise additional money to assist investigators. Lisa Topel described her son's death as a tragedy and said she's heartbroken that she won't hear his voice again. She and her ex-husband, Pete LaComb, have issued public appeals to help find the person responsible for their son's murder. His dad said life has been a struggle for him every day since the slaying. "It's hard to concentrate. We are all grieving." LaComb's best friend, Dan Buie, set up the private reward fund and friends and relatives have issued personal appeals urging anyone with information to help police find the killer. "We desperately want justice for our family," said the victim's sister-in-law Lea LaComb. "We are left with so many unanswered questions. If anyone knows anything, please, please come forward."

Lea's mother, Annie McLeod, also expressed outrage at LaComb's death. "When someone snuffs out a life, it's never a random thing," she said. "It's a direct, horrible violence that marks a family forever. It is never isolated to the person that is attacked. It shakes the very foundation of the entire family and extended family and each member will wear the scar of that loss for the rest of his or her life. The stronger the love in the family...the deeper the wound." The victim was a 13-year-old boy when McLeod first met him. "I've watched this young man grow tall, strong, warm and loving. My son-in-law, Peter, has now lost his brother – forever."

Amanda Nicole Lankey
White Cloud, Michigan

It was believed a 13-year-old girl had sneaked off to meet someone she'd been chatting with on the Internet, but when her body was found two weeks later police knew they were hunting for a killer. Amanda Lankey spent the night of Sunday, June 20, 2004 at a friend's house near White Cloud, Michigan in Newaygo County, but the next morning she wasn't there. A check of the computer showed that during the sleepover Amanda was chatting with someone who used the name "skit-zo killa" and investigators thought she'd left the house to meet the individual. She didn't appear to take any clothes with her and her backpack, money and shoes were still at the friend's house.

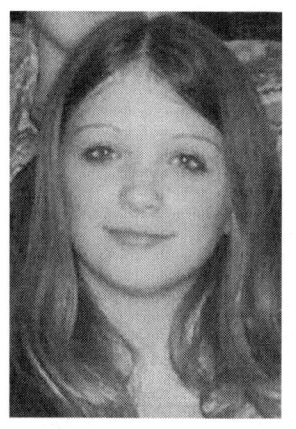

Deputies with the Newaygo County Sheriff's Department listed her as a missing person and made routine inquiries but the need for full scale searches was ruled out because they considered her a runaway. This view was fueled by the fact Amanda and her brother were to leave in a few days to be with their mother who had recently moved to Florida. The girl had objected to leaving her hometown friends and her mother agreed to let the pair stay a couple of more weeks with her grandparents to give them time to say goodbye to everyone. It appeared Amanda had climbed through the bedroom window to get out of the house without anyone noticing.

The family called Amanda's grandparents as soon as they discovered she was missing, but it wasn't until mid afternoon when the girl hadn't come home that police were notified. Over the next couple of days deputies talked to people who thought they had seen Amanda but everything changed on Monday, July 5, 2004 when mushroom pickers found the body of a young girl in a heavily wooded area of the Manistee National Forest some seven miles to the southeast from where Amanda had gone missing. The victim, who died from blunt force trauma to the head, was still wearing pajamas. Homicide detectives now believe the 13-year-old was killed somewhere else and her body dumped in the forest, probably by someone who lives in the vicinity of White Cloud or is familiar with the area. Based on the decomposed state of the body, it's likely Amanda was killed the same night she vanished. The murder weapon hasn't been found but it's believed to be some sort of metal bar or baseball bat.

Amanda was a typical young teen who enjoyed popular music and hanging around with friends and school mates. She played the trumpet and violin and had pretty good grades in school. She had also just turned thirteen and had very mixed feelings about leaving Michigan and starting a new life with her mother and brother in the Tampa, Florida area. Since switching focus from a teenage runaway to a murder investigation, detectives with the Newaygo County Sheriff's Department have interviewed hundreds of people and submitted material to the crime lab to uncover possible DNA evidence.

The Carole Sund/Carrington Foundation based in Modesto, California, has posted a $5,000 reward for information that solves this case and homicide detectives have consulted with investigators from the Federal Bureau of Investigation and the National Center for Missing and Exploited Children to determine what other avenues should be explored in the search for Amanda's killer. Her mother, Victoria Foster, also frequently travels to White Cloud to make appeals through the media or attend vigils to make sure people don't forget there's a killer on the loose in the community.

The family has also set up a web page in memory of Amanda who was born on June 7, 1991. "We will never forget," the message reads. "We live every day in spite of the loss, and we live every day for her life that was taken way too soon. She will always be in our thoughts every morning when we get up, during every meal we eat, every experience that we share, in every dream we have. We see her in every child's face, and we see what she would have been in every moment of every day. We want everyone else to think of her as much as we do and remember that whoever did this – is still out there. We need answers."

Bruce Lee
San Jose, California

A well known cable television host was shot to death after being confronted by three assailants at his grocery store in San Jose, California. The killing occurred around 11:50 p.m. on Sunday, August 13, 2006 while Bruce Lee was alone in the Hello Hollywood Enterprises Market he owned on Tully Road near McLaughlin Avenue. The body of the 49-year-old victim was found near the counter of mini-mart after people nearby heard shots and saw three individuals in dark clothing fleeing from the area. Although Lee operated the store, he was best known for a weekly television show on the local Comcast station called Hello Hollywood News. Police said they don't know if Lee was the victim of an attempted robbery or if his murder was related to the program he'd hosted for six years. Initially the cable show focused on the motion picture industry but just before the murder he had turned to interpreting dreams submitted by viewers. The show wasn't being broadcast through the summer, but was scheduled to resume in the fall. Lee considered himself an entrepreneur and his web site listed him as a director, screenwriter, acting coach as well as a tae kwon do third-degree black belt.

Detectives from the San Jose Police Department's homicide squad who are probing the murder suggest it's likely there are individuals who have information about the slaying, but are hesitant to speak with investigators. Detectives said even if someone thinks the information they have is trivial or not important they should still tell police about it. They said the tiniest detail might be the piece of the puzzle that is needed to solve the case. In hopes of encouraging people to come forward with information the Carole Sund/Carrington Foundation posted a $5,000 reward and the San Jose Crime Stoppers program will pay up to $1,000 to anyone who calls in anonymously with information that solves the murder.

Kristie Lynn Lee
Pompano Beach, Florida

At the moment police believed a young mother was being murdered in her Pompano Beach, Florida apartment, her in-laws were with her and say everything was fine. It was 9 a.m. on Thursday, March 31, 1994 when Kristie Lynn Gunderson Lee was knocked unconscious when bludgeoned with a heavy object and then strangled. Two young women living in a nearby apartment heard blood-curdling screams as they left for work but didn't call police. They assumed Lee and her husband were having an argument. However, Jeffrey Lee was already at work and it was his mother and stepfather, Kay and Joe Petralia, who were inside the apartment picking up their 20-month-old grandson, Zachary, who they looked after while the couple worked. Kristie Lynn was a hair stylist and would have left the apartment a short time after saying goodbye to her son. But that morning she didn't show up for work.

The scream was heard at precisely the same time the parents admit being in the apartment. A half hour earlier Kristie paged her husband but when he called the apartment there was no answer. At 10:30 a.m. the 911 operator received a call from the victim's mother-in-law reporting a tragedy. Petralia and his wife had returned to the apartment to get some clean clothes for their grandson and found their daughter-in-law on a bedroom floor. Investigators observed marks on her neck indicating she had been manually choked after being struck a couple of times on the head. Born September 4, 1973, Kristie was 20 when she died.

A friend described Kristie as a loving, vivacious young woman who didn't have an enemy in the world. She was a 15-year-old girl when she met Jeffrey in 1988 in Austin, Texas where she had lived with her parents since 1981. She became pregnant in 1992 and moved with her husband to Florida where they resided with his parents at their Pompano Beach home before moving into their own apartment in the 1400 block of SW 46th Avenue, just north of West McNab Road. A neighbor saw Kristie around 8:30 a.m. on the day she died answering the door when her in-laws arrived at the apartment. Jeff's mother told police that when they returned to the apartment the key wouldn't work in the door lock, but they were able to enter through an open patio door at the rear of the unit. She noticed blood on the floor and some things strewn around before finding Kristie in the bedroom. She said she attempted to revive her daughter-in-law and then called 911.

Homicide investigators were able to clear the victim's husband of any direct involvement after fellow employees confirmed he had been working at his office through the morning until police arrived to notify him of his wife's death. Investigators said it's possible an intruder attacked the woman, but they have not narrowed their focus in any direction. They also said examination of evidence failed to link anyone specific to the crime and are hoping there is someone with information that will allow them to make an arrest. Broward Crime Stoppers have posted a $1,000 reward and the victim's family has contributed an additional $1,000 to encourage people to come forward and name Kristie's killer.

Un Sam Lee
La Mirada, California

Homicide investigators are trying to determine what led to the killing of a woman who owned several massage spas in Los Angeles and Orange counties. It was around noon on Saturday, April 6, 2002 when the body of Un Sam Lee, a 47-year-old Korean businesswoman, was found in her residence at the luxurious Hillsborough condominium complex on Gainsway Court in La Mirada. She was last seen about 11 p.m. Thursday, April 4, 2002 leaving the upscale massage parlor facility known as the Happy Spa she operated on Wilshire Boulevard in Santa Monica. The clients were mainly doctors, lawyers and other well-to-do professionals. It's believed she drove her white 2002 Mercedes S class the 35 miles, mostly on freeways, from the spa directly to her home of Hillsborough Drive near South Beach Boulevard. Police were called when the woman failed to show up at her various business locations and they found her body while checking her condo unit. The victim was bound and gagged but investigators have never revealed the cause of death other than saying it was a homicide. Lee was well known in the Korean community and detectives want to know if she expressed any concerns to anyone in the days leading up to her death. Evidence indicates someone overpowered the victim after breaking into her apartment and it's possible the attackers believed she had a quantity of cash at her home from the businesses she operated.

Dominique Lewis
Brooksville, Florida

She was a 19-year-old student who made friends on the Internet and someone she met may have killed her just after the Thanksgiving holiday in 2007. The body of Dominique Lewis was located in a wooded section off Brooksville Rock Road in Brooksville, Florida on Tuesday, December 11, 2007. She lived in St. Petersburg and attended the Ultimate Medical Academy in Clearwater, Florida where she was studying nursing. Detectives from the Hernando County Sheriff's Office have teamed up with investigators from the St. Petersburg Police Department to probe the death and catch her killer. The life she was living, however, has complicated the investigation and many individuals she was associated with through Internet dating and social networking sites have been reluctant to cooperate with police. Investigators said many of her relationships were sexual. A railway worker found Dominique's body among trees beside the CSX Railroad tracks at the dead-end of Brooksville Rock Road, north of Budowski Road in Hernando County. After a description of tattoos and jewelry was released to the public, the victim was officially identified as Dominique Lewis. Police learned she lived at the Bay Breeze Motel at 3900 34th Street in St. Petersburg with her boyfriend until November 30, 2007 and may have spent time with friends or lived at other motels in the area after that date. Her family last spoke to Dominique on Thanksgiving Day, November 22 and a St. Petersburg police officer gave her a traffic citation four days later after stopping her car for an equipment violation and discovering she was driving with a suspended license. Detectives are still hoping to locate people who saw the victim anytime from November 26 to when her body was discovered.

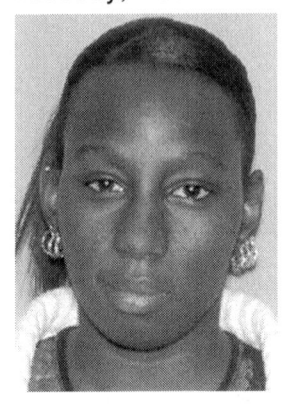

Dominique was born on April 7, 1988, the oldest of five children, and lived most of her life in St. Petersburg. She was five-feet, six-inches, 145 pounds with eight and a half inch extensions braided into her dark brown hair. She normally had four rings pierced into her ears, but only three were found with her body. Dominique also had the name Jeremy tattooed in Old English letters on her left wrist and the word Libra in the same style writing on her right foot. There was also a tattoo at the top of her left foot. She had been a student at Pinellas Park High School and had just started her nursing class at the time she was killed. Investigators learned Dominique moved from her parents' home in mid-December 2006 because they wouldn't allow her then 19-year-old boyfriend to come and live with her at their home. In the months since she left, the victim worked for some time with a company that provided adult chat and phone sex services. She also frequented a number of motels and strip clubs throughout St. Petersburg and Hernando County. Through the Internet she developed friendships with people in Pasco, Pinellas and Citrus counties as well as the Orlando area.

Pathologists believe the victim was dead four to five days before her body was discovered. Detectives learned she left her boyfriend around midnight on November 30 after some sort of disagreement and didn't show up for her nursing class the next day. Her parents didn't know she was missing until they heard the description of the body found along the railway tracks and realized it was Dominique. It was also only after her body was found that police located her white two-door 1994 Ford Probe at the Fat Boys Beauty Supply store at 301 34th Street North in St. Petersburg, some 70 miles south of where her body was discovered. The Hernando Crime Stoppers program has posted a reward of up to $1,000 for information that solves this case.

Investigators said they are hoping to hear from individuals who knew Dominique and can provide names of some of the people she knew. They said the victim may have said something to someone that could be very important to the case. Detectives believe the location where the body was dumped is likely an area that the killer knows and he may have taken other people in the past. The cold case investigators looking into the Lewis murder want anyone who thinks they have even what they feel is trivial information to call in because that detail could be what's needed to identify the person who killed Dominique.

Brittany Lynn Locklear
Hoke County, North Carolina

A young kindergarten girl was taken by a stranger while waiting for a school bus outside her family home in Hoke County, North Carolina and then sexually molested and murdered. Five-year-old Brittany Locklear was standing at the end of her driveway beside Gainey Road on Wednesday January 7, 1998, nine miles west of Raeford, when the driver of a pick-up truck offered her a ride. Her mother, Connie Chavis, kept peaking out the front window of their trailer home and when she didn't see her daughter, she assumed the bus had arrived. Moments later, a neighbor pounded on the door to tell Chavis a stranger had coaxed her daughter into his vehicle. Not believing her daughter had been abducted, Chavis and her father-in-law drove to West Hoke Elementary School, but little Brittany wasn't there. Police arrived from the Hoke County Sheriff's Department, the North Carolina State Police and the Federal Bureau of Investigation along with hundreds of volunteers to search the countryside for the missing girl. The only vital piece of information came from the neighbor who saw Brittany getting into a full size pick-up truck. Searchers discovered some of the girl's clothing and the hunt continued through the day and into the night. The following day, more than 24 hours after the abduction, searchers came across the girl's body in a drainage ditch alongside Ryan McBryde Road, about three miles south of where she had been abducted.

The Sheriff's department called in off-duty and auxiliary deputies to lead teams from the more than 600 volunteers who turned out after learning Brittany had vanished. Within a few hours they found the girl's backpack, her overalls and shoes. Early Thursday afternoon Hoke County Sheriff Wayne Byrd apologized to hundreds more people who turned out to help. The search was over. "It's sad news that I bring, said Byrd as he struggled to find the words. "I was hoping it would be a live body, but it's a lifeless body." The drainage ditch where she was found was adjacent to a farm lane, very much like the road leading to her home. Medical tests show she drowned after being held underwater in the ditch. She had also been raped by her killer.

The auditorium at J. W. Turlington School wasn't large enough to hold the thousands of people who turned out for the Sunday, January 11 funeral to say goodbye to the tiny victim. She was described as "God's little angel" during the service but there were no words that could console the grief that had been ravaged on residents of the rural farming region. Brittany was outside no longer than five minutes before the stranger approached. Her mother usually waited with her, but that morning she'd gone to use the washroom. She caught a glimpse or her daughter standing alone and when she looked out again moments later she was gone. Several neighbors standing some 200 yards away became concerned after seeing Brittany get into a truck and rushed over to tell her mother. Investigators believe that moments after the abduction, the killer drove south on Gainey Road near 3 Guy Loop where the family's trailer was located to a secluded area somewhere off Laurinburg Road, also known as state highway 401, where she was attacked. A short time later police say it's likely the victim was taken to the site of the ditch off Ryan McBryde Road where she was murdered. Investigators said all evidence suggests she was killed shortly after being abducted.

Police have obtained a variety of physical evidence including DNA from the attacker which has been compared to known sex offenders and other people living in the area. All were cleared of any involvement in Brittany's death. A $20,000 reward is being offered by the state's governor to anyone who comes forward with information that assists police in solving the murder. The State Bureau of Investigation also established a task force and through the years has tracked down countless leads. Many individuals, including people who were the closest to Brittany, came under scrutiny and several have been asked to take polygraph tests as well as submitting samples for DNA testing. People who came forward at the time with information have also been re-questioned to see if they can recall any other details that will assist the investigation.

Police prepared a psychological profile and have asked people if they remember any individual who showed signs of paranoia or irritability after Brittany was killed. They said the person may have attempted to change their appearance or excessively cleaning the interior of their vehicle. Police said these are little things that if someone remembers could become an important key to unlocking the mystery of the girl's abduction and killing.

Anthony Lombardi
Santa Clarita, California

A money machine service man was stalked before being killed outside his home in Santa Clarita, California. It was around 10 a.m. on Tuesday, September 16, 2008 when Anthony Lombardi was robbed and then gunned down in the driveway of the house on Undine Road in this community of 175,000 people some 35 miles north of Los Angeles. The bandit took a large amount of cash which the 55-year-old victim had just withdrawn from the bank to fill the various automatic teller machines that he serviced in the area. Investigators said the killer followed the victim and became familiar with his daily routine before confronting him. Lombardi was shot several times in the upper torso and died almost instantly. A group of children heading home from school in the late morning found the victim slumped in the driver's seat of his vehicle. There was no sign of the murder weapon. Detectives said Lombardi owned a company that serviced and replenished cash dispensing machines in convenience stores, restaurants and other independent outlets in Santa Clarita and neighboring area. Investigators are hoping to find anyone who saw anything suspicious while Lombardi was visiting the Wells Fargo Bank and Bank of America branches just before he was killed.

Lombardi was described as a friendly fellow who always had a wave and kind word for neighbors. He lived alone in the upper middle class neighborhood and was the father to three adult children. His daughter drove into the neighborhood several hours after the shooting occurred and collapsed in the arms of a police officer when told her father was dead.

Rewards totaling $20,000 have been posted for help in solving the slaying and investigators said they want to hear from anyone who noticed a vehicle following Lombardi or saw someone lurking around his home anytime leading up to the shooting. Police said they don't know if the killer followed the victim home or if he was waiting in the vicinity of the house located between Velan Drive and Tamarisk Place. The neighborhood isn't a gated community, but is only accessible by Golfcours Road off Tournament Road and police hope people who frequent the area might remember a stranger in the vicinity around the time Lombardi was murdered.

Steve Longoria
Austin, Texas

A 20-year-old man was shot and killed with a small caliber handgun after answering the door of his family's home in a four-plex building in the southeast area of Austin, Texas. Steve Longoria was confronted by a man at the home on Merritt Circle at Teri Road, just east of Interstate 35 at 2:23 a.m. on Sunday March 7, 1993. The victim's wife, young daughter, mother-in-law and several friends were in the house at the time. When the victim confirmed his name was Longoria, the person at the door pulled a gun and fired at close range into his chest. The gunman ran from the area after the shooting.

Homicide detectives from the Austin Police Department haven't revealed a motive but are urging anyone with information to come forward to assist with the investigation. The Austin Crime Stoppers program is also offering a reward of up to $1,000 to anyone who calls the tip line with details that help police capture the culprit.

Eduardo Lopez
Fort Worth, Texas

A teenage grocery clerk may have been murdered during a robbery in Fort Worth, Texas because he recognized the gunman. Eighteen-year-old Eduardo Lopez was shot in the head and back around 11:50 p.m. on Sunday, May 29, 1994 at Danal's grocery store on Hemphill Street after saying "what's up" to the bandit who was pointing a gun at the manager. Lopez died from his injuries two hours later at John Peter Smith Hospital. An employee of the store for only two months, Lopez had just graduated from Paschal High School.

Homicide detective from the Fort Worth Police Department suggest the victim may have recognized the suspect as someone from the neighborhood where he lived two miles away or possibly an individual he'd seen around the school. However, investigators say it's conjecture and there is nothing to positively indicate that Lopez knew the suspect because his face was masked.

Detectives said the bandit entered the store, located between West Fogg Street and West Drew Street, just before closing and threatened the manager with a gun while shoving him toward an office where the safe was located. Another suspect kept watch outside. Both were Hispanic males, but investigators were not able to get a detailed description.

Following the robbery the manager was locked in the store's freezer but escaped minutes later and alerted police. Another person called the 911 emergency number at 12:03 a.m. to report a shooting at the store, but detectives have never been able to locate that individual and are still anxious to speak with them to determine if they have additional information that will help solve the slaying. They are also appealing for anyone who may know who is responsible for the killing of Lopez to contact them. Crime Stoppers is offering a reward of up to $1,000 to encourage people to call the tip line if they have information that will assist the police.

Mayra Lopez
Stockton, California

A 14-year-old girl was killed and her friend injured when gunmen opened fire while driving along a quiet street in Stockton, California. Mayra Lopez was pronounced dead at the St. Joseph's Medical Centre less than three hours after the shooting which occurred on Dalewood Street around 9:30 p.m. on Saturday, May 3, 2008. She received a gunshot wound to her head. Her friend, 14-year-old Oscar Leon, was shot in the leg and later recovered.

The two honor students from Morada Middle School had been walking down the driveway near the triplex unit where Mayra's family lived on their way to a party when multiple shots were fired toward homes on the block-long street running north from Sandalwood Drive and turning west to link with West Lane Frontage Road.

Investigators said the four occupants of a white or gray colored sport utility vehicle were likely members of a gang but Mayra and her friend were not connected in any way with gang or gang related activity. They were innocent victims of a drive-by shooting. Described as a happy, fun-loving, bubbly young girl with a 3.1 grade point average, Mayra had lots of friends and just enjoyed life. Homicide detectives from the Stockton Police Department have not been able to establish a motive for the slaying or identify the gunmen.

Mayra's parents, Macario and Maria Lopez, went to their daughter's school Monday morning to help her classmates and others cope with the tragic loss. They talked about her always having a smile on her face, how much she enjoyed chatting with friends on the Internet and all the happy memories she had at school. It was a time to remember, a time for hugs and a time to cry.

Mayra was mischievous and a bit of a prankster, but she also helped out in the school office and was one of 35 students who maintained high grades and earned an opportunity to participate in the school's annual science trip to Santa Catalina Island.

She was a person who could have contributed something to society, but instead became the victim of a senseless killing on a street where, until that day, children rode their bikes and residents went walking without fear. Investigators said they are anxious to solve the murder and Stockton's Crime Stoppers program has offered a reward of up to $1,000 for anyone providing information that leads to the arrest of the killers.

Celia Loya
El Paso, Texas

The victim was just leaving for work when she was confronted by her killer at her home in east side El Paso, Texas. It was around 8:45 a.m. on Tuesday, February 7, 1995 when Celia Loya, 30, opened an inside door leading to the garage of the stylish executive home on Lake Champlain, just south of Pebble Hills Boulevard where she lived with her husband.

The attacker had entered the garage and was waiting on the other side of the door. She was pushed back into the house and savagely beaten in the living room. Minutes before Loya had called her office to let them know she would be a bit late for work but at that time gave no indication anything was wrong.

After making the phone call, investigators said it appears she took her purse and keys and was heading to the garage where her car was parked. Police were unable to find a motive for the slaying and it's possible the victim was attacked after unexpectedly encountering someone who was attempting to break into the home in the trendy Stanton Heights neighborhood.

After trying several times through the day to reach Loya, her husband became concerned and rushed home to make sure she was okay. He found her in a pool of blood on the bathroom floor. Before entering the house he noticed the garage door open and her car still parked inside. Police said the attacker entered and exited through the garage.

Nothing was stolen inside the home but there were signs of a violent struggle leading from the garage door to the living room and along a hallway to the bathroom. There were obvious injuries to her face and upper body and an autopsy showed she was brutally beaten and bludgeoned. Police did not indicate what she was hit with or if the murder weapon was recovered. Crime Stoppers has posted a reward for information that identifies Loya's killer.

Kimberly R. Mabry
Coleta, Illinois

The dismembered body of an exotic dancer was found in a creek in a rural area of Whiteside County near Coleta, Illinois some eight months after she vanished. The remains of Kimberly Mabry were discovered on Friday, April 14, 1995 but investigators have very little information to assist their homicide probe. The 27-year-old victim was five-feet, four-inches, 110 pounds with blonde hair and blue eyes. She was last seen on Thursday, September 1, 1994 in Rockford, Illinois, some 85 miles northeast from where her body was located. At that time she hung around Broadway Street, a rough area of town and sometimes frequented the Grand Hotel, a haven for drugs, alcohol and prostitution which has now been transformed into a 45 unit apartment building that serves as a permanent supportive housing facility for those who are destitute.

Investigators from the Whiteside County Sheriff's Department and the Illinois State Police are anxious to find out who Mabry associated with while in Rockford. They are also hoping to get a more comprehensive list of the places she frequented, individuals who were customers of crack houses in the vicinity and people who solicited sex acts from prostitutes. Crime Stoppers has a standard reward of up to $1,000 for anyone who calls anonymously with a tip that assists police in arresting Mabry's killer.

John Maclellan
New Orleans, Louisiana

After clinging to life for two months, a 38-year-old man succumbed from gunshot wounds received during an attempted street robbery in New Orleans, Louisiana. John Maclellan was shot when confronted by a heavy-set bandit around 2 a.m. on Friday, July 16, 2004 in the vicinity of Bellaire Drive and West Harrison Avenue. Maclellan, who worked as a bartender at the posh Smith & Wolenksy's New York style steakhouse, was walking to his Lakeview district home after meeting friends at a nearby establishment. When he told the bandit he wasn't carrying any cash, the gunman opened fire hitting Maclellan several times in the torso. He called for help on his cell phone and described the gunman to the 911 operator before collapsing. For two months family and friends donated blood and maintained a vigil at Charity Hospital, but Maclellan died on Friday, September 23, 2004. Detectives from the New Orleans Police Department's Third District Homicide Unit described the assailant as an African-American male, wearing a blue bandana on his head, a red cap and white t-shirt. They said he could have been accompanied by others, but the victim didn't recall anyone in particular in the vicinity.

Maclellan, a native of Massachusetts, had lived in New Orleans for a number of years. He was born in Weymouth and graduated from Boston College in 1989. His father, Dave, who lives in Norwell, Massachusetts, has vowed never to give up until his son's killer is captured. The murder took the life of his oldest child and impacted heavily on all those in the family. He has made personal visits to New Orleans to make sure the police continue to actively work on the homicide. He has also made appeals through the New Orleans Crime Stoppers program and over the years has encouraged local news outlets to highlight the hunt for his son's killer. Crime Stoppers has a reward of up to $2,500 for information that solves the case and Dave Maclellan is confident someone will come forward with details that will help police make an arrest.

Maclellan began working at Smith & Wolenksy's when he moved New Orleans in 2001. Many nights he carried cash from the restaurant, but it's not known if he was carrying any money when he was shot. The high-end steakhouse, one of 16 owned by the company across the United States, closed its doors after business dropped dramatically following the devastation of Hurricane Katrina. The catastrophic flooding experienced by the city also affected the momentum of the investigation since many people who may have information that would be helpful in solving the case have moved away and don't realize investigators are still looking for help to find Maclellan's killer. Detective Erbin Bush, one of the investigators working on the case, believes it's important to refresh people's minds about old cases and encourage them to contact police. Someone knows something and police are hoping that person will come forward soon to give them the name of the killer. Crime Stoppers executive director Darlene Cusanza is acutely aware of the vital role the program plays to get information about unsolved cases. She said they always hope someone has bragged to another person about their involvement in a crime and then an anonymous call comes into the tip line.

Julie Magliulo
Pompano Beach, Florida

It was a quiet neighborhood in Pompano Beach, Florida, and a place where parents weren't afraid to let their children play outside. There was hardly any traffic on the streets and bends in the roads ensured vehicles didn't travel too fast. It seemed the perfect place to bring up children. But Monday, June 8, 1987 became a nightmare for Brenda and Antonio Magliulo when their three-year-old daughter, Julie, vanished. The girl had been playing outside and at 9:30 a.m. told her mother she was going to a playmates home nearby. A half an hour later, Brenda saw her daughter's friend outside, but there was no sign of the blonde-haired, blue-eyed girl who everyone knew by the nickname JuJuBee. She frantically scoured a wooded area behind their home and enlisted other residents to search surrounding streets before calling the Broward Sheriff's department at 11:50 a.m. to report her daughter missing.

The home where Antonio and Brenda lived with their five children at 6201 SW 19th Street was soon buzzing with activity. It became the command post for a massive search that lasted for weeks. Local investigators got immediate assistance from the Florida Department of Law Enforcement and the Federal Bureau of Investigation. As police and volunteers fanned out to scrutinize properties in an ever expanding perimeter from the missing girl's home, helicopters searched from above and divers checked lakes and waterways, as well as a flooded rock quarry about two blocks from the house. They found no trace of Julie.

A deputy sheriff had been driving through the Broadview Estates neighborhood where the Magliulo family lived and saw Julie playing outside her house around 8:30 a.m. on the morning she went missing. Around 9 p.m. a garbage man saw Julie near her home and a neighbor told police he saw her about 9:40 a.m. walking on a pathway toward a nearby Circle K convenience store. That morning she was wearing red shorts and a blue t-shirt. She also never went anywhere without her purple Raggedy Ann doll. Investigators produced thousands of posters with Julie's picture and urged anyone who has seen the missing girl to alert the nearest law enforcement agency. The parents also made personal appeals for their daughter's safe return.

Despite organizing massive searches, the sheriff's department also had to conduct intensive investigations to determine who was responsible for Julie's disappearance. Antonio, who was better known to everyone as Tony, his wife Brenda and their oldest daughter, Camille, then 15, were questioned for several hours. Detectives wanted to know if anyone in the family might be involved. They asked if they knew of a hostile relative or acquaintance who took the child to punish the family for something. They couldn't think of anything to put the police on the track of someone who could have taken Julie. It was a complete mystery.

There was no sign of Julie on her birthday, Monday, August 31, 1987 when she would have turned four. It was a quiet day for the family, but the parents continued to have hope. Volunteers were searching fields, wooded areas, business sites, backyards, ditches adjacent to roadways and going door to door in the hunt for Julie. Miami Dolphin wide receiver Mark Duper also made a video appeal while clutching a large color photograph of the girl and begging for her return. The message was shown on news broadcasts across the country. "I think she'll be back," her Mom said. "I just don't know when. She's in God's hands."

Ten months after she vanished, two men who were out target shooting stumbled on Julie's skeleton remains in a marshy field flanking the Everglades some three-quarters of a mile south of Route 84 just east of State Highway 27. The site is about 20 miles southwest of the missing girl's home. It was a remote and undeveloped area of Broward County at the time, but today it's the site of the City of Weston, a community with a population of 64,000 built by the Arvidea Corporation, a subsidiary of Disney. Police were not able to locate a great deal of physical evidence when the remains were found on Thursday, April 21, 1988 beside Binocular Lake. Medical examiners said the body had been disturbed by animals and soaked by water and muck when the area flooded in the nine months before she was located. They also said a lot of things disintegrated when a wildfire ravaged the region six weeks earlier. It was by accident the men made the discovery. Their vehicle had got stuck in mud and they were scanning the marshy fields for rocks to construct a pathway to give some traction to drive the truck out when they spotted the skeletal remains. It took a week before forensic experts were able to confirm that Julie had been found. Pathologists determine her cause of death as asphyxiation.

Floral arrangements covered the alter at New Covenant Church when a memorial service was held for Julie on Friday, April 29, 1988. There was a large portrait of the little girl looking out at mourners. Antonio comforted his wife as they sat in the front row with their four other children. Their arms were wrapped around each other and they cried. Reverend George Callahan had no words to explain why such a tragedy had occurred. "Although we may not understand the circumstances, we celebrate that little Julie is home," he said. "That she's all right, that she is with Jesus." He beseeched God to hold Julie in His arms and protect her.

Investigators were never able to identify anyone as a possible suspect, but 20 years after the little girl's body was discovered, the Federal Bureau of Investigation has reopened the case and posted a reward of up to $25,000 for anyone providing information that leads to the arrest and conviction of the person responsible for Julie's kidnapping and killing. They are appealing for anyone with information that will solve the case to contact a local FBI office or the nearest American embassy or consulate. Cold case investigators said during a joint news conference by the Broward Sheriff's Office and the FBI they have reason to believe that there may be individuals who have information pertinent to the girl's disappearance that for unknown reasons have not yet come forward. "We are making an appeal to these people to contact the FBI as soon as possible."

The FBI has a special unit formed in 2006 called the Child Abduction Rapid Deployment Team or CARDT with some 60 agents assigned to teams in five regions across the United States. They assist local police departments whenever a child is abducted. In 2008 they implemented a special program to examine cold cases and the investigation into the disappearance of Julie Magliulo was one of the first five they selected. It was in November 2008 they announced the girl's abduction and homicide case had been reopened.

People are being asked to reach into the recesses of their minds and make every effort to recall if they remember anything suspicious around the time Julie was taken. Investigators said it's possible someone anywhere could recall something that is vital to the case. An individual who lived in the girl's neighborhood at the time of the disappearance could recall seeing a vehicle or someone suspicious, or a person living 2,000 miles away might remember thinking it was strange how someone made attempts to change their appearance.

Special Agent Jim Lewis of the FBI's Miami Field Office, who is working to develop new leads, said "this case may be cold, but it still has a heartbeat." Lewis and Detective Scott Champagne of the Broward County Sheriff's Office are working with former Detective Don Scarborough, a retired Broward County Sheriff's deputy and one of the original investigators when Julie vanished to probe any new evidence that surfaces as well as re-interviewing people who provided information around the time of the kidnapping and murder.

The FBI's Behavioral Analysis Unit has also provided indicators that might help pinpoint a possible suspect. They are asking if you know of someone who was visiting or moved to Pompano Beach just prior to the time Julie vanished and left suddenly after June 8, 1987. "Even if you think that your information is unimportant, or that someone else may have already reported what you know, please contact the investigation's hotline. Now is the time to come forward. It is never too late to give any information that might help. Your call may be the one that provides us with the information needed to solve this case." Investigators are seeking public assistance to identify anyone who started acting differently. They said this may not mean the person was involved in this crime, but if you know of someone experiencing a behavioral change at that time, police would like to question them to ensure they are not connected with the case. Some of the changes can include:
- A person unexpectedly leaving the area around the time the girl vanished even if they have a plausible sounding reason such as going away on business or visiting a relative or friend.
- Changes in a person's alcohol, drug or cigarette consumption, either an increase or decrease.
- Missing work or other appointments around the time of the disappearance.

- ➢ Showing unnatural interest in the case such as being absorbed in media coverage or talking about the incident even years later.
- ➢ Displaying nervousness or irritability.
- ➢ An increase or decrease in expression of religious beliefs.
- ➢ Changes in routine sleep patterns.
- ➢ Unexplained injuries such as cuts and bruises particularly on hands or arms.
- ➢ Making attempts to change ones appearance by cutting, growing or dying hair, shaving or growing a moustache or shaving or growing a beard.
- ➢ Someone who stopped using or stored a vehicle just after Julie vanished or a person who sold or gave away their car at the time.

Brenda Magliulo remembers Julie as a very independent little girl who loved walking to the local convenience store to buy her favorite candy. She also adored her brothers and sisters and would often follow them through the woods behind their home. Julie's mom has moved from the neighborhood to escape the memories of that day in 1987 when her daughter vanished but she still lives in hope that the killer will be caught. Her husband shared the same hope until his death in 2008. Investigators are also hoping to bring the suspect to justice. "Now is the time to come forward," said a joint statement released by the FBI and the sheriff's office when the case was reopened. "It is never too late to give any information that might help. Your call may be the one."

Find My Killer

Chapter 5 – Mann to Redmon

Annie Mann
Anchorage, Alaska

Her murdered body was found behind an abandoned industrial warehouse off a four lane roadway on the southern rim of the Elmendorf Air Force base in Anchorage, Alaska, but investigators don't want to reveal details of how she was killed. Detectives are, however, appealing for help to find who is responsible for killing 45-year-old Annie Mann, a resident of Kokhanok, a tiny village some 250 miles away and accessible only by air. The victim, a native woman, who was only five-feet, one-inch and weighed almost 100 pounds, was wearing green pants, a purple jacket and a gray t-shirt with the word Hawaii on the front. Her body was discovered behind the building at 1924 Post Road near Spar Avenue on Sunday, August 8, 1999 and homicide detectives are hoping someone will remember seeing her in the city anytime before that date. Anchorage Crime Stoppers has also offered a reward of up to $1,000 for anyone who provides information that solves this killing.

Pamela Lynn Mansell
Lexington, Kentucky

Homicide detectives are trying to trace the final movements of a 35-year-old woman who was smothered and strangled in Lexington, Kentucky. A newspaper delivery person found the naked body of Pamela Lynn Mansell on the morning of Thursday, November 8, 2001 in a grassy area beside a driveway off Briar Hill Road. Investigators determined the victim had been killed somewhere else and her body dumped at the entrance of a horse farm in Fayette County just east of Lexington. Mansell, the mother of two daughters, lived at 1229 Nice Drive, on the city's western boundary, some 15 miles away from where he body was discovered. Detectives have had only limited success in developing a timeline showing where the victim was in the days before she was killed and are anxious to speak to anyone who remembers seeing her. Investigators are also hoping to find people who knew the victim and can give them information about individuals she associated with around the time of her death. The Bluegrass Crime Stoppers program has posted a reward of up to $1,000 to the person who can assist investigators solve this killing.

Donna G. Martin
Boca Raton, Florida

A 53-year-old security firm worker was stabbed to death by someone in her Boca Raton, Florida apartment after she spent the evening at a local bar. Investigators believe Donna G. Martin was murdered by someone she knew in the early morning hours of Tuesday, January 12, 1999 at her one-storey apartment complex known as the Crystal Palms at 6902 Palmetto Circle South. She was last seen at 10:45 p.m. Monday, January 11 at the Porter House Bar and Grill, six blocks away, on Palmetto Park Road near Powerline Road. Witnesses didn't see her leave with anyone and police believe she may have encountered the individual when she reached her home. There was no sign of a forced entry or any type of struggle outside the apartment unit. Residents also didn't hear any sort of commotion. The victim's body was found on the kitchen floor around noon Tuesday when a colleague from ADT Security Services came to her home to find out why she wasn't at work. The victim, who died from multiple stab wounds, was still wearing the same clothes she had gone to work in the previous day which indicates she was killed shortly after arriving at the apartment. Restaurant employees told investigators the woman often came in and had some drinks after work. The night Martin was murdered, the staff remember that she was sitting alone and quietly sipping drinks until paying her bill and heading home. She left a bit later than usual that night but waiters and the bartender didn't recall her talking to anyone through the evening. Investigators from the Palm Beach County Sheriff's Department are hoping to find someone who might know who was with Martin in her apartment or if she went anywhere after leaving the bar. The local Crime Stoppers program has also offered a reward of up to $1,000 to help solve this case.

Sergeant Gregory Keith Martin
Jonesville, North Carolina

Although the only officer patrolling Jonesville, North Carolina on the night of Saturday, October 5, 1996, he felt very safe because nothing usually happened in this community of less than 1,500 people. Sergeant Gregory Keith Martin had just left an all-night restaurant after getting something to eat and was heading to a 24 hour convenience store to pick up a couple of newspapers for the staff at the dispatch centre. Around 2:30 a.m. while heading eastbound on Highway 67 toward Interstate 77, he spotted a red colored pick-up truck in the parking lot of a strip mall. He told the dispatcher he would be checking a suspect, but a few moments later reported the vehicle travelling toward the Interstate. Martin followed the 1996 Dodge Ram southbound for about a mile on the Interstate to an isolated section. It's not known if the vehicle was pulled over or the driver just stopped at that location after noticing the police car behind him. "I'm going to need some assistance," said Martin after radioing his location. A North Carolina State trooper arrived at 2:42 a.m. and found Martin dead on the shoulder of the roadway. The 30-year-old officer, who was married with three children, had been shot multiple times in the head. Martin had served with the Jonesville Police Department for three years and since a boy had dreamed of being a police officer.

The pick-up truck the killer had been driving was stolen from Ramey Motors in Princeton, West Virginia and the license plates were taken from a Chevy Blazer left for servicing at a transmission shop in the same community. The vehicle was located later that day at Lucia Incorporated, a company in Elkin, a couple of miles north of Jonesville, which manufactured sportswear clothing for women. One of the company's vehicles, a white 1980 Chevrolet sports van with the company logo and a red stripe was taken from the lot, but found at 6:30 p.m. in Gastonia, a community of 66,000 residents some 95 miles to the south. The Lucia vehicle was in the parking lot of the Home Depot store on East Franklin Boulevard near the Cox Road exit from

Interstate 85. Investigators believe the killer likely turned around at the next interchange after shooting Martin and stole the Lucia vehicle before continuing his trip southward. A 1982 red Toyota Land Cruiser, believe taken by Martin's killer from the Home Depot parking lot after dumping the Lucia van, has never been found. It is a long time ago, but investigators are hoping someone will remember seeing any of these vehicles on the day Martin was killed. At this point detectives do not know how many people were in the vehicles and have no idea what they look like.

A $30,000 reward has been posted for the capture and conviction of the killer and investigators are hoping there are people who remember details from that night that will assist them in putting together all the pieces. Police have utilized billboards and even hypnotized a witness in hopes they could recall information in a trance like state that was locked somewhere deep in the mind. Investigators haven't indicated if they got additional evidence through hypnosis, but they did get information from someone 10 years after the slaying that might be extremely valuable once the killer is caught. The Jonesville Police Department and the North Carolina State Bureau of Investigation are continuing to probe the killing and remain hopeful someone will come forward to help them solve the murder of Sergeant Martin.

Dale Tyrone Matthews, Jr.
Tampa, Florida

A 19-year-old man was shot to death while preparing a bottle to feed his four-month-old daughter in Tampa, Florida. A friend found Dale Tyrone Matthews Jr. collapsed on the kitchen floor of his mother's home at 3222 East Louisiana Avenue about 10:20 a.m. on Tuesday, February 26, 2008. He was clutching the baby bottle to his chest and, Lailah, his daughter was crying in a nearby bedroom. Investigation showed someone fatally shot the victim after confronting him in the house. The baby was not harmed. Homicide detectives from the Tampa Police Department haven't established a motive for the slaying and are continuing to interview family members and friends in hopes of identifying possible suspects. Police have not identified the person who found Matthews, but said he came to the house that morning to work out with his friend. There was no answer, but the doorway leading from the garage was open and he went inside and discovered the victim who lived at the home with his mother and sister.

He was unemployed and his 20-year-old girlfriend, Sierra Sam, would leave their baby with him while she went to work at a local day care center. She had dropped Lailah off on Monday and spent a bit of time with Matthews before putting the baby to bed. At the time of the killing Matthews was alone in the home with his daughter who was in a rear bedroom. Investigators believe the victim had put the baby in a crib and was preparing a bottle for her when the killer arrived at the home just west of North 34th Street. Although Matthews had been jailed for four months on drug possession charges he was described as a caring parent and willing to look after his child at anytime. Sam said they had known each other about two years after meeting at a local club. A reward of up to $1,000 is available from the Tampa Crime Stoppers program for anyone who can provide information that helps police solve this killing.

Dorian Jacques McCorvey
Austin, Texas

A 21-year-old man was killed by mistake when gunman in Austin, Texas opened fire on the wrong vehicle. The shooting occurred on Saturday, October 21, 1995 while Dorian McCorvey and his two passengers were stopped at a traffic light on Loyola Lane at Manor Road. He was in the far left turn lane when another vehicle stopped beside him. At that point a young man leaned out the passenger side window and fired some 10 shots over the roof of the car at McCorvey and the occupants in his vehicle. McCorvey was killed almost instantly and his two passengers wounded, but they later recovered from their injuries at Brackenridge Hospital.

The burgundy Oldsmobile that the victim was driving careered through the intersection and crashed into the office of a car wash on the southwest corner. The other car, described as a cream colored or dark Cadillac, sped off. McCorvey was a student at Austin Community College and worked part-time at Apple Computer. Although the area had become a magnet for gang members and drug dealers, investigation showed McCorvey and his two friends had no connection with criminal activity.

Police said it's likely the gunman was targeting someone who drove a similar vehicle. Homicide detectives believe there are people who know who is responsible for the shooting and are urging them to come forward. Austin Crime Stoppers has also posted a $1,000 reward for information about the fatal shooting.

Lisa Ann McCuddin
Fort Dodge, Iowa

Homicide detectives are still trying to ascertain the connection between the shooting death of a 23-year-old woman and a shootout a short time earlier at a Fort Dodge, Iowa hotel. Lisa Ann McCuddin was shot around 4 a.m. on Saturday, October 2, 2004 when a car pulled alongside the vehicle she was riding in on Kenyon Road, east of Highway 169. The 29-year-old driver, Fred Murray of Omaha, was wounded in the attack. McCuddin died from her injuries, but Murray recovered after hospital treatment. Shortly before Lisa, a mother of two children, was killed, police were called to the former Holiday Inn on Highway 169 where a man had been wounded in a gunfight. Detectives with the Fort Dodge Police Department said the two incidents are related but investigations so far haven't pinpointed the exact link.

It is believed the couple was heading to the hotel to attend a birthday party when the shooting occurred. After his car was ambushed, Murray raced a short distance down the road to the Holiday Inn to get help but McCuddin was dead before they reached the parking lot. Lisa was born on October 6, 1980 in Sioux City, Iowa and was killed four days before her 24th birthday. Her mother, Becky McCuddin, has never given up hope that the killer will be caught although she has faced a great deal of frustration as the investigation has dragged on through the years. Police said they have physical evidence and have narrowed the focus of the murder probe, but require additional information to secure some loose ends.

Through the years Becky has solicited help from students enrolled in the crime scene investigation class at Iowa Central Community College to hand out flyers in various neighborhoods to encourage people to come forward with information about her daughter's murder. She said there are people who know the killer but are afraid to speak up. A $10,000 reward has been issued and police have received some information, but the key pieces are not yet available. The Webster County Crime Stoppers program has also offered a reward for anyone who is willing to provide information without giving their name. Becky has been looking after her daughter's two children, Markasia, then 4, and Davontrez, who was only 10 months old when Lisa was murdered. The children give her strength to continue because she sees her daughter in their faces ever day. She has also written to everyone from the local mayor to the President of the United States to ensure the killing of her daughter won't end up as a forgotten file in someone's desk drawer. She now lives every day hoping for justice.

Thomas McKnight   Judy McKnight

Thomas & Judy McKnight
Lincoln County, New Mexico

The 1984 shotgun killings of Thomas "Cotton" McKnight and his wife, Judy, in the kitchen of their ranch in New Mexico's Lincoln County has baffled investigators and continues to be a complete mystery. The victims were found dead at the Upper McKnight Ranch on Thursday, November 15 and so far the Lincoln County Sheriff's Department, the New Mexico State Police and New Mexico Attorney General investigators have been unable to identify any possible suspects. The Crime Stoppers program in Ruidoso, the largest community in the county, has offered a $1,000 reward in the slayings and the State of New Mexico is offering $10,000 but through the years no one has come forward to provide information and collect the money.

Historically the area was the site of the 1878 Lincoln County War where Billy the Kid shot and killed Sheriff William J. Brady and Deputy George W. Hindman. During the conflict, which was actually a feud between cattle ranchers and the owner of the area's largest general store, dozens of people died and a truce wasn't arranged until U.S. Cavalry troops began battling both factions. Since the cowboy days there haven't been many killing in Lincoln County and consequently the murder of McKnight and his wife jarred those living in various communities between Ruidoso and Roswell in this sparsely populated area of New Mexico. The ranch was some 17 miles south of Picacho, a village of less than 100 people, on Highway 380. It's completely remote and whoever took the lives of the couple had to travel on rugged back roads to carry out their mission.

The pair had been dead about 48 hours when their bodies were discovered, so investigators have put the time of death as sometime in the late afternoon of Tuesday, November 13, 1984. Homicide detectives were unable to determine a motive for the slayings and have never found evidence to link anyone specifically to the murders. There was no sign of a forced entry into the home and it appears the couple was familiar and friendly with whoever drove out to the house on that day. McKnight had just opened a can of beer after coming home from a sheep pasture and a short time later his wife entered the house after doing some banking in Ruidoso. She had also stopped to have a drink at her favorite bar in that community, the Hollywood Lounge. McKnight was confronted by his killer when he walked into the kitchen of the ranch-style home and was shot in the chest and in the head just above his left eye. Judy rushed into the room and was kneeling over her husband when the gunman fired a shot into her lower back. While on the floor, both victims were then shot execution-style in the back of their heads. From 1978 to 1982, McKnight served as head of the Lincoln County Commission, but there were no controversial issues that would have led to his murder.

Police will not confirm if two weapons were used or if they believe one or two gunmen were involved in the killings. Despite the lack of a motive, investigators said someone drove deliberately to the couple's isolated home with the intent to kill. Investigators said it wasn't just a random act of violence, but very calculated and premeditated. Through the years investigators have reviewed the evidence and followed additional leads, but are no closer to solving the case than they were when first called to the murder scene. Whoever was responsible took time to wipe any objects in the house they may have touched and investigators were never able to find any fingerprints. It also appears as though some things were planted at the murder scene as false clues to point police in the wrong direction and interfere with the investigation process. Detective said they are now hoping someone will have talked about the slayings and police will get an anonymous call to put them on the track of the killer. McKnight's sister, Terri Bussey, is also anxious for the killer to be captured.

Donna Deanne Mills
Jacksonville, Florida

The death of Donna Deanne Mills is tragic and senseless. Asleep in her bed on Saturday, December 15, 2007, the 29-year-old woman was struck by a stray bullet fired randomly in an apartment complex, known as Preserve at Cedar River at 4301 Confederate Point Road in Jacksonville, Florida. The bullet went through a window of apartment unit 130 where she had lived for several years. She was killed instantly. Police do not know if someone was firing from a moving vehicle or walking through the trendy Westside neighborhood. It was around 3:15 a.m. when police received a 911 call about shots being fired at several vehicles.

Uniformed officers found a couple of cars that had been damaged, but there was no indication anyone had been hurt. At 11 a.m. police were called back to the area after residents discovered other vehicles with bullet holes and at that time an officer noticed a shot had gone through the window of an apartment unit. After getting no answer at the door, police forced their way in and found the woman dead inside. Investigation confirmed Mills was killed by a stray bullet fired from a private roadway inside the gated waterfront community.

Mills, known as "Dee Dee" to close friends, had worked for more than eight years at VyStar Credit Union and volunteered for a number of charitable organizations including the Leukemia and Lymphoma Society. She enjoyed her job and loved spending time with family and friends she had made since moving into her own place. It was 10 days before Christmas and that Saturday Donna had plans to attend a 25th birthday party for her younger sister, Sarah. She also had a passion for photography and had just established a wedding photo business with a friend. A cousin described her as a beautiful person, someone who was so full of life. She was a kind and giving person who touched the lives of so many. The cousin also made an appeal to the killer urging him to give himself up. "If you want to be brave, proud or whatever...turn yourself in," said the message on the Internet. "Be an honorable person not a coward who hides behind a gun."

Investigators say the shooting was random. It's likely someone passing by fired shots toward the vehicles and buildings in the complex. It was completely by chance the victim was killed as she slept in her bed. Her sister said she was in a place where she should have been completely safe, but instead her life was taken by someone acting reckless and senseless. They took the life of a person who was working hard to make the world a better place for others. They also devastated her family members and friends who no longer can hear her voice or see her smile. The Jacksonville Sheriff's Office is urging anyone with information to come forward. A $16,000 reward fund has been established and Crime Stoppers want people to call their tipline anonymously if they won't talk to the investigators directly.

Christy Ann Mirack
Lancaster, Pennsylvania

An elementary school teacher was murdered in her apartment on the outskirts of Lancaster, Pennsylvania four days before Christmas. The body of Christy Ann Mirack was discovered on Monday, December 21, 1992 by the school's principal who went to her apartment at 2071 William Penn Way when she didn't show up to teach her Grade 6 class. The 25-year-old victim, who was dead on the living room floor, had been raped, savagely beaten and then strangled. Detectives from the East Lampeter Township Police believe Christy Ann was confronted by her killer sometime between 7 a.m. when her roommate, Mary Lesko, left the apartment and 7:45 a.m. the time she usually headed to work. They also believe the murder occurred before 9 a.m. Residents at the Greenfield Estates complex reported seeing a white vehicle, similar to a Dodge Daytona, with black louvers on the rear window in the parking area around the time of the slaying. Forensic tests have also indicated the killer was a white male. Christy Ann was born in Sunbury, Pennsylvania, but lived most of her life in the nearby community of Shamokin and after graduating from college got a teaching position at Rohrerstown Elementary School. Investigators haven't indicated if someone had forced their way into the apartment but did say the victim may have known her attacker. They also said it's possible the assailant had watched the apartment unit from the parking lot and waited until the roommate left before going to the door. Although Christy Ann was five-feet, seven-inches, she weighed only 120 pounds and an assailant would have had no trouble overpowering her. Through the years police have extensively interviewed friends, neighbors and relatives but were never able to determine a motive or identify a possible suspect. They said there may be other people who have not been interviewed who have valuable information about the victim and are urging them to contact investigators immediately. They are also hoping someone who has heard something through the years will now be willing to come forward and tell investigators what they know. The Pennsylvania Crime Stoppers program is also offering a reward of up to $2,000 for anyone who can provide information anonymously on the tip line that helps solve the killing.

John Mitchell & Mary Mitchell
Fort Worth, Texas

The brutal deaths of a retired couple in Fort Worth, Texas are likely related to drug trafficking. When the bodies of 69-year-old John Mitchell and his 65-year-old wife, Mary, were found around 8 p.m. Tuesday, April 14, 1999 in their home on Hurley Avenue police discovered quantities of marijuana. Investigation showed the couple was selling drugs from their home and it's likely the killer was one of their customers who knew they usually had a considerable amount of cash in the house located between Mitchell Avenue and West Jessamine Street in Fort Worth's Fairmount neighborhood. Detectives from the Fort Worth Police Department homicide unit indicated there was a violent struggle and the house had been ransacked. The beatings the victims received caused blunt force trauma injuries and they were also stabbed repeatedly. There was no sign of a forced entry. The couple's daughter found the bodies when she went to check on them after getting no answer on the phone. The pair had operated a popular rock and roll bar on Magnolia Avenue at Hurley Avenue, seven blocks north of their home and investigators said it's likely they made underworld contacts through the business that enabled them to become neighborhood drug dealers after selling their bar and going into retirement. Detectives are hoping someone has overheard an individual bragging about killing the couple and will come forward with the information. If the person isn't comfortable talking directly to detectives, the local Crime Stoppers program is offering a reward of up to $1,000 for anonymous information that solves this case.

Colin Moaning
Oklahoma City, Oklahoma

The killer made a mistake when he shot the driver of a car in Oklahoma City. It was on March 24, 1999 when 27-year-old Colin Moaning was shot in the head while driving his friend's car on Highland Avenue near Smith Road in the northeastern area of the city. He died three months later. Investigators said the car owner was the intended victim but on that day he was sitting in the front passenger seat while letting Moaning drive. As he slowed the green Camaro to pass a maroon colored Chevrolet pick-up truck with an extended cab someone in that vehicle fired several shots. Moaning was hit in the head and his friend only grazed by a bullet.

Police surmise the shooting was in retaliation for the friend giving evidence three years earlier at a trial which led to the conviction of two people in connection with a 1994 double murder. Police said there are individuals who know Moaning's killer, but are convinced their lives will be in jeopardy if they cooperate with homicide investigators. At this point detectives are hoping they can break through the wall of fear and persuade people to come forward and identify the gunman. A reward is also available from Crime Stoppers to anyone who anonymously helps solve the killing.

Nolan Moi
Madisonville, Ohio

The 19-year-old victim was shot in the head while walking up the stairs of a home in the Cincinnati suburb of Madisonville in Ohio, but other residents didn't hear anything. It was just after 9:30 a.m. on Monday, March 11, 2002 when roommates found the body of Nolan T. Moi on the stairway of the house at 4412 Erie Avenue just north of Whitney Avenue. He died from a single bullet wound to the head. The roommates at first thought Moi had fallen down the stairs and carried him to his apartment unit, but called paramedics when they realized he wasn't breathing. Police have attempted to trace the victim's movements in the hours leading up to the slaying, but have not had a great deal of success in finding people who saw him Sunday night or in the early hours of Monday.

Investigators have not determined a motive and have been unable to identify any potential suspects in Moi's death. Investigation has shown the victim was a typical teenager who enjoyed getting together with friends and spending time watching television or playing video games. He made money working as a pizza delivery boy and occasionally smoked marijuana, but detectives found nothing in his background that would be a catalyst for his killing. His family put up a $10,000 reward for information that will help find the killer and the Greater Cincinnati Crime Stoppers program is offering up to $1,000 for an anonymous tip that leads to an arrest in this case.

The victim's mother, Lucy Logan, spearheaded a personal campaign to establish a reward fund to encourage witnesses to come forward and later worked with Cincinnati's television station, WKRC Channel 12, to produce a 45 minute video of various unsolved local homicides which was broadcast regularly on a closed circuit network to inmates incarcerated at the Hamilton County Justice Centre. The video showed the faces of victims and reenactments of the killing, including the one where her son was shot to death. The video also highlighted the local Crime Stoppers tip line number and encouraged anyone with information to make the call anonymously to the program. Logan also worked with relatives of other murder victims to set up a support group called "Who Killed Our Kids" with the aim of solving the cases. Logan said it's devastating when witnesses won't come forward to help get killers off the street. She is convinced someone knows who fired the gun that killed her son but just doesn't have the courage to speak out.

Reginald "Buck" Montgomery,
Lincoln Park, New Jersey

Homicide detectives are still trying to determine what was behind the killing of a 25-year-old man on a tree-lined stretch of road near the airport in Lincoln Park, New Jersey. The bullet-riddled body of Reginald "Buck" Montgomery was found in a ditch at the side of Beaverbrook Road around 10:38 p.m. on Tuesday, May 17, 1994, a short distance north of Bridgewater Lane. The victim, who lived on

East 159th Street in Bronx, New York, a street with older but well maintained apartment buildings, was last seen across the river in Harlem around 7 p.m. on the night he died. At that time he was with a friend in a burgundy-colored Toyota Land Cruiser with Connecticut license plates.

Montgomery was described as a black male, five-feet, nine-inches, about 150 pounds with short black hair and brown eyes. He was wearing dark green trousers, a white sweatshirt, white sneakers, white socks and a black leather cap. Homicide investigators are hoping to complete a timeline to show his movements in the final four to six hours in his life and are appealing to anyone who saw Montgomery or knows anything about his killing to contact them. Crime Stoppers is also offering a reward of up to $1,000 for anonymous information that will help investigator solve the case. It's likely that on the night the victim died he was driven across the George Washington toll bridge to the New Jersey Turnpike and Bergen Passaic Expressway before turning onto Highway 202 or the Boonton Turnpike which leads to the Lincoln Park Airport. There has been speculation through the years that the one runway airport mainly used by single-engine private aircraft has at times been used as a transit point to smuggle drugs to the New York area.

Troy Art Moross
Madison Heights, Michigan

A man with droopy eyes and his hair combed low across his forehead might be able to help solve the slaying of a 26-year-old local musician in Madison Heights, Michigan. The body of Troy Art Moross was found around 5:30 a.m. on Monday, February 26, 2001 outside the Borite Corporation on Sherman Avenue near East Whitcomb Avenue and Dequindre Road, in this community of 31,000 some 16 miles north of Detroit. Investigation showed the victim had been savagely beaten. Death was attributed to blunt force trauma to the head. Moross vanished after leaving Grumpy Joe's Sports Grill at 31660 John R Road around 2:30 a.m. on Saturday, February 24, 2001. The bar, now called Augie's, is less than a mile from where his body was found. He left the bar with a man and police are still trying to identify the individual in hopes he can shed additional information on where Moross went and who might have killed him. The individual was about 30 years, around five-feet-nine to five-feet-ten, 160 to 165 pounds with a medium build. He had light brown hair combed to the right across his forehead and partially covering his right eyebrow. He had on old faded jeans and a light gray zippered sweatshirt.

The victim, who was born on December 23, 1974 and lived in Troy, Michigan, eight miles away, was last seen by family members several hours before he vanished leaving the Astro Lanes on John R Road where he bowled every Friday night on a league team. He told them he was stopping at the nearby Sports Grill before heading home. Investigators want anyone in that area at the time of the homicide to think back and try to recall anyone matching the description of the man seen with Moross when he left the bar. Crime Stoppers is also offering a $1,000 reward to anyone who can provide information that helps solve this killing.

Kimberly Sue Morse
North Providence, Rhode Island

An exotic dancer was brutally murdered in her North Providence, Rhode Island apartment after coming home from work. The 32-year-old victim, Kimberly Sue Morse, was grabbed from behind and attacked with a knife when confronted by someone around 2 a.m. on Tuesday, January 18, 2000 at her basement apartment on Garibaldi Street, just north of Falco Street. Investigation showed she parked her Jeep Cherokee sometime between 1:40 a.m. and 1:50 a.m. in the lot outside the small apartment building where she had lived for almost three years. Detectives with the North Providence Police Department are not sure if someone followed her into the apartment or if they were waiting inside. Kimberly went to the kitchen area where evidence indicates a male attacker grabbed her from behind and slashed her throat. As the victim slumped to the floor she was also stabbed several times and likely died within minutes from severe blood loss. Sometime later the killer dragged her body to a bathroom where she was stripped naked and dumped into the bathtub. Before leaving the apartment the assailant draped towels across Kimberly's body and then used some flammable materials to set a fire in hopes of destroying any evidence that might help investigators identify her killer. The blaze smoldered for almost 15 hours before other residents in the building noticed smoke and called the fire department. Firefighters arrived a short time later and found the victim's body after forcing their way into her apartment.

Her sister, Sandra Estes, who spoke to her the day before she died, thinks it's likely someone who knew Kimberly very well is the killer. It's also possible that it was someone who fantasized about her while watching her at work. In the hours before her death, she was at the Foxy Lady, a gentleman's club featuring nude girls, private rooms and massages, until its 1 a.m. closing time. No one remembers seeing anyone acting unusual or in a suspicious manner with Kimberly that night. The four mile drive from the club in the Douglas Avenue and Chalkstone Avenue area would normally take a little more than 10 minutes and the timeline suggests she went directly home considering she probably lingered at the club for some time past closing waiting for customers to leave. Whoever the killer, her sister hopes he's tormented with what he has done and can't look at himself in the mirror. She hopes he will take responsibility and turn himself in. Police are hoping someone comes forward with information and are reminding people there is a $20,000 reward for anyone who assists police to solve this case.

Ronald Morton
Amarillo, Texas

A killer set a fire in a second story Amarillo, Texas apartment complex to conceal a murder. The victim, Ronald Morton, was discovered in the early morning hours of Friday, November 6, 1992 after someone noticed smoke coming from unit 203 of the two-storey building on South Polk Street, just south of 24th Street. Firefighters immediately searched the smoke-filled apartment and found the unconscious victim. He was brought outside where emergency crews realized he was the victim of a homicide. Investigators from the Amarillo Police Department have followed up on a number of leads, but have never been able to determine a motive for the slaying or identify the suspect. The local Crime Stoppers program is also offering a reward of up to $1,000 for information that solves this case.

Sharalyn Movonne Murphy
Sacramento, California

In her early 20s she drifted into prostitution to survive but it also led to her death. It was mid-September 1994 when Sharalyn Movonne

Murphy left the apartment on Watt Avenue in Sacramento, California where she was living with her boyfriend to find clients on the street nearby. She told him she would be back shortly but she never returned. Three months later the remains of a young woman, with the head and hands missing, were found on the banks of the New Melones Reservoir off Camp 9 Road, some 100 miles to the southeast. The remote location where the body was discovered could indicate the killer is familiar with the area. In fact, Camp 9 Road runs off Parrotts Ferry Road and follows a winding mountainous route before passing the dam at Yea Hoo Gulch on the Stanislaus River and continuing to a power plant in a valley area. The body was located a distance past the dam which creates the reservoir at a point where the road is closest to the water in Calaveras County.

It's likely the 24-year-old victim was killed and dismembered shortly after being picked up by the killer and the remains dumped some time later. The badly decomposed body was discovered around 3 p.m. on December 13, 1994 and a subsequent autopsy revealed she'd been stabbed multiple times in the chest.

A month earlier the Tuolumne County Sheriff's Department was notified when two hands washed up on the south shore of the reservoir and on December 22 testing began which confirmed they were from the remains found on the other shore. It was more than a year later through laborious searches of fingerprint records that investigators were finally able to identify the murder victim as Sharalyn Movonne Murphy. At that point detectives were able to build background on the victim and start tracing the final moments in her life. She was born in Washington but moved to the Carmichael area of Sacramento near where her mother lived. She dated one man for a while and after breaking up she started going out with another person and moved into an apartment with him. She never found a job in Sacramento and started performing sex acts whenever she needed money for rent and food.

Investigators could not confirm if she was hooked on drugs. They have also ruled out any possibilities that her old boyfriend or the man she shared an apartment were involved in her death. Detectives said the killing was likely a crime of opportunity after the individual randomly picked up Murphy while out looking for a prostitute. Investigators have also ruled out any connection with a couple of serial killers who had murdered a number of young women in that part of California but said it's possible the person who took Murphy's life may have killed others and not yet been arrested. Detectives are still anxious to find any information that will move the investigation forward and urge anyone who has heard or remembers something about Murphy or her possible killer to contact police. They said it's not unusual for someone to brag about murdering someone even years after the event.

David "Ray" Ninemire
Westwood, Kansas

A store manager, who was filling in on the overnight shift, was shot to death while trying to foil a robbery at a small supermarket in Westwood, Kansas. The killing of David "Ray" Ninemire at 6 a.m. on Friday, August 15, 2003 shocked the town of 1,700 people which hadn't had a murder in nearly 60 years. Ninemire, described as a "gentle giant" who was friends with everyone, was at the rear of the Westwood Apple Market on Mission Street near West 47th Street when he heard one of his cashiers screaming for help. She had been confronted by a thin man with a fake beard and dressed like Abraham Lincoln who was holding a 9 mm black semi-automatic handgun to her head. As the bandit attempted to pull the 70-year-old clerk toward the customer service window she tripped and stumbled to the floor. At that moment, the 68-year-old manager who had rushed to the woman's aid made a move to intervene. The robber spun around and pointed the gun in Ninemire's direction and fired a volley of shots. One bullet ruptured the femoral artery in the victim's upper right leg and he bled to death before help arrived. After the shooting the gunman walked calmly to the front of the store where he came face to face with a female customer. At this point the suspect fired more shots and one slug ricocheted off a wall and fragments struck woman near her ear and in her arm. She recovered from the injuries.

The victim, who had worked at the store for years, was remembered as a church-going man and someone who gave freely of his time to help others. He also loved woodworking and sometimes fashioned toys for his grandchildren. When the woman screamed, he wouldn't have thought about his safety, but just that someone needed his help. His killer wasn't very tall and had a slim build. Investigators said it's possible the black trench coat, black pants, fake beard, shaggy black wig and the wide-brimmed black top hat were being used to disguise a woman's identity. Everyone who saw the killer described the person as young looking and very calm. When last seen the killer was turning onto Lloyd Street from West 47th Street. Westwood Police said some people suggested the person was white or Hispanic, but after interviewing all witnesses investigators were unable to distinguish the killer's age, gender or race. By contrast Ninemire was known to everyone. He stood tall and was always ready for a friendly chat. His wife, Phyllis, said he was a strong and kind man and she expressed anger that his life was cut short. Her hope is that someone will come forward with the killer's name. The couple was a month away from celebrating their 45th wedding anniversary when Ninemire was killed. Rewards totaling $35,000 are available for anyone who provides information that helps police arrest and convict the killer.

An executive order from Kansas Governor Kathleen Sebelius to contribute $5,000 to the reward fund described Ninemire as a hero. "He came to the aid of a female friend and coworker and was killed in the process," the governor wrote in the January 2006 proclamation. "Mr. Ninemire's coworkers and responding police officers did what they could to save his life. He bled to death while lying on the floor before medical help could arrive." She then included the following from Westwood Deputy Police Chief Dan Brewster. "Ray has a loving family and a community that demands that this case be solved. Anything that I could write about, this man, the Christian path he lived, the imprint he left on those who knew him would fall short in describing the person he was before 6:00 a.m. on August 15, of 2003." In various appeals Brewster has said police are a phone call away from solving this case. He suggests someone is carrying around the burden of knowing who is responsible for the killing of Ninemire and urged them to come forward and reveal the secret they are holding.

Isaac Newbill
Cincinnati, Ohio

Homicide investigators want to know who killed Isaac Newbill and why. The 23-year-old man's body was discovered around 9:30 p.m. on Thursday, December 17, 2003 in an alleyway off Charlotte Street, between Central Avenue and John Street. It's a ram-shackled neighborhood with boarded up buildings, dilapidated factories and vacant lots overgrown with weeds. Members of a band practicing on the third floor of a mostly unoccupied building called police when they heard gunfire somewhere in the vicinity. The street where the victim was found is basically a driveway, wide enough for one vehicle, and tunneled between five storey 1940-style factory structures. It's been called by some the "path of death" because so many people have been murdered through the years in the vicinity. Detectives from the Cincinnati Police Department haven't yet determined a motive for the shooting death.

Newbill grew up in the west-end neighborhood and didn't associate with gang members and other petty criminals who consider local streets their territory. He'd just become a new father and was hoping to enroll at Cincinnati State Technical and Community College in January. Despite growing up in an at-risk neighborhood, he got his high school equivalence certificate and had recently completed some technical classes through a federal government program aimed at helping disadvantaged young people. Relatives said Newbill was loved by everyone in the family and they are all saddened that his child will grow up without knowing him. The Greater Cincinnati Crime Stoppers has offered a $1,000 reward for information leading to the arrest of Newbill's killer.

Chau Nguyen
San Jose, California

He was a Buddhist living a simple life and investigators are baffled as to why someone would want to kill him. Chau Nguyen didn't appear to have an enemy in the world, but around 2 p.m. on Sunday, January 14, 2006 he was shot to death while sitting in his car outside the home where he lived on the south side of Pettigrew Drive immediately west of Plumstead Way in San Jose, California. It was first thought that the 43-year-old victim had been in a car accident, but when neighbors ran over to help, they found Nguyen with a gunshot wound to his head.

Robbery doesn't appear to be a motive and investigators are baffled as to who may be responsible. He was a quiet, peaceful man who spent lunch breaks meditating. Normally lots of people would have been outside in the mid afternoon, but it was raining and no one saw the gunman. Katie Ho, the home owner who rented the room that Nguyen shared with his girlfriend, was told something had happened and rushed outside to find the victim dead in his car.

Born in Vietnam, Nguyen and his brother, Tich, had lived in San Jose since 1980. He graduated from Mission College in Santa Clara and was a design engineer in the telecommunications industry. Since 2000 he worked as a senior radio frequency technician with a close-knit team at LGC Wireless. Company representatives said he was highly respected both personally and professionally and although somewhat of a loner, he would attend office parties and other social functions with colleagues. Mostly when away from work, he preferred spending time at home, reading or watching television. He tried to maintain a simple lifestyle as a vegetarian in the Buddhist tradition. He also contributed considerable amounts of money to the less fortunate, including victims of the December 26, 2004 tsunami which devastated the Phuket region of Thailand and the Hurricane Katrina disaster on August 29, 2005 which displaced millions of people and destroyed thousands of homes along the Gulf Coast.

Police went door to door through the neighborhood but didn't find anyone who could suggest a motive for the murder. Everyone knew Nguyen as a kind and gentle individual. There have been several Crime Stoppers appeals related to the killing and a $10,000 reward posted for information leading to an arrest.

Barbara "Bobbie" Jo Oberholtzer
Alma, Colorado

Hours after celebrating her promotion to office manager, a 29-year-old woman was shot and killed while hitchhiking home in rural Colorado. Barbara "Bobbie" Jo Oberholtzer left the Village Pub at the old Bell Tower Mall on the main street of Breckenridge, around 7:50 p.m. on Wednesday, January 6, 1982 and made a brief stop at the nearby Minit Mart before walking towards Highway 9 to thumb a ride to Alma, some 16 miles to the south. She never arrived home.
Born on Christmas Day in 1952, Bobbie Jo was enjoying life with her husband in the tony and picturesque ski resort community of 2,500

nestled in the mountains of Colorado. She stood five-feet, three-inches and weighed only 100 pounds but had piercing blue eyes and flowing blond hair stretching past her shoulders. When she left the restaurant she bundled up to face the 20 degree weather and bitter winds that were whipping through the mountainous region. She had called her husband, Jeff, to let him know she was with friends and assured him she'd be getting a ride home. When she hadn't arrived by 11:30 p.m. he became upset. But the anger turned to concern when she wasn't home at 1:30 a.m. and he drove to Breckenridge and searched through the night looking for her. He contacted friends in the morning and search parties were organized to check the route from the mall to their home. At 3 p.m. her body was discovered on a snowy embankment 20 feet off Highway 9 and some 300 feet from the Hoosier Pass summit parking lot. She had been shot in the chest with a .38-caliber or 357 Magnum handgun firing hollow point bullets. Death was attributed to exposure and blood loss. There was no indication she'd been sexually assaulted.

Summit County sheriff's investigators discovered the victim had struggled with her attacker and inflicted scratches that left the killer's blood at the scene. They also felt she had made an attempt to run for her life after the assailant tried to bind her hands with an 18-inch plastic flexi-cuff, similar to what police sometimes use to handcuff prisoners. The cuff was looped around one of her wrists, but the killer wasn't able to secure her other hand. She was most likely in his vehicle while struggling with him and made an attempt to flee across the parking lot and then down the embankment but had difficulty making her way through the knee-deep snow. Several shots were fired, one grazing her upper body and another penetrating her chest. She was shot at a range of one to two feet and after falling on her back she slid a short distance down the slope. A key ring with a hook that her husband had fashioned to help fend off anyone who might threaten her, was found in the parking lot. A number of other items, including her driver's license, backpack, a bloody woolen glove and some bloodstained tissue were located later that day 20 miles away off U.S. 285, a highway running from the community of Fairplay through the mountains to Denver. An orange colored sock was found beside Bobbie Jo's body, but it wasn't until July 3, 1982 when the matching sock was discovered on the body of another woman who vanished the same night that Oberholtzer disappeared. That victim, Annette Kay Schnee, was face down in Sacramento Creek when spotted by a man and his 11-year-old son who were fishing in the remote mountain valley area outside Sacramento, Colorado, some three miles west of Highway 9 and about 10 miles south of the Hoosier Pass summit. The Schnee murder site is also close to where some of Bobbie Jo's belongings were located. Even though the sock links the two deaths, evidence obtained from both crime scenes have revealed DNA material from separate males who have not yet been identified. Investigators believe the orange sock was planted near Bobbie Jo's body to substantiate a connection between the two killings, but detectives are of the opinion each killing was carried out by a different person. Even though the Summit County Police Department set up a task force to probe both killing, the specific details regarding the murder of Annette Kay Schnee are contained in the section of this book related to her death. In connection with the Oberholtzer slaying, detectives want to hear from anyone who saw the victim after she left the variety store and specifically if they can recall seeing her hitchhiking or a description of the vehicle that may have picked her up. The Summit County Crime Stoppers program has a standing reward of up to $1,000 to anyone who anonymously calls their tip line with information that solves this case.

Alexander Michel Odeh
Santa Ana, California

A million dollars reward is available for anyone who can assist the Federal Bureau of Investigation solve the bombing death of a Palestinian spokesman in Santa Ana, California. Alexander Michel Odeh died instantly and several other people were injured when an explosive device detonated as he opened the door to the American-Arab Anti-Discrimination Committee offices at 1905 East 17th Street in Santa Ana. The blast occurred at 9 a.m. on Friday, October 11, 1985 when the booby-trap device exploded as Odeh opened the door.

The FBI classified the homicide as a domestic bombing and has spent hundreds of hours tracking leads to identify those responsible. Forty-one-year-old Odeh, the ADC's western regional director, left three young girls without a father. He came to the U.S. in 1972 from Palestine and was considered a moderate voice in the Arab-American community. A day earlier, Odeh had condemned terrorism in a television interview but praised the then Palestine Liberation

Organization leader Yasser Arafat and described him as a man of peace.

The blast heavily damaged the ADC's offices and showered debris onto the street injuring several people. Through the years the FBI has undertaken a number of initiatives to track down those responsible including placing ads in Jewish newspapers to publicize the reward. A separate $100,000 reward has been posted by the Arab-American community.

Howard Curtiss Olson
Portland, Oregon

A renowned glass artist who had one of a kind art pieces displayed in galleries across the American Northwest was beaten to death in his Portland, Oregon home. A neighbor found the body of 67-year-old Howard Curtiss Olson at the house where he lived on Northeast 143rd Avenue on December 15, 2008 after not seeing him for a few days. Police were called to the residence at 8:13 a.m. and found what they described as evidence of homicidal violence. Investigation by detectives from the Portland Police Bureau showed Olson was savagely beaten but police haven't revealed the exact cause of death. The victim was on the floor next to the stove in the kitchen and blood splattered about the room. Detectives called the slaying senseless and suggest it might have occurred during a robbery attempt. Olson, who moved to Portland at the age of 18, owned and operated the Bad Attitude Art Glass Company.

Olson, who went by the name Curtiss, was born on December 5, 1941 in Spokane, Washington but spent a lot of his childhood and teen years in Pendleton, a city of 16,000 in Oregon some 200 miles east of Portland. Following an auto accident that left him suffering from amnesia, Olson had to learn how to function in life. He started a business producing copper foil stained glass in 1978, but five years later took classes at the Fusing Ranch and Multnomah Art Centre in Portland and later in Seattle at the Portcon Glass show to perfect his technique of fusing glass into unique, whimsical and one-of-a-kind art pieces. He created face masks and fish design wall plaques and trays as well as kitty faces and star pins. Just before his death he encased some of his art pieces in glass and produced a number of table tops. Although sometimes cantankerous, friends said he was extremely artistic, very generous and loved making people laugh. His kitty face creations showed his lighter side with their wide eye stare and smile. And apart from expensive art pieces he produced an assortment of pins and fridge magnets so everyone could afford to own one of his works.

He also made no secret that he used marijuana for medical use to relieve the pain he still suffered from his near fatal car crash 30 years earlier and sometimes shared home-rolled cigarettes with friends. He was known to keep quantities of marijuana at his home and often had quite a bit of money strewn around. People who knew him can't believe any of his friends would have killed him, but speculate someone who found out what he had in his house may have thought the eccentric artist would be an easy victim for robbery. He never locked his door and would welcome strangers into his home to chat about his art which today decorates many offices and private homes along the Western Seaboard. Detectives from the Portland Police Bureau are urging anyone with information about Olson's death to contact them or call Crime Stoppers which is offering a reward of up to $1,000. They are anxious to hear if anyone recalls seeing anyone around the victim's home located between East Burnside Street and Northeast Glisan Street or have overheard someone who indicated they were with Olson around the time he was killed.

Ralph Osburn
Tulsa, Oklahoma

As 57-year-old Ralph Osburn stood talking to his daughter and 9-year-old grandson in the parking lot of the Tulsa, Oklahoma bar he owned, a man approached and clubbed him over the head with a two-foot-long tree branch. The attack happened at 10:40 p.m. on Tuesday, May 24, 1988 and police are still trying to identify the assailant. After being struck, Osburn slumped to the ground and the assailant rifled through his pockets of his pants before taking his wallet. The victim was admitted to hospital with severe head trauma and died the following day. His daughter, Jennifer, and her son were not injured. Osburn owned the Tiki Lounge at 4325 East Apache Street where the robbery occurred and investigators with the Tulsa Police Department hope some of the patrons who knew him will come forward with any information they may have heard through the years to identify the killer who ran off in a northerly direction.

The victim's empty wallet was found a few days later outside a vacant house at 2443 North Quebec Avenue. The house backs onto the west side of a park located directly south of Osburn's bar. Investigators believe the killer, a black male described as in his early 20s, 5-feet, 10-inches and around 170 pounds, is probably familiar with the area. At the time of the attack the assailant had a medium length moustache and shoulder length "jeri curl" hair. A $1,000 reward is available from Crime Stoppers and the Citizen Crime Commission is continuing to appeal for information about this homicide. In the moments leading up to the robbery, police said the thug attempted to intimidate the victim, but then seemed to have second thoughts and walked away. Seconds later, after Osburn turned his back to reassure his daughter and grandson that everything was okay, the attacker knocked him unconscious with the tree branch.

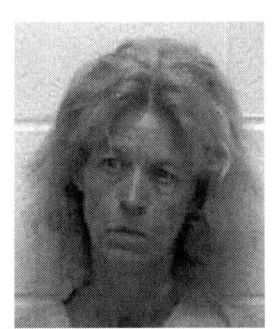

Ann Outz
Elbert County, Georgia

For six years she struggled to recover from a near fatal accident only to have her life taken away by a killer in Elbert County, Georgia. The body of Ann Outz was discovered around 2 p.m. on Saturday, June 24, 2006 in a wooded area near the Red Minnow Lighthouse Restaurant on Brewer's Bridge Road, just south of Lawrence Cecchini Road, north of Elberton. The 48-year-old victim, who had been reported missing on June 12 by her mother, Edna Goodwin, lived alone in a two-storey duplex on Highland Drive, a few blocks from the main street in Elberton. A neighbor heard some sort of argument at the woman's home in early June but didn't think anything about it until he learned of the killing. Investigators said it's likely the five-feet, seven-inch, 120 pound woman was dumped in the woods after being murdered at another location. The cause of death hasn't been made public but authorities did say it was a homicide by violent means. Outz was described by her mother as a good person who had difficulty with drugs and had battled to rebuild her life after being almost killed in a 2000 traffic mishap. Goodwin said her daughter was left disabled by the crash and had to learn to do everything again, including cooking, talking and walking. She checked on her every day and last saw her June 2 before leaving to attend a grandson's graduation in North Carolina. When she wasn't able to locate her daughter after she got home, Goodwin called police to report her missing. After the victim's body was found investigators from the Elbert County Sheriff's Office, the Elberton Police Department and the Georgia Bureau of Investigation teamed up to probe the slaying. A $1,000 reward has been offered by the Georgia governor's office for information leading to the arrest and conviction of the person responsible for the woman's murder.

Carnell Parker   Shontae Peterson

Carnell Parker & Shontae Peterson
Coatesville, Pennsylvania

A $10,000 reward is being offered to anyone who names the people responsible for the slaying of 24-year-old Carnell Parker and his 21-year-old girlfriend, Shontae Peterson, in Coatesville, Pennsylvania. It was Sunday, July 6, 2008 when the couple was executed in the dining room of a three-floor home at 206 Charles Street. Both victims were shot in the head. Coatesville, a community of more than 11,000 south of Route 30, some 46 miles west of Philadelphia, has been plagued with violence in recent years mainly through gang and drug activity.

The street where the shooting happened is two blocks south of the West Lincoln Highway between South Church Street and Strode Avenue. Investigators with the Coatesville Police Department have indicated Parker's killing wasn't a random violent act, but detectives suspect he was targeted for death. Most likely his girlfriend was killed because she was just in the wrong place. No motive has been officially determined for the slayings, but police said there was damage to the windows, screens and doors indicating the gunman had staged some sort of home invasion. There were several other people at the duplex when the shootings occurred, but fled before police arrived. The 911 call came in at 9:10 a.m. reporting two people shot dead and blood all over the place. The victims were last seen alive around 2:30 a.m. but police believe the killings occurred shortly before the 911 operator received the call for help. Peterson recently graduated from college and had been friends with Parker for some time.

Investigators said they are anxious to speak with anyone who can give a clear picture of what happened inside the house. Neighbors called the murders senseless and described the couple as "good people" who were caught in a bad situation. The reward was posted by the Citizen's Crime Commission and they want anyone with information to call the tipline.

Robert S. Parrish
Fort Wayne, Indiana

It's the only home on the block and sits on the south side of the street. The surrounding homes are situated on corner lots at each end of Vermont Avenue and face the intersecting streets in the Northside District of Fort Wayne, Indiana. Those living in the neighborhood really didn't have a clear view of the yellow frame house where Robert S. Parrish lived alone. It was around 6:30 p.m. on Wednesday, March 29, 2006 when relatives found the 49-year-old man dead in the bathroom of his single-storey home. He had been shot several times. There were some shell casings on the floor, but no sign of the murder weapon.

Family members made repeated attempts to reach Parrish after learning he didn't show up for work and had missed an appointment through the day. They located his body when they went to the home at 1112 Vermont Avenue, between Crescent Avenue and Kentucky Avenue. An autopsy indicated the victim died as a result of a bullet wound to the head.

Investigation by the Fort Wayne Police Department showed Parrish did not commit suicide, but was killed after an intruder or intruders entered his home. Although there isn't much traffic in the area, the street is very accessible from the east and west as well as from a north-south alleyway directly east of the victim's home. There are no suspects and Crime Stoppers is offering a $1,000 reward to anyone who can provide information that allows police to make an arrest.

Frank George Perzel
Lexington, Kentucky

A 52-year-old man was beaten to death in his Lexington, Kentucky apartment, but no one heard a commotion or calls for help. It wasn't until 4:21 p.m. on Tuesday, July 2, 1996 when a neighbor checked the apartment at 445 Davidson Court that the body of Frank George Perzel was found on the floor of his living room. Even though the body was badly decomposed pathologists were able to determine that he died as a result of blunt force trauma. The four-plex where Perzel was killed is the last home on the dead-end street running off North Broadway Street between West 6th Street and Delcamp Drive. It is mostly obscured by several large trees and homicide detectives from the Lexington Police Department couldn't find anyone who saw or heard anything through the weekend up to the time the victim's body was found in the ground-floor unit.

Perzel was last seen Friday afternoon when he left the Michael's Warehouse where he worked as a laborer. Fellow workers didn't call police to check on his welfare when he failed to show up Monday and area residents has no sense anything was wrong since they rarely saw Perzel around the neighborhood.

Police are appealing for anyone who has information about the slaying or knows where the victim went after work on Friday or anytime through the weekend. It's not known if he brought someone to his home or if he was confronted by someone who came to his door. Crime Stoppers is offering a standard $1,000 reward to encourage people to come forward and assist investigators in solving this case.

Edward Pieron
Coral Gables, Florida

Edward Pieron came from Southern California in 2005 to study biology at the University of Miami, but ended up dead in the living room of a rented three bedroom Coral Gables home he shared with three other students, a day after celebrating his 21st birthday. Pieron's girlfriend discovered the body around 2:45 p.m. on Saturday, July 5, 2008 sprawled in a pool of blood on the floor of the home in the 8000 block of Southwest 62nd Place between SW 82nd Street and Davis Road, in

South Miami. It's normally a quiet neighborhood and not an area anyone would expect this type of violence. After finding Pieron motionless on the floor, his girlfriend went hysterical and ran screaming to the home of neighbor Ricardo Silva to get help. After calling 911 Silva and his wife grabbed a first aid kit in hopes of treating the victim but were met with a scene of horror.

There was a lot of blood on the floor and on furniture, including the couch, some blood spattering, bloody footprints and smears. Investigators from the Miami-Dade Police Department have ruled the death a homicide, but at this point they don't know where the killing actually occurred. Evidence found at the scene showed that Pieron had made a purchase at a the CVS Pharmacy a few blocks from his home at 6456 South Dixie Highway at the corner of Davis Road about two hours before his body was discovered. There is an entrance off Davis Road into the drug store parking lot directly across from Fuchs Park and surveillance video confirms the victim was alone when he came into the pharmacy. Police examined video recordings from all the security cameras in the vicinity but didn't identify any possible suspects.

There was an Independence Day party and a celebration of Pieron's birthday on July 4 which continued to the early morning hours. It wasn't particularly rowdy but partygoers did set off fireworks in the backyard and on the street during the barbecue. Police haven't found any links with the death and the party, but are keeping an open mind. It's more likely an attacker followed Pieron from the pharmacy to the house. There was no evidence of a break-in, but investigators did say there were signs of a struggle inside the home.

The victim called his girlfriend around 1 p.m. Saturday to invite her over for a late afternoon lunch. When she arrived she found him on the floor. All his roommates were away and had not attended the party, but police have not yet said if anyone else had stayed overnight at the house. Investigators have been tightlipped about the cause of death and haven't indicated if a motive has been determined. Pieron, a native of Los Angeles who lived with his mother in Woodland Hills,

California before enrolling at the University of Miami, was known as "Eddie" by his friends. He also listed interests on his MySpace computer profile as drinking, smoking, parties, working out, crazy hot sex, clubs, chilling with homies, hackey sack, going to the beach, occasionally laying out in the sun and he loved trying new things. "I live for nights I won't remember and friends I'll never forget," he wrote.

In media interview after the slaying, Pieron's mom, Pamela Bailey, said the killing left her devastated and shocked. "I feel like I'm cried out and yet nothing will bring him back. I knew things like this happen and I never expected it to happen to me. I want him to be remembered as a kid who was just so loving and so full of life." She also called him gregarious and outgoing and said he was "sociable almost to his detriment."

Bailey spoke to her son on his birthday but there was nothing in his voice that hinted of trouble. He was making plans to come home and then travel with his mom to a cousin's wedding in Hawaii. "He just has such a zest for life. He was just a bright, sweet adorable kid." His friends described him as a typical student and enjoying his time in university. Ironically, one of the items purchased at the pharmacy was a case of beer. The video shows him in a white short sleeved shirt showing identification to the dark haired female sales clerk proving he'd turned 21 and legally entitled to buy alcohol in Florida.

A $25,000 reward has been posted for Pieron's killer and investigators are hoping someone will come forward with critical information that will help them solve the slaying. A separate $1,000 reward has been issued by the Miami-Dade Crime Stoppers for information from an anonymous caller that identifies the killer.

Detectives said they are not sure if they have spoken with everyone who attended the birthday barbecue and are urging anyone who was not interviewed to make contact with them. They also hope people who were in the neighborhood of the pharmacy will review the surveillance video on the internet and think back and recall if they saw anything that can assist the investigation. There is no suggestion Pieron was involved in anything sinister or that he had any enemies. He was well known on the campus and considered by fellow students and faculty as someone who was friendly and sociable as well as being a great guy.

Carnell Pittman
Coatesville, Pennsylvania

A young man who had just graduated from high school and was hoping to start a life for himself in Virginia was shot to death in a Coatesville, Pennsylvania alleyway. It was around 5:30 a.m. on Thursday, August 7, 2003 when police responded to a call regarding gunshots in the vicinity of North 7th Avenue and East Chestnut Street and found the body of Carnell Pittman. The 18-year-old victim was in a garage alcove against the brick wall of an abandoned home. He had been shot in the left arm and upper chest and was pronounced dead at Brandywine Hospital.

Pittman, who lived on Maple Avenue some 20 blocks away, was known to police and it's possible the shooting was drug related, but investigators have not been able to come up with a firm motive. They also don't have any idea who is responsible for the killing. Neighbors reported hearing two shots which police believe were fired from a .38-calibre or 9mm weapon. A man wearing a black hooded sweatshirt and blue jeans was seen running away from the area moments after the gunshots were fired. He was also described as being short, heavy set and hunched over.

The victim, who was also known as Booda, played football while attending Glen Mills High School. He was well known and someone who could make people laugh. He was very close with his family and lived off and on with his sister, Syretta, and her five children several blocks from where he was killed. He has a twin sister, Carnisha and an older brother, Steven, who has criminal convictions for drug dealing. His father had recently died and his mother, Cherry, had moved to Pittsburg. Investigation showed the victim had stopped to urinate in the alleyway when someone approached and began firing from a handgun. Detectives with the Coatesville Police Department are confident Pittman was targeted for death and there are people in the community who could provide a lot more information. There is a $15,000 reward for anyone who can help police identify the gunman.

A task force has been set up by the Chester County District Attorney's office to find Pittman's killer and individuals responsible for the killings of four other people in Coatesville, a town of 11,000 residents about 46 miles from Philadelphia. The task force comprised of investigators from the Coatesville Police Department, Chester County, the Pennsylvania

State Police and the Federal Bureau of Investigation is also probing the murders of Brian Keith Brown, Charles "Corey" Jennings, Carnell Parker and his girlfriend, Shontae Peterson. Parker, 24 and Peterson, 21, were shot to death, July 6, 2008; Brown, 29, was murdered April 1, 2006 and Jennings, also 29, was gunned down on October 19, 2005. In recent years, Coatesville has become a very violent community and during a Mother's March for Peace rally participants were told it's only a five minute walk from where Pittman was murdered to the site of the various other killings.

Jamie Mahalani Plabico-Davis
Honolulu, Hawaii

She had chestnut brown eyes and jet black hair which flowed to the middle of her back. At 20, she was the mother of a 15-month-old daughter but crystal methamphetamine was running her life. The family of Jamie Plabico-Davis hoped she would start getting things under control but on Saturday, December 11, 2004 her body was discovered on the North Shore near Velzyland, a popular surfing spot near the northern tip of Hawaii's Oahu Island. She was last seen a week earlier around 2 a.m. walking along the Sand Island Access Road from the Keehi Boat Harbor to the home of a relative in Kalihi. At the time she was wearing a white t-shirt, short denim overalls and black slippers. Although an autopsy didn't definitively determine the exact cause of death, she was officially listed as a homicide victim because her body was partial buried. Jamie was located a day after she was reported missing in a sheep grazing area on the University of Hawaii's Waialee Livestock Research Farm on the Kamahameha Highway, between Kalou Marsh Road and Waialee Beach Park Road. Because of the advanced stages of decomposition, it was determined she died on Monday, December 6.

Jamie was five feet tall and weighed less than 100 pounds. She was a listed as Filipino but also had Caucasian and Japanese heritage. Relatives said she was a happy-go-lucky girl, but recently had fallen in with the wrong crowd and her life was on a downward spiral. She had been raised in the government subsidized housing area of Palama near Honolulu's downtown. She dropped out of school in Grade 9 and had lived on the streets with her sister for a while. When investigators removed the victim's body from the sandy soil they noticed her nails were painted pink, she had a small ring on the little finger of her right hand and a red hair band on her left wrist. Toxicology tests revealed deadly levels of methamphetamine and there were signs she may have been suffocated.

She was last seen alive on Friday, December 3 when she visited her mother, Hisae Davis, who was looking after Jamie's young daughter, Emary. The young woman had lived with her boyfriend, but they broke up when he was sent to prison on forgery and auto theft charges. At that time she started associating with what were described as "the wrong people" and became heavily addicted to drugs. There are a lot of unanswered questions about the homicide and investigators from the Honolulu Police Department are particularly interested in hearing from anyone who saw Jamie between December 5 and December 6, 2004.

Karen Pretty, Scott Pretty & Mark Pretty
Houston, Texas

A contract killer went to the wrong house and murdered three innocent victims. It was on Wednesday, May 10, 1978 when Robert Pretty came home to find his wife and his two young sons dead in their home in a northern suburb of Houston, Texas. His 28-year-old wife, Karen, was in a water-filled bathtub off the master bedroom with her hands and feet tied with telephone cord. Their sons, Scott, 7 and 5-year-old Mark, were in a bathtub in another room. A post mortem showed all had died as a result of strangulation and drowning.

Robert knew something was wrong when he arrived home and heard water running in a front bathroom. Both children were face down and dressed in their pajamas. He pulled them from the water and ran to another bathroom adjacent to the master bedroom where he found his wife's lifeless body. She was wearing a flowered bathrobe. Dr. Joseph Jachimezek, the pathologist who performed the autopsies on the victims, said Karen was choked with a telephone cord and the boys with bare hands. The youngest boy was also beaten and there was evidence all three had been held underwater. He described the deaths as very slow and agonizing.

Both robbery and sexual assault were ruled out as a possible motive and investigators concluded the victims were likely mistakenly killed by a hit-man who went to the wrong house. Police concentrated on this theory after finding the Pretty family car, a 1978 Mercury Marquis, parked near a Goodson Drive apartment building where a well-known drug dealer had lived before being arrested on evidence provided by an informant who lived near the Pretty family. Investigators said an out of town contract killer may have been hired to take revenge on the informant and his family but instead went to Robert Pretty's home where he killed the man's wife and two sons. Although many years have passed, detectives from the Houston Police Department are still anxious to solve this crime and are hoping someone will come forward with information.

Bruce Allen Price
Lexington, Kentucky

Homicide detectives are trying to determine why a 32-year-old man was shot to death four blocks from his home in Lexington, Kentucky. The victim, Bruce Allen Price, was shot by a heavy set man around 10 p.m. on Thursday, February 10, 2000 outside a home on Elm Street near Charles Avenue. He was pronounced dead a short time later after being transported to an area hospital. Nearby residents told investigators from the Lexington Police Department that a man went up to Price – an imposing man of six-feet-one and 190 pounds – and shot him several times. The gunman and two other people standing nearby jumped into a dark colored Cadillac and sped from the area. Price, the son of Brutus and Rosie Price, lived four blocks away at 549 Ash Street and police have been unable to ascertain the connection he may have had with his killer and what he was doing on Elm Street. The Bluegrass Crime Stoppers program is offering a reward of up to $1,000 for information that leads to an arrest in this killing.

Osbaldo Quintana-Reves
Lexington, Kentucky

Five days before Christmas a 22-year-old man was fatally shot on a country road on the outskirts of Lexington, Kentucky. The body of Osbaldo Quintana-Reves was discovered around 10 p.m. on

Monday, December 20, 2004 after police were called to the vicinity of 2200 Muir Station Road, a rural horse farm area in the city's east end. The site of the shooting is about eight miles from where the victim lived at 2100 Carla Court, a quiet cul-de-sac off Lisa Drive on the east side of Interstate 75. Quintana-Reves, who was born on June 10, 1982, was last seen earlier in the evening at a Hispanic grocery store in the vicinity of the Continental Inn on East New Circle Road at Eastland Parkway opposite the Eastland Shopping Centre. He was with an individual described as a Hispanic male, five-feet, nine-inches, about 150 pound and wearing a dark baseball hat and a red sweatshirt. Homicide detectives from the Lexington Division of Police are hoping to get any information people might have about the murder of Quintana-Reves including the reason he was killed. The local Crime Stoppers program is also offering a reward of up to $1,000 for information about his murder.

Anita Elizabeth Redmon,
Stone Mountain, Georgia

After serving 25 years as a police officer in Doraville, Georgia, the grandmother of seven was fatally shot while working as a gate attendant at Stone Mountain Park. She thought it would be a much safer job, but around 12:30 a.m. on Saturday, July 16, 2005, Anita Redmon was murdered during a robbery attempt. The 63-year-old part-time employee called the Stone Mountain Park Police communication centre sometime after midnight to advise that a woman was at the west gate kiosk seeking permission to retrieve a pair of shoes she'd left in the park. Moments later when the dispatcher called back to make sure everything was okay, Redmon said she had a "Signal 44" the police code indicating an armed robbery. The dispatcher also heard a pop sound which investigators believe was the shot that took Redmon's life. One police officer was less than half a mile from the gate and arrived within a minute but saw no sign of any suspects.

Redmon, who had worked at the park since April, was pronounced dead on arrival at the DeKalb Medical Centre eight miles away in the Atlanta suburb of Decatur.

She was a trailblazer. The first female employed by Doraville Police Department, initially as a dispatcher and then as a full-fledged police officer. She was promoted to a sergeant but forced to retire in 1999 when surgery for a brain aneurysm left her slightly incapacitated. Friends and colleagues described her as a being a beautiful bright light in the world and someone full of humor. She always put others ahead of herself and was just a great person. For 25 years she carried badge number 221 and was proud of the time she spent serving and protecting people. Her daughters were also proud of her accomplishments, but worried each day she put on her uniform to patrol the streets of Doraville, a city of 10,000 located 13 miles northeast of Atlanta. There was the concern Redmon could face a life and death situation as a police officer but her daughters never dreamed she would be fatally shot working as a gate attendant.

Rewards totaling $55,000 are being offered to help solve the slaying, the first ever violent death of an employee in the history of the park which serves as a monument to Confederate leaders in the Civil War. The park features a relief sculpture on the face of Stone Mountain showing President Jefferson Davis along with Generals Robert E. Lee and Thomas "Stonewall" Jackson. Witnesses told of seeing two black males acting suspicious at the park a day before the shooting. One was in the vicinity of the Stone Mountain Park Inn and the other hiding among some trees near the west gate entrance at the end of James B. Rivers Road at East Mountain Street. It's believed Redmon's assailants ran into the park after the shooting, but investigators were not able to determine if they headed along Robert E. Lee Boulevard, the roadway running through the park, or made their way through a treed area for some distance before hopping a fence and escaping onto East Mountain Street.

Police combed the park through the night and for several days following the shooting but they didn't find the murder weapon or any other evidence that would help identify the suspects. They received numerous tips but none of the leads have panned out so far. Chief Chuck Kelley of the Stone Mountain Park Police said it's a case that must be solved and vowed to never give up. He said Redmon fought for justice most of her life and it would be fitting to make an arrest in her killing. Kelley said the priority of the park is the safety of both visitors and staff and it's a tragic loss that someone who devoted her life to public safety was killed in a senseless crime. He said she was shot just doing her job. Since the slaying they have installed bullet proof glass and security cameras at the kiosk. There's also a memorial to Redmon at the kiosk where she died.

Find My Killer

Chapter 6 – Reed to Stephens

Crandall Jack Reed
Jacksonville, Florida

The world for a devoted wife changed in the blink of an eye on Friday, November 16, 2007 when her husband of 13 years was shot to death. Crandall Jack Reed, a driver for Yellow Cab in Jacksonville, Florida, was killed while sitting in his vehicle around 3:30 a.m. in the rear parking lot of the Boy Scouts of America building at 521 Edgewood Avenue South, just south of Lenox Avenue. The 51-year-old cabbie would often park behind the building on slow nights to reduce gasoline costs while waiting for calls from the dispatcher. Detectives from the Jacksonville Police Department determined a car pulled beside Reed's cab and someone asked for a ride. When the person approached the taxi, they brandished what appeared to be a high powered rifle and forced the victim to hand over his wallet. Shots were then fired striking Reed in the back and through his heart. Despite the injuries, the cab driver floored the white colored 2005 Mercury Sable across a vacant lot adjacent to the Boy Scout's North Florida Council building and made his way southbound toward the Quick Trip Food Mart about a block away on the other side of the street. People in the area had called police immediately after hearing gunfire and the first responding officers found Reed in his car which was stopped near the driveway of the convenience store, just south of Roselyn Street. He was pronounced dead at Shands Jacksonville Medical Center a short time later.

Reed, who retired from the Navy, was known as Jake to colleagues at Jacksonville Transportation Group, the business that operated Yellow Cabs in the city. He had been a driver for four years and was in unit 3488 when shot. Investigators said the gunman wore a white t-shirt, dark pants and a baseball cap, but since the incident happened in an industrial area in the early morning hours when most businesses were closed, there were not a lot of people around to describe exactly what happened.

The couple celebrated their 12th anniversary on November 1 and 15 days later his wife found her life turned upside-down. She said he wasn't bothering anyone and randomly became a victim of murder. "He was just making a living...an honest living," she said. "He was just trying to get away." Terri, who has become a volunteer with the Justice Coalition in Jacksonville, said she wants the case solved. "I want to know who did it and I can't rest until I do. I have to have peace."

The owners of the Yellow Cab company put up money to bring the Crime Stoppers reward to $11,000 for information leading to an arrest in the killing. Reed's widow was at the news conference in March 2008 when the reward was announced and had a message for the killer. "If you're the one that did, I told you, I ain't stopping," she said. "We will get you." The executive director of Crime Stoppers Wyllie Hodges also urged anyone to come forward who knows the killer. "Someone out there knows who done it," he said. "Someone out there has some information that can solve this crime. You're looking at $11,000 to come forward."

Sergeant Christopher Reyka

Sergeant Christopher Reyka
Pompano Beach, Florida

He was a deputy sheriff in Broward County for 18 years and at 1:20 a.m. on Friday, August 10, 2007 his life ended in a hail of bullets outside a 24 hours drug store. Sergeant Christopher Reyka positioned his police car near two suspicious vehicles in the parking lot of the

Walgreen's store at 960 South Pompano Parkway at Cypress Bend Road in Pompano Beach and was preparing to check the license plates when someone emerged from one of the vehicles. As Reyka, the father of four children, stepped from his car, the person immediately began firing shots in rapid succession from a handgun. Ten shots were fired. The 51-year-old police officer was hit five times and pronounced dead a short time later at a nearby hospital. Security cameras set up in the parking lot of the pharmacy recorded an image of what appeared to be a late 1998 to early 2000 Ford Crown Victoria or a 1995 to 2004 Mercury Grand Marquis speeding away after the shooting.

His Sheriff's Department badge identified him as officer 9463 but friends knew him as Chris. They described him as a good son, brother, father, husband, friend and hero. Colleagues are also anxious to find the person who ended his life. They want justice. A reward of up to $267,000 is currently available to the individual who provides information that leads directly to the arrest and conviction of Reyka's killer.

The "officer down" alert was broadcast after customers and staff called the 911 emergency number to report a police officer was bleeding profusely after being shot. Police cars descended on the all night pharmacy after racing down South Pompano Parkday, a six lane divided street also known as Powerline Road. There is an entranceway off Cypress Bend Road and another directly off South Pompano Parkway. Sergeant Reyka was alive when the first deputy arrived on the scene but almost immediately lapsed into a coma and wasn't able to give fellow officers any details that would help them track down his killer. He is survived by his wife, Kim, and their four children, Ashley, Sean, Autumn and Spencer.

Born on April 28, 1956 into a family of 10, Sergeant Reyka enlisted in the United States Marine Corps and got married before spending 18 years with the Broward County Sheriff's office. He also ran a lawn and landscaping business for 23 years in his spare time. As an officer he was assigned to general patrol, the tactical unit and the detective office before being promoted to sergeant. His wife said he loved to serve and protect others and was a proactive, diligent, careful and a blessing to humanity. He also had a great love for his family and enjoyed many trips through the years to various places in the United States. Kim called him her hero and best friend.

Resident set up a makeshift memorial in the parking lot of the Walgreen's store to honor Sergeant Reyka. They placed teddy bears and American flags. There were flowers and cards. Someone tacked a police cap to a post and hung a cross from a chain. There was also a note: "It's not how this officer died that made him a hero, rather it was the way he lived." Investigators described the killing of Sergeant Reyka as an ambush. He didn't have a chance to pull his gun.

Broward Sheriff Ken Jenne, Captain Wayne Adkins and Reverend Rick Braswell, a Sheriff Department chaplain, went to the officer's home at 3 a.m. to inform the family of the death. Kim sat with her daughters, Ashley, then a 22-year-old senior at the University of Florida and Autumn, 16, who was enrolled at a Palm Beach high school, as Jenne told them Reyka wouldn't be coming home. Her oldest son, Sean, 20, was at the U.S. Marine Corps boot camp in Pensacola, and 13-year-old, Spencer, the youngest, was still asleep upstairs. A police car raced Kim to the North Broward Medical Centre but he didn't survive long enough for her to say goodbye.

They were married in 1985, four years before Reyka joined the Pompano Beach Police Department. He became a deputy sheriff's when the Broward County Sheriff's took over the department in 1999 and promoted in 2004 to sergeant. She knew being a police officer was a dangerous life, but she didn't expect that knock on the door. He was a good cop, just like her father had been, and he was well trained and very safety conscious. When she kissed him goodbye and walked him to the door around 9 p.m. on August 9, 2007, she had no inkling it would be the last time she would see him alive.

Some 5,000 police officers and other mourners attended the funeral service for Reyka in the community of Sunrise, just west of Fort Lauderdale and an hour south of their home in Wellington. It was a police and military funeral with burial at the VA National Cemetery at Lantana in South Florida.

His colleagues have vowed not to forget Sergeant Reyka and will continue investigating until the killer is brought to justice. They know there's a cop killer out there and they won't stop hunting until he's behind bars. "Somewhere, somebody knows," said Broward County Sheriff Al Lamberti, who took over the department three months after Reyka's killing.

Teresa Carol Richardson
New London, North Carolina

Teresa Carol Richardson was found murdered on Thursday, August 25, 2005 in her home at 112 Bluebird Land in New London, North Carolina. She had 16 cuts and stab wounds to her neck, chest, arm and back. There were two slash wounds across her throat which cut her jugular and carotid artery and eight inch stab wounds that damaged her vertebra and spinal cord. The attack occurred in the basement on the evening of August 24 when the victim confronted someone who broken into the house. She was last seen around 8 p.m. riding a golf cart around the condominium property where she had worked as operation's manager until June 2003 when improprieties were uncovered. She pleaded guilty in September 2003 to larceny but later launched a law suit against the Montgomery County Sheriff's Department and the Badin Shores Resort Owners Association for making false accusations.

Clarence "Moses" Riffle
Jimtown, West Virginia

Robbery was the motive for the killing of a retired coal miner who lived alone in his home near the hamlet of Jimtown, West Virginia, some 80 miles south of Wheeling. The 76-year-old victim, Clarence "Moses" Riffle, was murdered between 11 p.m. and 11:30 p.m. on Tuesday, November 18, 1980 at his home off Route 33, about 12 miles west of Elkins. His body was found by his son two days later in the front room of the house, just inside the door. Detectives from the West Virginia State Police said some money and a number of items were stolen, including a .410 gauge Westernfield bolt action shotgun with the victim's name hidden under the buttplate. Although the victim was found at 9:30 a.m. on Thursday, investigators have pinpointed the time of death to a period sometime before midnight on Tuesday. Detectives learned he spoke to someone just after 10:30 p.m. and since the television was still on he hadn't yet started getting ready for bed. It's likely the killer stopped at the home after pulling off the well travelled roadway and shot Riffle three times with a small caliber handgun before rummaging through his five-room, one storey home. Police are hoping someone will contact them who knows who is responsible for the slaying or anything about the gun that was taken from the house.

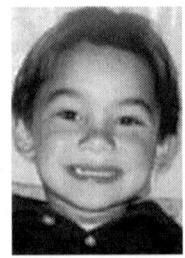

Kimberly Riley   Jeremy Britt-Bayinthavong

Kimberly Riley & Jeremy Britt-Bayinthavong
Tacoma, Washington

A 19-year-old university student and a five-year-old boy were killed when a gunman crept through the fog and fired numerous shots through a window of a house during a Thanksgiving celebration in Tacoma, Washington. It was around 10 p.m. on Thursday, November 28, 2002 when family and friends had just finished dinner at a split-level home on South 75th Street and L Street. The teenagers and children were in the lower level recreation room while the adults cleared away dishes and cleaned up after the celebration. Gunfire erupted and about a dozen shots came through the blind and curtain covered window. Jeremy Britt-Bayinthavong was struck in the upper body and Kimberly Riley was shot twice in the chest. The boy breathed his last breath as his father, Eric Britt, attempted life-saving efforts before paramedics arrived. Kimberly, who had moved to Tacoma from Hawaii two months earlier to attend the University of Washington, underwent surgery but died a few hours later at the Madigan Army Medical Center. Her boyfriend, 22-year-old Jeff Spencer, was shot in the leg and his sister, 20-year-old Harmony, received gunshot wounds to her stomach, back and arm. They later recovered from their injuries. Investigators were never able to identify a suspect or come up with a motive. Police have also been unable to determine if a March 3, 2000 incident where a gunman fired 23 rounds into the home is connected to the slayings. The home was owned by Joseph and Evangeline Britt, the little boy's grandparents, who were also in the house when the March shooting occurred. They weren't hurt in either incident.

Joseph has joined other family members to make numerous appeals for people to come forward with information. He also made a vow to his grandson at the funeral home that he wouldn't rest until the killer was found. Joe told authorities they were upstairs when the gunshots rang out. At first it was thought they were firecrackers but when they realized shots were being fired everyone ran to the recreation room to make sure things were okay. Instead, he saw it was a scene of horror with blood all over the place. "People dying in your arms." His son was cradling little Jeremy and giving mouth to mouth. He screamed out that he was breathing, but Joe said they were his grandson's last breaths. Joe's nephew, Jeff Spencer was on the floor with his arms around Kimberly, the young woman he'd known for only a few weeks. He told her that he was sorry and he loved her. "I love you," were words he had never spoken to her since they first met. There were up to 40 people, including some neighbors, at the Thanksgiving celebration, but a few left prior to the shooting. Jeff's father and Joe's brother-in-law Leonard Spencer recalled how the house was always full of laughter and joy but following the tragedy was so sad. "It just cries," he said. The family moved from the scene of the nightmare and now lives in Federal Way, a community 12 miles northeast of Tacoma.

Kimberly grew up in Volcano, Hawaii, a town of 2,200 people on the outskirts of the Hawaii Valcanoes National Park on the Big Island some 26 miles southwest of Hilo. She graduated in 2001 from Waiakea High School and spent a year at the Hilo Campus of the University of Hawaii before transferring to the University of Washington. She was studying liberal arts but had her sights set on some day owning her own business. While at home she volunteered with the Aloha Veterinary Centre and was a member of the Christ Lutheran Church in Hilo. Her father, Mike Riley was at home with his wife, Carol, when he received a call from his son, James, 22, telling him that Kimberly had been shot. James, who knew Jeff and introduced him to his sister when she moved to Tacoma, was also at the party but not hurt. Shortly after the phone call from his son, a doctor at the medical center telephoned the family in Hawaii to formally tell them their daughter had passed away. He wanted to know how something like this could have happened to his daughter. "Two months after sending our daughter to school, she is murdered," he said. "This is not the way we live in America. What's happened is an attack not only on the Britt family and the Spencer family, it's not only an attack on our family…this is an attack on the way we live in America." Mike wants the gunman caught. "The people who did this are murderers…they're monsters…they are not human. They are going to come back. They have taken my daughter. They are going to come back and take other daughters. They are not through yet. They are in our community."

Mike Riley said his daughter was absolutely thrilled when accepted at the University of Washington. She had grown up in a small town and was going to live in another area of the United States to learn and prepare herself for the future. But her dreams will never be realized. Mike also won't get his dream of seeing his daughter at her graduation and will not be giving her away on her wedding day or seeing her children. His daughter was the light of his life and would have been a wonderful mother, but her life was snuffed out with a senseless act of violence. Jeremy was also robbed of the opportunity to grow up and make his mark in life. He was a sweet kid who celebrated his fifth birthday a month before he was killed. When the gunshots ripped through the lower-level recreation room, Jeremy was sitting on the lap of Harmony Spencer. She pulled herself into a ball and used her body to shield him from harm and was hit three times. However, she wasn't able to protect her little nephew from a gunshot wound and he was officially pronounced dead on arrival at the Mary Bridge Children's Hospital.

Police reconstructed the crime scene and determined the killer walked across the lawn and fired at least a dozen shots through the ground floor window where most of the young people from the Thanksgiving celebration had gathered after the meal. Some were watching the big-screen television and others grouped around a pool table, but mostly they were chatting. The gunman, who was concealed by a thick fog which blanketed the neighborhood, couldn't see anyone through the window because of a closed blind and pulled curtains. But that didn't stop him from pulling the trigger on the semi-automatic handgun. Although he couldn't see, police do not think it was a random act of violence and believe the gunman had a gripe with someone inside the house. Someone was the intended victim. Seconds after the volley of shots were fired a teenage girl in the neighborhood saw a figure in dark clothing running from the Britt house and drive off in a pick-up truck. The vehicle was described as a dark-colored late 1970s to mid 1980s full size Ford pick-up with a light colored canopy. It had a loud exhaust system and raced away at high speed with its lights out. The families of the victims have organized a $25,000 reward fund to help police identify the killer and want anyone with information to call Crime Stoppers. "There's got to be someone out there that knows something," said Joe Britt. "They've got to come forward. This is not something to ignore. They have to have a conscience. If you know something, please call."

Daniel Rodriguez
Brooklyn, New York

A young man, described by his mother as a person who wouldn't hurt a fly, was found brutally murdered in Brooklyn, New York. The severed head of Daniel Rodriguez was discovered Thursday, November 30, 1995 at the Empire State Recycling, a private garbage transfer station at 110 51st Street near 1st Avenue in Brooklyn. He had been killed with a single gunshot to his right temple. It was almost two weeks later at 5:30 a.m. on Tuesday, December 12 when a patrolling police officer found the 21-year-old victim's torso in a parking lot of the Riviera Plaza at 3295 Amboy Road in Staten Island. The arms and legs have never been located and investigators have no idea where the killing occurred. The remains in the parking lot were frozen and wrapped in several layers of plastic before being bound with duct tape. Detectives from the New York City Police Department said the victim was dismembered after being killed and the head and limbs placed in garbage containers, but they have no idea where the torso was kept before it was discovered. No clothing was ever found and police can't determine any reason why someone would want to kill Rodriguez.

The victim was last seen on Tuesday, November 21 and his mother officially reported him missing five days later. However, it wasn't until January 10, 1996 that the head and torso were matched to the missing person report. Rodriguez was a mechanic at an auto repair shop and still living at home with his mother in the Bensonhurst area of Brooklyn. He was hard working and would sometimes be away from home for several days to pick up cars that were purchased from vehicle auctions in various states. On occasion he would stay at a friend's house but most of the time he would watch television and help his mother around the house. Rodriguez didn't drink and when out with friends was always the designated driver. He had been looking forward to a Thanksgiving meal his mother was making and when he didn't show up she knew something was wrong. When another two days passed and still no word from her son, she went to the police and filed a missing person's report.

Investigators said trash collected in all five boroughs by a number of private garbage companies is taken to the transfer station to be compacted into bales and bound with metal bands before being shipped to a dump in Virginia. It was when one of the bales burst open that the head was discovered. The slaying of Rodriguez has puzzled police and the New York Crime Stoppers program is offering a reward of up to $1,000 for information that will help solve the case. His mother is also hoping the killer is found to find out why someone wanted to kill her son. "I want justice for this," she said. "We have no answers."

Edna Marie Rodriguez
Fort Worth, Texas

A father in Fort Worth, Texas awoke in the middle of the night to find his eight-year-old daughter was missing. The police search began immediately, but a day later, on the afternoon of Sunday, July 12, 1998, the tiny body of Edna Marie Rodriguez was found in the driveway of a home a block away. She was wearing her nightdress and an autopsy revealed she'd been strangled. It was shortly after 2 a.m. on July 11, 1998 when Fidencio Rodriguez made a frantic call to the Fort Worth Police Department. He'd fallen asleep on a bed with his two daughters, but now one was missing. She wasn't in the house...she wasn't anywhere. Rodriguez hadn't heard any unusual sounds and didn't hear eight-year-old Marie leave the family's well kept bungalow at 3536 Travis Avenue, just north of Ripy Street. Police converged on the area within minutes and began searching street by street through the early morning hours. At first light officers from the day shift arrived but police who'd searched through the hours of darkness wouldn't go home. There was a little girl who needed to be found. About 120 police officers began a systematic house by house canvass covering numerous blocks without finding any sign of Marie. There was no sign of a struggle or any indication she'd been kidnapped. Investigators considered the possibility she was sleepwalking and encouraged searchers to check any area the child may have found to spend the night. By noon, some 10 hours after Maria had gone missing, it became clearly evident to detectives that there was a strong possibility of foul play and a criminal investigation which was being quietly conducted during the search effort became a top priority. The house became a crime scene and painstaking interviews were conducted with the parents.

Police dogs were utilized to make a systematic check of properties starting with the home where she lived and expanding throughout the neighborhood. By Saturday night extensive searches had been conducted over a half mile radius and media appeals asked people to make checks of their properties across Fort Worth. All police officers and other emergency workers, cab and transit drivers, delivery people and members of the public were asked to keep their eyes peeled for any sign of Maria. Through the night police cars patrolled the streets and at daybreak Sunday the search was intensified covering much of the same ground that had been checked the previous day in case anything had been overlooked. At 3 p.m. Maria's body was found in the driveway of a vacant home at 3604 Lipscomb Street. The street is one block to the west from the Rodriguez residence and the house situated just to the south of Ripy Street. She was on her back and no attempt had been made to conceal the body. The driveway, basically around the corner from the home where she lived, had been searched several times on Saturday and Sunday and had been examined by a police dog and its handler. There was no doubt, the brazen killer had dumped the girl's body a block from her home while police and others were scouring the neighborhood. Detectives questioned area residents but no one saw anyone near the house. Investigation showed the girl had been murdered at another location and her body carried to the spot where she was found.

The parents were shattered upon learning their little girl had been found dead. Fidencio and Juana Rodriguez had been clinging to the hope that Maria was safe. They were praying she would be found and they could walk her to her Grade 3 class at George C. Clarke Elementary School. But now they had to make plans for a funeral and to take her little body for burial in Minas Barroteran, Mexico, the mountain region village where she was born, 110 mile west of Laredo, Texas. The Schepps Dairy posted a $10,000 reward for the arrest and indictment of the killer. The Tarrant County Crime Stoppers program also made available a reward of up to $1,000 for anyone who provides anonymous information that solves the case. Detectives from the Fort Worth Police Department have continued to follow up leads through the years since she vanished, but have not yet identified a suspect. They acknowledge there are probably people who know who is responsible and are urging them to call in with the information.

Robert Rodriguez
Fort Worth, Texas

Shortly after getting involved in an altercation at a Forth Worth, Texas bar, a 32 year-old man was shot to death in a nearby parking lot. Warehouse employees found the body of Robert Rodriguez around 6 a.m. in their company's parking lot when they arrived for work on Friday, May 14, 1993. He had been shot in the head. Fort Worth homicide detectives learned Rodriguez had got into a fight at Johnny's Bar and was confronted by someone while opening the door of his car in the parking lot at 3446 May Street between West Bewick Street and West Biddison Street. Crime Stoppers is offering a reward of up to $1,000 and investigators are hoping someone will come forward and identify the killer.

Ann Saephan
Anchorage, Alaska

Gang violence is believed behind the shooting death of a 15-year-old girl outside a video arcade in Anchorage, Alaska. Ann Saephan, a sophomore at Bartlett High School, was shot in the head while a front seat passenger in a red Honda Civic that was leaving the parking lot of the Space Station arcade at 2710 Spenard Road on November 8, 2003. She was killed instantly. Another person, Steven Keoviengthong, 14, was wounded but recovered from his injuries. The shooting occurred just after 9 p.m. and police said it was linked to a recent emergence of gang activity in the city. Ann, who was born in Portland, Oregon on January 21, 1987 moved to Alaska with her Laos-born parents, Cheng Saechoa and Loun Saephan, in July 1998. She has two married sisters and three brothers. Friends described her as a fun-loving person who put others ahead of herself. The summer before she died, Ann wrote a poem describing how she someday wanted to be a wife and mother. She was also a person who loved to sing and dance and be around family and friends. At her funeral she was remember as someone with a warm, open and loving heart. Police said the victim wasn't a gang member but some of those in the parking lot were associated with gangs. Detectives from the Anchorage Police Department were unable to find anyone who could adequately describe the vehicle carrying the gunman.

Joshua J. Salyer
Fort Wayne, Indiana

Homicide detectives are still trying to determine who dumped the body of a former pet store owner at a recycling plant in Fort Wayne, Indiana. The 28-year-old victim, Joshua J. Salyer, was found at 10:10 a.m. on Monday, November 24, 2003 at the Community Action Recycling Enterprise facility on New Haven Avenue between Meyer Road and South Coliseum Boulevard. Death was attributed to multiple gunshot wounds to the head. Investigators said the killing has the earmarks of a gangland slaying but they have been unable to determine a motive or identify the person responsible. Through the years police have worked to develop a time-line to trace the victim's movements but still need people to come forward and provide details to fill in several gaps. Salyer was once the co-owner of the Fins and Feathers Pet Store in Bluffton, a town of some 10,000 people about 27 miles south of Fort Wayne. At the time of the murder Salyer was working as a tow truck driver for the Blue Eagle Towing Company. Detectives have been unable to ascertain where the murder occurred, but evidence shows the body was wrapped in cardboard and dumped at the recycling plant. A worker spotted the body after the contents of a large garbage bin were deposited onto a conveyor belt for sorting. Investigators want anyone with knowledge of the killing to come forward and the Greater Fort Wayne Crime Stoppers program has posted a $1,000 reward for anyone who is willing to call in anonymously with information.

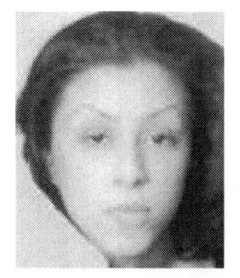

April Marie Sanchez
San Jose, California

She decided to end her ties with gangs and pursue an education, but the dream for a better future ended with her murder. It was on Saturday, April 19, 2003 when the partially clothed body of sixteen-year-old April Marie Sanchez was discovered on the bank of Coyote Creek in the vicinity of Phelan Avenue and Roberts Avenue in San Jose, California. The petite teenager was last seen around 12:30 a.m. walking home from a friend's house in the area of Keyes Avenue and South Sixth Street, some 20 blocks from where her body was found. There were suggestions she would have followed Story Road, the continuation of Keyes Street or made her way to McLaughlin Avenue in the area where her boyfriend lived. Whatever the route, April was accosted by someone or a group of people who ended her life. There were no witnesses and police did not find anyone who heard anything so investigators were unable to pinpoint where she was confronted. The last anyone saw of the girl was her walking along Keyes Street wearing a backpack. The cause of death has not been revealed but authorities did say the girl received visible injuries not inflicted by a bullet or a knife. Her wallet was also missing indicating she could have been the victim of a robbery.

April had been rebellious but wanted to change her life around and a couple of weeks before her death drew up a personal plan of learning after enrolling at the Foothill Continuation High School. Principal Jackie Guevara said she completed a battery of tests and set a goal to earn her high school diploma. She should have been a student at Yerba Buena High School, but had dropped out after getting involved with a rough crowd from the Nortenos street gang. The gang's symbol was tattooed on her arm. But she wanted to give that life up and get away from the tough, criminal-like existence that she had become embroiled in. Going to school and getting an education was her first step. She also wanted to reunite with her mother and the family she turned her back on when she became associated with the Nortenos. She was hoping she could make her family proud of her. Most of all she wanted to be the happy teenage girl she had been before her life as a street gang member.

A man walking his dog found April's body around 7 a.m. partially hidden by weeds on the bank of the creek. She was a young woman who cared more about others than herself and had struggled hard over the past few weeks to escape the violence that was all around her in the street gang environment. There is also the possibility that her affiliation with the Nortenos gang led to her death. When walking home she would have passed through territory claimed by the Surenos street gang, a rival of those in the gang that April had associated with. Police did consider involvement by the Surenos, but have found nothing to directly link any members of the street gang with her killing. A $10,000 reward was issued for information that will help police make an arrest and investigators are still appealing for people to come forward. Ron Gonzales, who was the San Jose mayor when April was killed, said every day a case goes unsolved the trail gets colder. He urged people to come forward with tips to help police solve the slaying. "I join every family in our community to help make sure that criminals, who prey on our children, can be caught and locked up as soon as possible," he said. The then police chief, William Lansdowne, also appealed for help from the community to bring justice for the young victim. "We do our best work to prevent and solve crime when we work in partnership with our residents," Lansdowne said during the April 30, 2003 news conference where the reward was announced.

Ricky San-Nicholas
Stockton, California

An 18-year-old man was fatally shot while trying to drive away from a fight that had broken out in the parking lot of a Stockton, California gas station. The victim, Ricky San-Nicolas, Jr., got into his car and was attempting to drive away around 11:46 p.m. on Saturday, September 15, 2007 after six to eight people became embroiled in a melee at the Arco Gas Station on the northeast corner of East Washington Street and South Wilson Way. One of those involved in the fight pulled a gun and fired at the victim's car. San-Nicolas was killed almost instantly but his vehicle continued about a block westbound on Washington before crashing into a wooden power pole. The group involved in the fracas, described as in their late teens, fled in a white Ford Taurus. Detectives said they were unable to find out why the group was fighting and if San Nicolas was actually involved or an innocent person trying to get away from the ruckus. Investigators said they would like to speak with anyone who witnessed the incident or who can identify those taking part in the fight. Stockton Crime Stoppers is also offering a reward of up to $1,000 for anyone who can help solve the case but who wishes to remain anonymous.

Francisco Santoni, Maria Villa & Dante Santoni
El Paso, Texas

Homicide investigators are still trying to find out who killed a family on a quiet cul-de-sac on the eastern boundary of El Paso, Texas. It was on Thursday, August 11, 1994 when a relative arrived to babysit and found the bodies of Francisco Cliv Santoni, 59, his wife Maria Concepcion Villa, 28, and their 3-year-old son, Dante Santoni Villa. All had been stabbed multiple times at the home on Garden Gate Way in this Mexican border city of some 600,000 people. There are only eight homes on the quiet street that runs eastbound off Saul Kleinfeld Drive, one block south of Bob Mitchell Drive. Maria's sister had agreed to look after Dante, who was born on July 20, 1991. Once inside the house she found a scene of horror. There was blood all over the place from the victims being stabbed repeatedly during the attack. Police haven't given any information regarding a motive but have indicated that investigators don't have any idea who may be responsible for the killings. Crime Stoppers has made several appeals but investigators said they haven't received a lead that has brought them close to making an arrest.

Jamie Santos
Wheeling, Illinois

The 911 caller may have been the man who killed the 27-year-old exotic dancer in Wheeling, Illinois, but police haven't found anyone who recognizes the voice. It was 11:35 a.m. on Monday, October 28, 1991 when emergency personnel found the body of Jamie Santos in her townhouse unit at 1765 Stonehedge Court, a cul-du-sac off Arlington Drive near the intersection of South Buffalo Grove Road and Dundee Road in this community of 36,000 some 25 miles northwest of Chicago. She had been smothered with a pillow. There was no sign of a struggle but the victim was on the floor of her bedroom dressed in a knee length nightshirt and underwear. The door to her apartment was also unlocked. Investigators believe the person who killed Jamie left the trendy townhouse complex and made his way to a shopping centre on the west side of North Buffalo Grove Road, north of Dundee Road where he used a coin operated telephone to alert authorities. It is not known if the person was a friend visiting Jamie or if she just answered the door and her killer overpowered her.

Jamie lived most of her life in that area and attended Buffalo Grove High School before graduating from Harper College in nearby Palatine, Illinois. She lived alone but was very close to her family and considered her sister, Laurie, her best friend. Once a week she had her parents over for dinner and while at home with her two cats, Bandit and Prince, she tended to the numerous plants that she grew. She also enjoyed making ornaments to put on her tree during the Christmas season. She was described as a caring, energetic and generous person with a wide variety of interests. Crime Stoppers has issued two separate rewards in this case, one for the identification of the 911 caller and another for the indictment of Jamie's killer.

Stacy-Ann Sappleton

Stacy-Ann Sappleton
New York, New York

A 26-year-old Canadian woman was murdered after traveling to the affluent area of Brookville in Queens, New York to visit her fiancés family and finalize plans for their upcoming wedding. Stacy-Ann Sappleton didn't arrive at the home on 226th Street and three days later on Monday, May 10, 2004 her body was found stuffed in a garbage dumpster some seven miles away. She had been shot several times and injuries to her body indicated she was involved in a violent struggle with someone shortly before her death. The pathology report also showed Stacy-Ann had been dead less than 24 hours indicating she had been held captive somewhere after being abducted. However, investigators from the Queens South Detective Bureau of the New York City Police suggested other forensic evidence indicates the victim was murdered shortly after she went missing. Investigation shows the victim was sitting on a chair dressed only in underwear when shot at least three times. She had wounds to her torso, neck and limbs from bullets fired at very close range. There was no indication she had been sexually assaulted. Sappleton, a group benefits specialist with the Great-West Life insurance company in Windsor, Ontario, a community directly across the Canadian border from Detroit, had flown to New York's LaGuardia Airport on Friday, May 7, 2004 and travelled the 13 mile distance by taxi to the home of her future in-laws.

Her flight landed at 8:30 a.m. and less than an hour later she called her boyfriend, Damion Blair, at their home in Canada to let him know the cab was on his family's street and nearing their house. Blair's parents would be at work when Stacy-Ann was scheduled to arrive but were leaving the door unlocked so she could get in. Police have found no evidence that Stacy-Ann ever reached the front door and they are completely baffled how a young woman could be overpowered and spirited away in broad daylight without anyone noticing.

Blair drove Sappleton from the home where they were living in Tecumseh, a community on the outskirts of Windsor, to the Detroit airport for the early morning flight. She was wearing blue pants, a long sleeve blue top with a gray vest, a dark blue jean jacket and a multicolored handbag. She also had a carry-on bag with clothing and other items needed for her visit. Blair received a phone call from Stacy-Ann when she arrived at the airport and another a short time later when the cab driver became lost on route to his parent's home. He spoke to the cab driver and at 9:18 a.m. received a final call from Sappleton telling him she was almost at the house. Police located a video recording from a security surveillance system showing the taxi pulling onto 226th Street from 147th Street around the same time. The cab driver also confirmed that he dropped the woman off at the front door but drove off before seeing her go inside. Damion's younger brother, 20-year-old Marc, an art student at Hunter College, was at home, but sleeping in the basement and didn't hear anything. He was questioned by police and also provided DNA samples but nothing was found to implicate him in the slaying.

Damion and Stacy-Ann were to be married September 3 on Long Island and she was in New York to make sure nothing had been overlooked and to finally see the hall where the wedding ceremony would take place. The couple met in California where Blair, who was two years older, was serving with the United States Marines in 1997. They had planned to get married in 1999, but he was assigned to Japan and the wedding was postponed until the completion of his military service. After being discharged he got a job as a computer engineer in Detroit and they virtually lived together since that time. Sappleton was born in Jamaica and at the age of eleven moved to Canada with her mother, Marcia Thomas. They lived in Toronto until Stacy-Ann left to attend the University of Windsor where she graduated in 2000 with a degree in history. She had kept in constant touch with Blair through the Internet while he was stationed overseas and at the time of her disappearance was counting off the days until she would become his wife. Thomas, who officially identified her daughter's body at the New York City morgue, told investigators that Stacy-Ann had made three phone calls after getting out of the cab. Two calls were to her and the other to a cousin who lives in New York, but none were answered. The last call was made at 9:50 a.m. In each call Stacy-Ann left a message saying she'd arrived safely and there was no hint she was in any sort of danger.

Damion's mother, Valerie Blair, called her home at 11 a.m. but didn't get an answer. There was also no response on Stacy-Ann's cellular phone and her call went directly to the answering system. She started worry when her son called at 3 p.m. and confirmed Sappleton was in New York and had taken a cab from the airport. When she got home a couple of hours later and there was no sign of her son's fiancée, she called the police emergency number. There was confusion during the call to police and Mrs. Blair was left with the impression she couldn't file a missing person report until 24 hours had passed. They called the airport and airlines, some cab companies and searched neighboring streets while waiting until 11 a.m. on Saturday the time Stacy-Ann was officially reported missing to the New York City Police Department. Both Damion and Sappleton's mother immediately flew to New York and had missing posters printed up with Stacy-Ann's picture after failing to have media outlets carry stories about the disappearance. With no evidence of a crime, police could do nothing more than issuing a state wide alert, adding Stacy-Ann's name to the list of people in the national missing person computer data bank and broadcasting the description of the slender young woman, who wore glasses, had braces on her teeth and her hair in braids, to all New York City police officers.

The disappearance became a murder investigation on Monday morning when a sanitation worker with the Ragonese Carting Company saw the body of an almost naked young woman when he attempted to dislodge a discarded display rack that was jamming the compacting mechanism on his garage truck. He was in the midst of collecting garbage from the Key Food supermarket on 73rd Avenue in Oakland Gardens after emptying dumpsters at another Key Food store located in the vicinity of Braddock Avenue and Hillside Avenue. Investigators believe Stacy-Ann's body had been stuffed in the dumpster behind the store at Braddock and Hillside, almost eight miles from the Blair home, sometime on Sunday and less than 24 hours before she was found. A search of the dumpster didn't turn up any of the victim's clothing or the luggage she had with her when she got out of the taxi. Investigators also said the killer went to great pains to dispose of the victim and didn't intend for the body to be discovered. Had the mechanism not jammed, the young woman's remains would have been crushed among the garbage collected throughout the day and dumped at one of numerous landfill sites used for the countless tons of refuse gathered each day throughout New York City. Although there was no official crime scene, police were able to gather a treasure trove of information, including DNA evidence, from her body which will assist in convicting the killer once an arrest is made.

Police conducted a forensic examination at the Blair home but were unable to determine whether or not she entered the house on the Friday she vanished. There was no sign that a struggle had occurred anywhere around the home. Police knew almost immediately that the body in the dumpster closely resembled the missing Canadian woman, but it wasn't until the next day when her mother and her fiancé went to the morgue that she was officially identified. Her mother took her to Toronto for burial and each year since the slaying work colleagues who described her as "a very smart, responsible and well-liked young woman" have held a golf tournament in her memory to raise funds for charitable organizations, including the Windsor and Essex County Crime Stoppers program. A $12,000 reward is available through the New York Crime Stoppers program for information that leads to the arrest of Stacy-Ann's killer.

Suzanne Sayles
Minneapolis, Minnesota

A 24-year-old secretary at the University of Minnesota Dental School was murdered in her Minneapolis apartment. It was on Wednesday, May 23, 1979 when the body of Suzanne Sayles was discovered in the tiny one-bedroom at the three storey apartment building. She had been raped and strangled. The victim grew up some 112 miles away in Austin, a town of 23,000 in the southeastern part of the state where Highway 218 and Interstate 90 connect. Police have been unable to determine a motive for her slaying or focus on a particular suspect. Suzanne took a secretarial job at the Dental School after finishing college and had just started going out with a student at the university when she was killed.

She spoke to her mother by telephone on May 22 but when she didn't show up for work the next morning a close friend and a fellow employee went to the apartment to make sure nothing was wrong. The door to unit 305 where she lived was unlocked and inside they discovered Suzanne's body on the floor. Nothing was stolen and police said the victim's purse, which was near her body, had not been touched. Suzanne did put up a struggle and bit the attacker, but there is no indication anyone had forced their way in. She was an outgoing person and investigators assume she knew the killer, possibly someone she had recently befriended. Detectives from the Minneapolis Police Department interviewed many of the people she had met during the short time she lived in the city but no one was able to suggest anyone who could be responsible for killing her.

Investigators have spent hundreds of hours tracking leads on the case and most recently have renewed efforts to find her killer by utilizing improved DNA technology to examine evidence collected at the time of the slaying. Her mother, Marilyn Sayles, still lives with her husband at the home where Suzanne grew up and has kept her daughter's bedroom the way it was when she left in 1979.

She described her daughter as a beautiful young lady who loved life and hopes she lives long enough to see police bring Suzanne's killer to justice. A standard Crime Stoppers reward is available for anyone who provides anonymous information that will assist police in making an arrest.

Annette Kay Schnee
Sacramento, Colorado

The 21-year-old victim was last seen hitchhiking along Highway 9 after picking up a prescription at a drug store in Breckenridge, Colorado. Annette Kay Schnee hadn't felt well on the afternoon of Wednesday, January 6, 1982 and booked off early from her job at the Holiday Inn. She was heading to the cabin where she lived just outside Breckenridge but didn't arrive. She also failed to show up for an 8 p.m. shift at a second job she had as a waitress at the Flipside bar at Breckenridge's Beaver Run.

Annette was reliable and it was surprising she wasn't at work, but no one immediately reported her missing. Friends became concerned when they found she hadn't been home and the uniform that she would have worn at the bar was still on the hanger. Investigators took a description of the five-foot, three-inch, 102 pound woman with long light brown and blond hair and brown eyes, but there was no sign of foul play. When no one heard from her within a few days police intensified their efforts to locate the young waitress. Investigation turned up someone who remembered seeing Annette hitchhiking on Highway 9. It was the same day and the same road where 29-year-old Barbara "Bobbie" Jo Oberholtzer was picked up by a killer.

Annette was born on January 16, 1960 and if killed the same night she vanished, her death came 10 days before her 22nd birthday. Around 4:45 p.m. on January 6, 1982 she was at The Drug Store where she chatted with a woman she appeared to know, telling her not to forget to pick-up cigarettes. The woman, who police have never found, bought a package of Marlboro cigarettes from the clerk. She was five-feet, four-inches with a slim build and looked like she had just returned from a camping trip. The two women left the store minutes apart and did not appear to be going anywhere together. Sometime later Annette was seen hitchhiking.

Despite intensive police investigations into the disappearance, it wasn't until July 3, 1982 when the young woman's body was found face down in Sacramento Creek by a father and his 11-year-old son who were fishing in the remote area south of Alma. Annette had been shot in the back with a .38 caliber, .357 caliber or nine millimeter handgun. The bullet passed through her body and was not recovered. Although it was summer when the body was located the fact she was mostly immersed in the ice-cold mountain stream prevented rapid decomposition and allowed forensic experts to obtain valuable evidence. They were, however, not able to determine if she had been sexually assaulted.

Detectives said the victim was fully dressed but there was indication some of the clothing was put on the body after Annette's death. At this point investigators are still seeking people who may have seen the victim after she left the Breckinridge pharmacy or anyone who has information that Annette Kay Schnee and Barbara "Bobbie" Jo Oberholtzer knew each other. Detectives obviously want to identify the woman who spoke to Annette at the drug store as well as anyone who can recall anything suspicious or something that peaked their interest around the time of the two murders.

Police located an old Colorado license plate ZD-25 and would like to find the owner or anyone who had possession of the plate through the years. Detectives also learned about two brothers who rented a house in Placer Valley around the time Annette and Bobbie Jo were killed. The pair may have been from Kentucky or Tennessee, drove a gray Chevrolet or Dodge van and worked for a local plumbing company. Detectives want to hear from anyone who believes they has information that will help solve the killings and also remind people that Crime Stoppers is offering a reward of up to $1,000 for anyone who provides the tip that solves either case.

Shamika Donise Scott
Amarillo, Texas

When owners of a small motel in Amarillo, Texas went to find out why a 24-year-old woman hadn't paid her daily rent, they found her dead on the floor. Shamika Donise Scott was discovered at 11:50 a.m. on Friday, June 9, 2000 at the Wagon Wheel Motel on East Amarillo Boulevard, just east of North Grand Street, and investigators determined she had been dead no more than 12 hours. An autopsy showed her death was caused by smothering. Laxmi Nathu, wife of the motel owner, found the victim on the floor beside the bed in room 27 when Scott failed to show up at 11 a.m. to pay the daily rent of $24 plus tax. Scott had rented one of six larger units contained in a separate building behind the main motel on the south side of the street.

Investigators from the Amarillo Police Department's Special Crimes Unit have interviewed dozens of people to determine where the victim went and who she was with during the final hours leading up to the time of the slaying. At this point police haven't determined a motive and haven't focused on any particular suspects. A woman living in a nearby unit visited Scott in the early afternoon but left around 2 p.m. when a man came to see the victim. Police said they also have confirmation that Scott was alive at 11 p.m. on June 8.

Her mother, Joyce Ivory, has made several appeals through the Amarillo Crime Stoppers program to help find the killer as well as distributing posters. Shamika was her oldest daughter and she now lives for the day when police solve the case. She said it's agonizing knowing that a killer is walking free and vows to do whatever she can to help find whoever is responsible. Ivory said she's haunted every day with not knowing who killed her daughter. "I need justice for Shamika." Billboards have been posted in both Amarillo and Lubbock, some 125 miles to the south, announcing a reward from Crime Stoppers in this case. Police are convinced someone is aware of who killed Scott and are urging that individual to provide investigators with the culprit's name.

Donald Edward Seebold III
Selinsgrove, Pennsylvania

An air of mystery surrounds the slaying of Donald Edward Seebold III in the early morning hours of Sunday, July 13, 1997 near the mid Pennsylvania farming community of Selinsgrove. The 21-year-old left a pig roast around 2 a.m. and walked some three miles east along Troxelville Road when confronted by one or more assailants. He was savagely beaten and received what medical experts defined as blunt force trauma to his head and face area.

Friends who left the party a short time later found Seebold face down in the middle of the roadway and assumed he'd fallen after passing out. They told police he was alive and put him in the rear seat of the car, but he was dead when they went to wake him the next morning. It's believed several attackers were involved and Seebold was beaten with some sort of object. A $1,000 reward has been offered by Pennsylvania's state Crime Stoppers program for any information that leads to an arrest in this case.

Jennifer Servo

Jennifer Lynn Olson Servo
Abilene, Texas

The trail for the killer went cold before the bludgeoned body of Jennifer Olson Servo was discovered in her Abilene, Texas apartment. Although the petite blonde failed to show up for her shift as a news reporter with television station KRBC, it was two days before friends and colleagues called the manager of the Hunters Wood apartment complex in the 5500 block of Texas Avenue to determine if she was okay. It was 1:30 p.m. on Wednesday, September 18, 2002 when the 911 operator received a call that a young woman had been seriously injured in apartment 427 and there was blood all over the place. The first police officer responding to the apartment complex on the north side of Texas Avenue at Quail Run Street made a cursory check of the victim and found no sign of life. "Possible DOA," – police jargon for dead on arrival – the officer radioed to the dispatcher. "Contact Major Crimes police immediately…"

Born, Jennifer Lynn Olson, in the resort town of Whitefish, Montana on September 23, 1979, she legally adopted her mother's maiden name in 2001 while studying for a journalism degree at the University of Montana. After graduation she worked part-time at television station KECI, Channel 13 in Missoula, Montana and for the National Public Radio network before being hired as a general assignment reporter in Abilene. Her killing likely took place in the early morning hours of Monday, September 16, a week before her 23rd birthday. There was no sign of a break-in at the one bedroom apartment where she'd lived since moving to Texas from Montana in July. Although she had worked at the television station for only a couple of months, Jennifer Servo was a popular personality and had become well known to the 115,000 residents of the central Texas community on Interstate 20 half way between Midland and the Fort Worth-Dallas metroplex. Keenly aware of the victim's status as a local celebrity, a special police team headed by Detective Jeff Bell was assembled and the investigation given top priority status. To this day police remain under enormous pressure to solve the slaying.

Known as Jen to her friends, she was dressed in shorts and a t-top when her body was discovered. They were the clothes she normally slept in and it's possible she was just about to go to bed or was already sleeping when her killer arrived at the apartment door. Friends say she wouldn't have opened the door to a stranger so some of her acquaintances were added to the list of possible suspects. Her death was also very brutal. She was hit repeatedly and received blunt force trauma injuries to her head. Police said there was also evidence of a sexual assault.

Jennifer grew up in Columbia Falls, Montana, a community of 3,700 known as the gateway to Glacier National Park. The town was only a few miles from Whitefish were she was born and her childhood was filled with small town innocence. She was outgoing, very curious and enjoyed music. She played the flute, was extremely creative and enjoyed writing stories. She was a cheerleader from her first year at Columbia Falls High School until graduation in 1998. She was also on the school's swim team, played volleyball and managed of the boy's basketball team. During school years she had a part-time job at the former Gary and Leo's grocery store and in the summer worked at Big Sky Waterslide at the local theme park on Highway 2, just east of Columbia Falls and at the Marina Cay near the village of Bigfork on Flathead Lake.

At 17, Jennifer called her mother from the Army Reserve office to say she was enlisting to get money for college tuition but needed parental permission to sign up. She began basic training as a reservist that summer. Later in high school she was a national award winner in history and government from the United States Achievement Academy which recognizes academic performance, interest and aptitude, leadership qualities, responsibility, enthusiasm, motivation to learn and improve, citizenship, attitude and cooperative spirit as well as dependability. She was recommended for the award by teacher Dan Fairbank who thought she was an incredible kid. During the six years she spent as a specialist in the 347th Quartermaster, she went to Missoula every month for training. She learned how to fire automatic weapons and propel grenades. She also became skilled in the operation of water purification systems and in her freshman year at the University of Montana her Army Reserve Unit was mobilized and dispatched to El Salvador to provide safe water for residents after Hurricane Mitch, a category five storm, which devastated vast areas of that Central American country as well as Honduras and Nicaragua. The storm, which raged across the Caribbean Sea with sustained winds of 180 miles an hour, killed almost 20,000 people. Some 59,000 people were left homeless in El Salvador which normally isn't impacted by hurricanes forming in the Atlantic Ocean. Jennifer's unit saved thousands of lives by providing water to some of the half million people who were evacuated in the region.

Investigators said the victim was found dead on the bathroom floor but there was a trail of blood from the living room where she was first attacked. There was no sign of a forced entry into the apartment but several items were missing, including a Kyocera cell phone, a Guess purse with a picture of Anna Nicole Smith on the side, a three-season DVD series of "Sex in the City" and a "Saving Private Ryan" video disc. Even though the items were taken from the apartment, police said robbery is not thought to be the motive for the slaying. Crime Stoppers has offered a $1,000 reward for anonymous information leading to the arrest of the person responsible and a private organization has offered an additional $5,000 to encourage someone to come forward and identify Servo's killer.

In 1998, after finishing high school, she enrolled in the journalism program at the University of Montana. The following year she started working part-time at KPAX, a local television station in Missoula and later got a weekend reporting job at KECI-TV, the NBC affiliate station in the area. When she graduated in 2002, Servo was invited to join the staff at the Abilene television station. Her goal was to become the national anchor with one of the networks and working at a major Texas television station was a stepping stone that could give her the break she needed to fulfill her ambition. Although she loved small time life and the openness of Big Sky Country, she wanted the fame and fortune that New York City can bring and all those who knew her believed she would achieve her dream. Her mother, Sherry Abel, drove with her the more than 1,500 miles to Texas and then spent a week buying furniture and helping get her apartment in order.

It's not known if the victim attempted to escape to the bathroom or was dragged their by her attacker, but she was a slightly built person and wasn't able to put up much of a struggle. An autopsy showed she was struck at least three times over the head with a heavy object, possibly a ceramic frog statue that was also missing from the apartment. Family members, including her mother and father, have been frustrated through the years that the case hasn't been solved and hope someday someone will come forward with information that will allow police to arrest Jennifer's killer.

Todd Siemens
Kansas City, Missouri

A security guard was shot and killed when an unruly patron grabbed his gun after being ejected from a Kansas City, Missouri restaurant. The incident occurred shortly before 4 a.m. on Saturday, May 3, 1997 when 28-year-old Todd Siemens got into a physical altercation with a man outside the Taqueria Mexico Restaurant at 910 Southwest Boulevard. Siemens, an employee of MP Security, had driven from a store in Shawnee where he worked as a security officer to visit a guard assigned to protect the restaurant. A customer became enraged when the manager told him the restaurant was closed and they wouldn't be serving any more drinks. After being led outside, the man attacked Siemens and during the struggle pulled the guard's gun from its holster. The victim was shot several times and later succumb to his injuries at the hospital.

Homicide detectives from the Kansas City Missouri Police Department said the killer was a Hispanic man who speaks only Spanish and is known by the names Morgan, Nelson and Mortal Combat. He is between 22 to 30 years, five-feet, six-inches to five-feet, eight-inches, about 180 pounds with a stocky build and short black hair and a medium to dark complexion. Shortly after the shooting, witnesses reported seeing the suspect hopping a Santa Fe train after telling them he needed to get out of town and was heading to Texas and then to the Chihuahua area of Mexico. Investigators believe the suspect could also be in Juarez, Mexico where he has a number of friends. Police learned the man had been in the Kansas City area for only a month and worked part of that time at a Mexican business close to the restaurant where the shooting occurred. He has what are described as numerous large visible scars on his right arm, a grim reaper tattoo on his right inner forearm and the initials RMP or MRP tattooed at the top of his left arm or on his left shoulder. The Greater Kansas City Crime Stoppers has posted a reward for anyone who can provide information that will help police identify this individual and make an arrest in this case.

Brenda Sierra
Crestline, California

A 15-year-old sophomore was abducted by gang members while walking to school in East Los Angeles, California and her body later dumped some 75 miles northeast in an area known as the Valley of Enchantment. It was sometime between 7 a.m. and 7:30 a.m. on Friday, October 18, 2002 when Brenda Sierra may have been enticed or forced into a car after leaving her home at 1061 Leonard Avenue, off Whittier Boulevard between Simmons Avenue and South Hendricks Avenue. Police have not established a motive for the slaying, but investigation has linked the violent LOTT gang to her disappearance. Most days Brenda walked to a girlfriend's house to be driven to school by her mother. When she didn't arrive between the usual times of 7:15 a.m. and 7:20 a.m., they assumed she wasn't going to school that day and left without her. The school also made no attempt to find out why she wasn't in class and her parents had no idea she was missing.

It wasn't until she failed to come home by 6 p.m. from an after school hair appointment that her family realized something was wrong and called police. It took officers three hours to respond and on arrival made no attempt to look for Brenda suggesting instead that she'd voluntarily left and like most runaways would show up in a day or two. Her frantic parents called her friends and any others they thought might have some idea where their daughter was, but no one had seen or heard from her through the day. When investigators returned the next day to get a detailed description the family discovered there were no plans for a massive search and their daughter's disappearance didn't meet the criteria for issuing an Amber Alert to let the public know she was missing. The police did prepare a news release to notify the media but Brenda's disappearance received only limited coverage on local broadcast stations and in area newspapers.

Frustrated with what appeared to be a minimal effort to locate their daughter, Raphael and Emelda Sierra launched their own campaign with friends and other volunteers to distribute leaflets across a wide area urging people to help bring Brenda home. Their light colored stucco home with three palm trees in the front yard became the command centre with people on cell phones trying to track down anyone in the area who had seen Brenda anytime after 7 a.m. Friday. Other volunteers headed to various neighborhoods in the vicinity to put up the missing person flyers in store windows, on hydro poles or any other locations were they would easily been seen by passersby. Everyone worked through the weekend unaware that a body of a teenager girl was found around 10 a.m. on Saturday, October 19 by two people out for a walk on Skyview Lane near Crestline, California in the Valley of Enchantment. The victim wasn't identified until Monday when police took Brenda's mother and Fabiola Saavedra, the oldest of the couple's five children, to the morgue. Brenda had been savagely beaten and died from blunt trauma to the head. She was also sexually assaulted.

Brenda attended Schurr High School in Montebello and was described by classmates as a good student and a great friend. They said no one deserves to die the way she did, but they had no idea who was responsible for her murder. The Sheriff's Department requested a $5,000 reward, but County Supervisor Gloria Molina recommended the amount be raised to $150,000 as a commitment to the family who was initially let down by the response from law enforcement. Molina said Brenda was a beautiful young woman from the East Los Angeles community who did nothing to deserve her terrible fate. "We remain firmly committed to solving this case and we will not give up until whoever is responsible has been brought to justice." Through the years there have been vigils at the school on the anniversary of Brenda's disappearance where students talk about the 15-year-old girl who left her home with her blue backpack and walked into a nightmare death. Investigators have also never forgotten the teenage victim and recently the official homicide file was transferred from the San Bernardino Sheriff's Department to the Los Angeles County Sheriff's

Department where it remains an active homicide investigation. Until the file was transferred both law enforcement agencies had worked jointly on the case since the abduction occurred in the Terrace neighborhood of Los Angeles County and her body located in San Bernardino's jurisdiction. Her parents have also prayed for justice since the killing, her father adding: "The people who did this have no heart."

Hector Solorzano-Silverio
Killeen, Texas

The 45-year-old man collapsed and died inside his Killeen, Texas home, but investigation confirmed the death was a homicide. It was on Saturday, October 12, 2002 when Hector "Titor" Solorzano-Silverio was involved in a street fight with a group of people near his home on Adams Avenue between Henderson Street and North Root Street, a few blocks east of Fort Hood. Police were called to the altercation but it had broken up by the time they arrived. They were directed to the victim's home after someone noticed he wasn't breathing. An autopsy showed he died as a result of injuries received in a beating. A funeral mass was held for Solorzano-Silverio at St. Joseph Catholic Church in Killeen and he was buried in his native Mexico. Killeen's Crime Stoppers program has offered a reward of $1,000 for information that solves the killing.

James Richard Sinkhorn
Lexington, Kentucky

Investigators are convinced someone in a 20-year-old college student's circle of friends knows who is responsible for his shooting death in Lexington, Kentucky. James Sinkhorn was found dead about 2 p.m. at the rear of an apartment complex at 2001 St. Michael Drive on Saturday, April 24, 2004. He was face up on the ground and his body riddled with bullets. Sinkhorn had visited his mother, Carla Lyttle at her Florida home a couple of weeks before the killing and she told police he appeared frightened. She suggests he knew people implicated in a drug ring at Lexington Community College, but homicide detectives said they haven't determined what led to the victim's death. Known as Jamie to friends, he was a popular student but quite imposing at six-foot-three and 210 pounds. Investigators speculate those connected with the death were afraid of him and fired numerous bullets to make sure he couldn't retaliate. Sinkhorn, who was born on January 14, 1984 in Cincinnati, was last seen at 2150 Richmond Road, an apartment building near St. Ann Drive and a short distance from Shriner's Hospital. It's five blocks from where his body was discovered. A $50,000 reward was initially offered for information leading to the killer and the Bluegrass Crime Stoppers program in Lexington has up to $1,000 for anyone who wants to anonymously give details to help police solve this case.

Sukhpal Singh Sodhi

Sukhpal Singh Sodhi
San Francisco, California

Homicide inspectors are trying to determine if a San Francisco, California cab driver was shot to death while dropping off a passenger or the innocent victim of gunfire between rival gangs. Investigation has shown that Sukhpal Singh Sodhi was shot at 3:52 a.m. on Sunday, August 4, 2002 on 24th Street just after passing Lucky Street.

It appears he stopped at Folsom Street while heading to his home and that's when gunfire erupted. As the shots rang out, the taxi sped four blocks to the area of Mission Street where it knocked over a couple of parking meters and a utility pole before crashing into a parked car. Arcing wires ignited leaking fuel and the 50-year-old victim was trapped inside the blazing cab until firefighters arrived. He was pronounced dead at the scene and an autopsy later attributed death to a bullet wound to the head. Sukhpal immigrated to the United States in 1990 and worked to support his wife, two daughters and a son living in Passiwal, a village in India's Punjab. An examination of the crime scene indicated the person responsible for killing Sukhpal was on the street to the rear of the cab. The fatal shot went through the window of the vehicle and struck the victim. Bullets had struck some parked vehicles and also hit the wall of a nearby building. Forensic investigators from the San Francisco Police Department found blood droplets trailing along the sidewalk from a pool of blood from someone else who had been wounded in the shooting incident. Detectives have never located the injured person who likely has vital information regarding Sukhpal's death.

Robbery was ruled out as a motive since the victim had $322 in his wallet. The probe also focused on the possibility the shooting was a hate crime since Sukhpal's younger brother, Balbir Singh Sodhi, was murdered almost a year earlier in Mesa, Arizona, four days after the 9-11 terrorist attacks in New York, Washington and Pennsylvania. Balbir was the first victim of what was described as a retaliation backlash after September 11, 2001 which resulted in the deaths of 16 people across the United States. The person who killed 51-year-old Balbir also attempted on the same day to murder two men from the Middle East. He was sentenced to death by lethal injection for his savagery, but the sentence was later commuted to life in prison in a unanimous decision of the Arizona Supreme Court.

Sukhpal, a resident of Daly City, a diverse multicultural community some seven miles south of San Francisco, had shared an apartment with Balbir when they first came to the United States and got jobs as cab drivers. But his brother didn't think San Francisco was a safe city and moved to the Phoenix area where he opened up a gas station in Mesa. Sukhpal and four of his eight brothers were part of an extended family group which came to the U.S. starting in 1984 to earn money to support their home village in the Punjab state, an area that at the time was embroiled in political and religious turmoil in involving Sikh and Muslim factions. Reports indicate the group sent a "small fortune" that not only provided assistance for their family, but gave the village paved roads, schools, a water system and lighting.

Sukhpal had been employed less than a year with United Taxi but had worked with another firm for an extended period and was very familiar with the various neighborhoods of San Francisco. The area where the killing occurred was on the fringe of a well known Latino gang stronghold but investigators have been unable to determine if the gunman who fatally shot Sukhpal was associated with a gang. At the time Inspector Joseph Toomey indicated it looked as though the cab driver was in the wrong place at the wrong time through no fault of his own.

Co-workers described Sukhpal as a decent guy and an easy going person. They said he worked hard to support his family. David Singh, a cousin who lived in Phoenix, portrayed him as a cool guy who never had any problems with anyone. Detectives believe the cab driver's shooting is a solvable case and are urging anyone with information to contact the city's homicide unit or provide details to the police department anonymous tip line. The San Francisco mayor's office has posted a $100,000 reward for information that leads to the arrest of Sukhpal's killer.

Richard Sopsher
Baton Rouge, Louisiana

A robbery attempt led to the death of a man in the parking lot of a Burger King in Baton Rouge, Louisiana. It was on Thursday, January 26, 2006 when two black males approached Richard Sopsher who was sitting in a car with his uncle waiting for a friend at the drive-in restaurant located at 6244 Airline Highway between St. Katherine Avenue and St. Gerard Avenue. When Sopsher refused a demand to hand over cash one of the assailants pulled a handgun and shot him at close range. The 22-year-old victim died almost instantly. Investigators have so far been unable to identify the attackers who fled from the Burger King which neighbors the Family Dollar store and a car wash operation. It's not known if the bandits had a car parked in the vicinity but no vehicle was seen. Baton Rouge Crime Stoppers is offering a reward of up to $1,000 for information leading to the arrest of Sopsher's killer.

Stasny/Villegas Slayings
Port Charlotte, Florida

Two killers shot an elderly couple to death after bursting into their Port Charlotte, Florida home and then drove almost four miles to North Port where they murdered a man and three children. The same guns were used to kill all the victims but investigators haven't found any connection between the two families. The shooting spree began sometime after midnight on Thursday, December 19, 1991 when intruders raided a home on Frisco Terrance, located among a network of streets which are nestled in heavy tropical overgrowth on the western outskirts of Port Charlotte. After cutting the telephone line the gunman confronted Paul Stasny, a 71-year-old U.S. Army veteran who earned a Purple Heart during WWII, and his 69-year-old wife, Rita, in the master bedroom. They were both shot multiple times. The couple's aging dog, Pepsi, a golden retriever, was also killed.

Paul Stasny   Rita Stasny   Luis Villegas

Revonda Peay   Billy Ray Hall   Richard Peay

The assailants ransacked the single-storey home stealing a number of items including two unique war-era German-designed three barrel guns. The weapons, manufactured by Drillings, have a rifle underneath a double barrel shotgun and are engraved with outdoor scenes. The weapons are quite unusual and if they can be tracked down, investigators are convinced it will put them directly on the trail of the killers.

A couple of hours after murdering Paul and Rita Stasny, the gunmen arrived at the home of Luis and Donna Villegas in the 3400 block of Chamberlain Boulevard. The couple had lived in North Port about a year after moving to Florida from Charlotte, North Carolina. Detectives determined the assailants again cut the telephone line and went room to room after forcing their way into the small concrete block home. Donna Villegas awoke when the gunmen opened fire in the bedrooms of her children and after grabbing a cordless phone ran outside. She called 911 at 2:41 a.m. screaming that someone was shooting her family. Thirteen-year-old Revonda Peay, eleven-year-old Billy Ray Hall, nine-year-old Richard Peay and his eight-year-old brother, Juantis, were shot numerous times. The gunman then chased down 36-year-old Luis Villegas and fired numerous shots into his head and body. Juantis was the only victim to survive the murderous shooting rampage and his mother escaped unhurt after fleeing to a neighbors. Although the gunmen had cut the phone line, the couple had a second telephone line which operated the cordless that Donna used to summon help.

The North Port Police Department teamed up with the Charlotte County Sheriff's Office and the Florida Department of Law Enforcement to probe the slayings. A $10,000 reward is being offered to anyone who provides information that leads to the arrest and conviction of the killers. Investigators have never established a motive for the murders but there are many theories ranging from a thrill killing to Villegas being targeted because he owned money to drug dealers. At the time of the murder Luis was working as a cook at the Quality Health Care Center in North Port and his wife a nursing assistant at the Life Care Centre, a nursing home in Punta Gorda, south of Port Charlotte.

Police did learn that Luis had worked as a guard from 1981 to 1984 at the Hillsborough Correctional Institute and was disciplined a couple of times for rough handling inmates. It is possible the killings were totally random but police are continuing efforts to find a link between the Villegas family and the elderly couple. Investigators are also working to identify the gunmen who are thought to be white males of average weight and height. They were wearing ski-masks and carrying automatic pistols, but police said at least one of them was wearing high top sneakers that sold exclusively for $12.99 in area K-Mart stores at the time of the murders. Although many years have passed since the six victims were killed, investigators said it continues to be an active case and they hope someone will come forward with information that will allow them to make arrests.

Christy Lea Cuzzort Stephens
Chattooga County, Georgia

She didn't go to school because she had a sore throat, but when her father checked on her a couple of hours later the 13-year-old girl was missing. It was around 9 a.m. on Monday, October 1, 1990 when Billy Stephens returned after driving his mother to work and discovered his step-daughter, Christy Stephens, wasn't in her bed at their home on Farmersville Road in Chattooga County, some seven miles east of Summerville, Georgia. His wife was asleep and didn't hear Christy leave, but her running shoes were found at the end of their driveway. It appeared as though she had dropped them and investigators initially treated the disappearance as a runaway case. A description of the girl was issued, but it was another two days before police began full scale searches in the area and other parts of the county. Three weeks later on Thursday, October 22 a deer hunter came across her remains in a wood-covered ravine some 300-feet off the road and about a mile and a half from her home. She was still wearing the blue jean shorts and blue t-shirt with a palm tree design that she was believed wearing when she vanished. Investigation showed the girl had been strangled and then her body dragged to the ravine area off Farmersville Road and covered over with small pine tree limbs and some brush. Because of the advanced stage of decomposition forensic experts determined she was killed soon after she went missing.

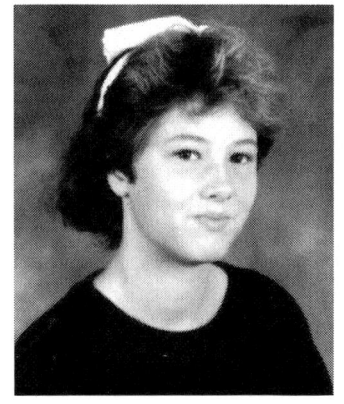

Christy was a Grade 8 student at Summerville Middle School and not experiencing any difficulties. It's possible she made arrangements to meet someone, but investigators have never been able to substantiate anything to reinforce that scenario. She was friendly and outgoing and never suggested to any of her classmates that she might run away. She did take some things when she left the house which bolstered the original theory that she was a runaway, but investigators said it's also possible she went out for a walk and was abducted by someone who saw a young girl walking alone on a two lane rural roadway in a fairly isolated area of the state. Her biological father, Tommy Cuzzort, who now lives in Alabama, is hopeful Christy's killer will be caught.

Recently the Georgia Bureau of Investigations posted the case as an unsolved homicide on their web site and appealed for people to come forward with information. Larry Kellett, the chief investigator with the Chattooga County Sheriff's Department has arranged to submit fluid samples taken during the autopsy to the state's crime lab for analysis with equipment for DNA testing that wasn't available at the time of the murder. Solving Christy's killing remains a top priority.

Find My Killer

Chapter 7 – Steward-Hill to Zywicki

Beverley Ann Steward-Hill

Beverley Ann Steward-Hill
University Place, Washington

A 20-year-old woman was found dead in her apartment after someone deliberately set at a fire which swept through the complex in University Place, a city of some 30,000 residents five miles southwest of Tacoma, Washington. It was around 6 a.m. on Saturday, June 24, 2006 when firefighters found the body of the victim, Beverley Ann Steward-Hill inside her apartment unit in the 2600 block of 70th Avenue West, just north of 27th Street West. Investigators haven't indicated if she was murdered and the apartment set ablaze by the killer to cover up the homicide or if she died of smoke inhalation through the work of an arsonist. Her pet dog, Zeus, also perished. Some 58 other residents of the two-storey Castellan West Apartments were forced to flee the flames and lost most of their belongings.

Crime Stoppers has posted a $1,000 reward for information in the death and an additional $9,000 is being offered by other people to assist detectives with the investigation. Only days after the blaze, Beverley's mother, Nellie Hill, was out raising money for the victims of the 35 fire damaged units. Most didn't have insurance and church and community groups joined forced to find donated clothing and other items needed by the residents to start rebuilding their lives. Beverley's mother did whatever she could do to help and spent time at a rummage sale organized in her daughter's honor at a local church. She said her daughter would have been one of the first out to help her neighbors if she was still here. Beverley, who studied to be a medical technician, was also a fan of the local hip-hop community and performers from the Tacoma area organized a benefit to bolster the reward fund.

Phillip T. Stewart
Fort Wayne, Indiana

A man nick-named "Bamm" was shot to death during a disturbance at a Fort Wayne, Indiana home. The 23-year-old victim, Phillip T. Stewart, was found just after 10 p.m. on Thursday, April 14, 2005 with a gunshot wound to the chest after police were called to 4333 Reed Street, between McKinnie Avenue and Senate Avenue, regarding a possible shooting. The victim remained in critical condition after surgery at Parkview Hospital and died four days later. Homicide detectives from the Fort Wayne Police Department have received very little cooperation in their attempt to identify the person responsible for Stewart's death and are appealing for anyone with information to contact them. Crime Stoppers is also offering a reward of up to $1,000 to encourage anyone who knows the killer to call the program's tip line anonymously.

William Stormo
San Diego, California

The San Diego Crime Stoppers program is offering the standard reward of up to $1,000 for anonymous information that leads to the arrest of the individual who killed a 33-year-old man in his Broadway Street apartment. William Stormo was found dead on the living room floor about 11:30 a.m. on Thursday, February 8, 2001 and police said there were signs of an obvious struggle. Investigation showed the victim had been strangled. Police responded to the man's apartment after someone called the 911 emergency number from a restaurant on Adams Avenue to report the death. The caller said he found the door of his friend's unit open and the victim's body inside. Stormo was described as a friendly and outgoing person who entertained many visitors at his apartment. Investigation by homicide detectives from the San Diego Police Department showed he was likely killed late the night before or in the early morning hours of the day his body was found. Detectives also determined the residence had been ransacked and many items stolen. The three storey apartment building where the victim lived was at 2930 Broadway, just east of 29th Street in the Golden Hill area of San Diego, and the restaurant on Adams Avenue where the 911 call was made is more than four miles away. Detectives have never been able to find the man who made the call and they are very anxious to speak with him to see if he can provide any further information.

Priscilla Lee Strole
Fairfield, California

A woman was possibly raped before being beaten to death at a home in Fairfield, California, a community of 100,000 people some 50 miles northeast of San Francisco. The attack occurred between 9 p.m. and 9:45 p.m. on Wednesday, August 31, 1993 when the victim, Priscilla Lee Strole, was alone at her home in the 1000 block of Buchanan Street, between Utah Street and Kentucky Street. The 38-year-old victim, who was unemployed, finished a phone call to a friend around 9 p.m. and 45 minutes later was found dead by her son on the living room floor. Investigators said the son arrived at the house but couldn't get in because the door was locked. When there was no response to his knock, he told authorities he went to the rear of the single-storey home and saw his mother sprawled naked on the floor. He ran to a neighbor's home to summon police and rescue units. The woman was pronounced dead at the scene and an autopsy showed she had been beaten to death. Forensic experts also determined the woman had sexual intercourse just before she was killed but there was nothing conclusive to indicate if it was consensual or she was raped. Detectives from the Fairfield Police Department found evidence the victim had been struck repeatedly over the head with a number of heavy objects located in the home. Investigators are hoping someone will come forward and indicate a possible motive and identify the individual who killed Strole.

Phillip "Brian" Sweat
Gainesville, Florida

He was stabbed seven times in his front yard in Gainesville, Florida, but before dying described his attacker to a 911 emergency operator.

Phillip "Brian" Sweat was confronted by someone at 2:33 p.m. on Monday, June 27, 2005 outside his home at 4024 SW 38th Street near Interstate 75 and Archer Road. Although having trouble breathing, the 40-year-old victim said his killer was a black male wearing jeans and a long sleeve blue shirt. The murder took place in broad daylight at the end of a secluded cul-de-sac and there were no witnesses. Detectives from the Gainesville Police Department theorize Sweat was attacked after someone came to his door or he noticed an individual near his car, a red 2000 Toyota MR2 Spyder convertible. When police arrived at the house moments after the victim's call for help, they found Sweat unconscious with his two dogs, a cocker spaniel and a Shih Tzu, cuddling beside him just inside the front door. Both dogs were caked with his blood. Sweat was pronounced dead at 3:45 p.m. in the emergency room at the University of Florida's Shands Hospital, about three miles from his home. There was no attempt to steal anything from the house and the victim's car was still parked in the driveway. Investigators have never been able to substantiate a motive and continue to hope someone will come forward who can identify the killer.

Sweat, a computer programmer, had worked with the Bank of America for many years in Pennsylvania, but in 2000 took a job in Jacksonville, Florida. His father died in 2002 and when his mother was diagnosed with cancer in June 2004, he moved back to the family home to care for her. Since her death in October, Sweat, who wasn't working, had lived alone at the house. Although investigators are confident a stranger was responsible for the slaying, they are still looking into the possibility he had invited the individual to his home. He spent a lot of time on his computer and may have been in contact with someone through the Internet. It's also possible that the killer wandered into the area from SW 40th Boulevard, the street running behind the victim's home which is lined with various hotels catering to travelers from Interstate 75 or the nearby commercial area on Archer Road. Police canvassed the neighborhood but failed to find anyone who believed they had seen anything suspicious around the time Sweat was murdered. Investigators also erected a flashing electronic sign urging people to come forward with information, but that effort didn't turn up anything of significance. Although Sweat kept to himself, he wasn't reclusive and went out regularly for dinner with a number of friends. He didn't drink or smoke and never took drugs. He also enjoyed sports and loved attending Gator games. Apart from the car he drove, Sweat wasn't a flashy person and didn't do anything out of the ordinary that would make him a target for bandits. He was dressed only in a pair of shorts when the attack occurred but the killer didn't even take his wallet from his pocket, indicating to detectives that robbery wasn't a prime motive. If he did confront someone trying to steal his car, investigators suggest there is a possibility the person pulled a knife and lunged at the victim to avoid getting into a struggle. The Alachua County Crime Stoppers program has offered a $1,000 reward for information leading to the indictment of the individual who killed Sweat. Investigators are hoping the reward money will persuade someone to divulge details that for one reason or another they haven't disclosed to anyone about the killing.

Rosie Tapia

Rosie Tapia
Salt Lake City, Utah

A six-year-old girl vanished from her parent's Salt Lake City, Utah apartment complex but investigators don't know if someone came in and took her or if she was abducted after crawling out the ground floor window. A nearby resident heard a scream about 4 a.m. on Sunday, August 12, 1995, but it wasn't until 5:30 a.m. that anyone realized Rosie Tapia was missing. At that time, Lewine Tapia went to check her children and found Rosie wasn't in bed. The window was open and the screen missing. She searched the apartment and then called police. A baby-sitter put the Tapia children, Rosie and four-year-old twins, Angelica and Robert, to bed at 9:30 p.m. while their parents were out for the evening. The children slept in the same room. Lewine got home with her husband, Roberto, at 2:30 a.m. and found the children fast asleep. When she awoke three hours later and looked in on the children, Rosie wasn't there.

The call for help came as dawn was chasing away the nighttime darkness and police wasted no time in launching a search of the neighborhood around the Hartland apartments at 1601 West Snow Queen Place. There was no sign of the little girl and nothing to indicate where she had gone. Apart from the open window and missing screen, detectives noticed the venetian blinds on the floor. The crime scene gave every indication that the girl had been abducted but there was no evidence suggesting anyone had gone into the room. Soon after the police search began a jogger making his way along a bicycle path only a short distance from the Tapia home found the victim's little body floating in a surplus canal of the Jordan River. An autopsy showed Rosie had been sexually assaulted and then drowned.

Detectives from the Salt Lake City Police have continued tracking down leads through the years but have never got the lead necessary to make an arrest. The FBI's behavioral science unit in Quantico, Virginia produced a psychological profile on the individual who may have taken the Tapia girl, but it hasn't yet helped to isolate a suspect. Investigators believe the crime was more than just a case of opportunity and if the killer entered the room, they are convinced he knew Rosie was sleeping there. It is also a brutal way to kill someone and indicates the person is quite callous. Although many years have passed since the slaying police are still hopeful someone will remember something and come forward with the clues that will help them make an arrest. So little evidence was ever recovered from the crime scene that investigators suggest it will only be through the direct assistance of someone that this case will ever be solved. A $30,000 reward has been offered to encourage anyone with information to come forward.

Alex Teehee
Port Charlotte, Florida

A sports utility vehicle purposely ran over a 20-year-old man out for a walk in Port Charlotte, Florida and the driver made a u-turn to go back and look at the victim's body, possibly to make sure he was dead. Alex Teehee was struck by the dark colored vehicle around 11 p.m. on Sunday, July 13, 2008 on Sibley Bay Street near Central Avenue.

Teehee, a single father with two children, was gravely injured, but lived several hours before being pronounced dead at Lee Memorial Hospital in Fort Myers, Florida where he had been airlifted with massive head and internal injuries.

Charlotte County Sheriff's Department investigators located evidence which showed the northbound vehicle, occupied by two men, veered from the east side of the roadway and intentionally hit the victim who was walking northbound on the west side of Sibley Bay Street.

The victim had received threatening text messages a couple of days before he was killed. Investigators initially kept details of the death secret and asked the family to delay a public memorial service and the publishing of an obituary for almost two weeks while they attempted to flush out the people responsible for the killing.

The tactic didn't work and the victim's parents, Tab and Carol Teehee who live in nearby North Port, began flooding the neighborhood with posters and appealing through the media for assistance to solve the killing of their son. They posted a $20,000 reward for information about those responsible for his death. The Florida Highway Patrol has teamed up with the sheriff department's investigators, but no possible suspects have been identified. The local Crime Stoppers program is also offering a reward of up to $1,000 for anyone who wishes to provide information anonymously regarding Teehee's hit-and-run homicide death.

Teehee was born in Broken Arrow, Oklahoma and moved to North Port with his parents in 2001. He graduated in 2006 from North Port High School and less than a week before his death moved with his sons to a home in Port Charlotte. A web site set up in his memory describes him as an individual who had taken full responsibility to care for his young children, Kaden, who was three at the time of his death, and Eli, then two years old. The site also allows the victim to speak.

"My name is Alex Teehee. I was a 20-year-old single father with physical custody of my sons," his message begins. "All of that changed on July 13, 2008 when I was struck by a vehicle intentionally and left to die. On July 14, 2008 I died of severe brain injury leaving behind my children, my family and my friends. To this date there has been no major progress in my case. Basically in my case it is easy to get away with murder. It seems like those people I called my friends, and trusted, are not. They have continuously lied to my family and the police to hinder the investigation. At this point if you aren't famous or your case doesn't get a lot of media attention it seems that no one cares that your life was taken by someone else. I wasn't a drug dealer whose house got raided, I wasn't kidnapped, and I am not important enough to the community for anyone other than my family and a few friends to really care what happens to the people who are responsible." His words obviously reflect the pain and frustration of his family and friends who are waiting for justice. The message continues. "There are murderers in our town on the loose and no one is doing anything about it. What is this world coming to and why isn't my life just as important as the last person or the next person. Check my record, I was a good kid, a great Dad. I tried to stay out of trouble and do what was right. Guess I just trusted someone I thought cared about me and look what happened." His family is now hoping justice for Alex will come soon when police finally arrest those responsible for his death.

Genevieve Tetpon
Anchorage, Alaska

She was one of a number of young women murdered in the Anchorage, Alaska area over the span of a few years and investigators have considered a serial killer may be responsible. The body of Genevieve Tetpon was discovered around 10:30 a.m. on Wednesday, March 22, 2000 in brush and snow along a frontage road some 25 feet from Arctic Valley Road on the eastern outskirts of Anchorage. The 28-year-old victim had been repeatedly stabbed but homicide investigators were unable to conclusively confirm that she had been sexually assaulted. Seminal fluid was found but police said it could have resulted from a consensual relationship prior to her death. Detectives said they are still trying to develop a timeline and determine where Tetpon was in the days leading up to the point she was murdered.

Born in La Grande, Oregon on May 5, 1971 she had lived in Alaska for a number of years and had three children. Her mother, Pat Milkowski, last saw Genevieve three weeks before her body was discovered, but she told police it wasn't unusual for her daughter to go away for periods of time. She became concerned after hearing news reports that an Aboriginal woman's body had been found by a motorist in a remote area just outside Anchorage. Police were able to put a name to the unidentified body the next day when Tetpon showed them a photograph of her daughter. Anchorage Crime Stoppers will pay up to $1,000 for information that leads to Tetpon's killer and the city has authorized a $20,000 reward for the arrest and indictment of the person or persons responsible for the slayings of at least six victims, mostly Native women, over a span of two years. The other murder victims are Vera Haphof, Annie Mann, Tina Shangrin, Michelle Butler and Della Brown.

Ivy Lynn Thomas
Baton Rouge, Louisiana

Homicide detectives are trying to determine a motive for the shooting death of a 32-year-old man in Baton Rouge, Louisiana. The gunman fired numerous shots while chasing Ivy Lynn Thomas through a grassy field just after 7 p.m. on Saturday, September 20, 2008 in the vicinity of Kaufman Street and the Scenic Highway. The victim fell to the ground after being hit by a bullet outside 1638 Kaufman Street and the gunman then stood over him and fired multiple shots into his body before fleeing. Thomas, the father of three sons and two daughters, lived three blocks away on Scenic Garden Avenue and it could have been somewhere near his home where the victim was initially confronted. Witnesses said they first saw Thomas being chased by the man in a field on the north side of Kaufman Street, between the Scenic Highway and Sanchez Street. The gunman was a black male, but witnesses were unable to provide a detailed description of the killer. Thomas, a graduate of Alcee Fortier High School, had lived in Baton Rouge all his life. Investigators from the Baton Rouge Police said the shooting occurred in a residential neighborhood and they suspect a number of people saw the incident but haven't yet come forward with their information. The Baton Rouge Crime Stoppers program is offering a reward to encourage anyone who is reluctant to speak directly to investigators to call to the tip line and identify the killer without giving their name.

DaNydia Thompson

DaNydia Betty-Jacqueline Thompson
Killeen, Texas

A seven-year-old girl was murdered after being piggy-backed away from a school by her abductor in Killeen, Texas. It was on Wednesday, April 30, 1997 when a man lured DaNydia Thompson from the playground of the Marlboro Heights Elementary School at 902 Reverend R. A. Abercombie Drive in the vicinity of East Veterans Memorial Boulevard and South 38th Street. The girl took the man's hand and walked from the school situated on the west side of the street between the Marlboro Heights Baptist Church and a small office building. Moments later witnesses saw the girl getting a piggy-back ride from a man in the vicinity of Veteran's Memorial Boulevard and Jefferies Avenue, some three blocks from where she was abducted. That was the last time anyone saw the little first-grader alive. Eight days later, on Thursday, May 8, 1997 her body was found stuffed in a plastic bag in a ditch alongside Highway 195, about 10 miles south of the city near the community of Florence.

DaNydia, who was called "Nee-Nee" by her family, was born on March 5, 1990 and was three-feet, six-inches, around 50 pounds with brown eyes and brown hair which she wore in ponytails. She had gone to school for breakfast and then went to the playground with other children before classes started. Her two cousins had walked with her the four blocks to school from her grandmother's home where she was staying, but they didn't notice the man approach. He called her by name and then casually led her away. It wasn't until DaNydia failed to come home after school that she was reported missing. She was a little girl with a small mole on her arm and a little scar on her forehead. Her front tooth was larger because the permanent one had grown beside the baby tooth. That day she was wearing a purple and white checkered short sleeve shirt with a white t-shirt, black denim jeans, a black belt and green LA Gear tennis shoes. She also carried a book bag with a floral design and turquoise trim. The missing person report went on with as much detail her grandmother could provide and more than 1,000 volunteers turned out during the next few days to search a vast area around the school.

Police were also putting out a description of the man who took DaNydia. He was black, about 25 years, five-feet, 10-inches, 150-pounds with an afro hairstyle, about three inches in length. He had a slender nose and thick moustache which reached the corners of his mouth. He was dressed in a black waist length jacket, baggy black jeans and wearing light colored tennis shoes. Investigators prepared a composite drawing of the suspect which was displayed in newspapers and on television across central Texas along with pictures of the missing girl. A reward of up to $6,500 is available for information leading to the capture of DaNydia's killer.

Christopher John Tillman
Portland, Oregon

Investigators are mystified by the baffling death of a 22-year-old man on the third floor of a small apartment building in Portland, Oregon. It was 8:22 p.m. on Wednesday, April 16, 2008 when the body of Christopher John Tillman was located near an elevator in the hallway of a four-storey building known as the Hazelwood Station apartments on East Burnside Street at NE 148th Avenue. Evidence indicates the victim was confronted by someone in the elevator and died from a single gunshot wound to the head. He crawled from the elevator and collapsed in the third-floor hallway.

Investigators from the Portland Police Bureau said Tillman lived in North Portland and they have no idea why he was visiting the neatly kept yellow and green building steps away from the TriMet Max light rail transit station. The neighborhood is well away from Portland's downtown area and not a locality where you have this type of violence.

Residents of the building called police after hearing gunfire. They found Tillman dead but haven't been able to determine a motive for the slaying. It's not known if the victim had arranged to meet someone at the building or was followed there by a stranger. Portland Police have reward money available to help solve this crime.

Harold & Joan Tillman

Harold & Joan Tillman
Yucaipa, California

The faithfulness of a white fluffy Maltese dog named Teddy helped police find the graves of two murder victims. Harold "Skip" Tillman, 55, and his 51-year-old wife, Joan of La Cañada Flintridge, California, vanished on Sunday, February 6, 2000 after meeting friends for dinner at the JJ Steak House and Seafood Grille on the third floor of a building on Colorado Boulevard and Delacey Avenue in Old Town Pasadena. They drove their dinner companions' home from the opulent restaurant around 9 p.m. and then went to their house on Bramblewood Road, a quiet dead-end street with about a dozen posh homes backing onto the Angeles Crest Highway near the La Cañada Flintridge Country Club. Tillman, a certified public accountant, was scheduled to meet with several clients the following morning, but didn't show up. A neighbor said he noticed the couple's car pulling into the garage about 10 p.m. when his dogs started barking but he didn't see them go into the house. That night Tillman's wife washed the clothes he'd been wearing. She put on a nightdress and robe before transferring the freshly-washed clothing to the dryer. At that point the events began that would eventually lead to the deaths of the couple.

Investigators said the murders appear to have been carried out by a professional killer or someone who desperately wanted them dead.

Every detail was planned. The person who took their lives may have slipped into the home through an unlocked sliding glass door or could have confronted them after ringing the doorbell. There was no sign of a struggle and it's possible some sort of ruse may have been used to lure them from the house. Joan, better known to friends as Joni, got into the car while still wearing the robe and they brought the dog with them. Police said there seemed to be some urgency as they left but no indication of fear or a reluctance to leave the house. It is possible they received a phone call telling them something had occurred or a request to meet someone right away, but any record of incoming numbers was wiped out by the more than 30 people who tried to telephone them in the ensuing days after they vanished. Among the phone messages was a call on Monday, February 7 from a man who found their pet Maltese while walking in a desolate tract off Oak Glen Road at 5th Street in Yucaipa, California, some 75 miles almost directly east from the couple's home. Unfortunately, he was calling to advise Teddy was dead.

Tillman was a respected businessman, but he and his wife did get involved in a couple of controversial financial transactions and a complicated business deal that all ended up in court litigation. Investigators said they were not the type of civil disputes that would likely result in a contract killing. One involved the failure to fulfill obligations of a promissory note related to an unsuccessful land deal in Georgia. Another stemmed from an allegation that $370,000 had been embezzled from a Hollywood fashion designer. And the third civil lawsuit followed a disagreement between Tillman's wife and a relative. Investigation showed the matters were close to being resolved and would not stand up as a motive for murder.

Someone familiar with the desolate landscape on the northern outskirts of Yucaipa, a city at the time of slightly more than 41,000 residents in the foothills of the San Bernardino Mountains, could be responsible for killing the couple. The person went earlier to a water runoff area on the north side of Oak Glen Road near 5th Street and dug two separate four-foot deep graves. The site was just off a paved service road at the bottom of a 25-foot rocky incline. Police stressed the killer had devised an elaborate plan to execute Tillman and his wife. After the couple left their home they somehow met someone who took their lives. Tillman was stabbed in the neck and they were both strangled. The killer drove their vehicle to the isolated community with the hope of burying their bodies in a spot where they would never be discovered.

It's believed Teddy jumped from the couple's silver-colored 2000 Dodge Durango when the assailant pulled off Oak Glen Road at the pre-dug gravesite and ran off into the darkness. The killer dragged the two bodies a short distance along the service road and across rocks to bury them. Tumbleweed was put over the fresh soil and dirt sprinkled on the roadway to conceal blood that dripped from Tillman's body while being dragged to the burial site. When the killer drove off, the couple's pampered dog scampered to the graves to keep vigil. Through the night or sometime the next day, Teddy fell asleep and didn't wake up. Death was attributed to shock and exposure, possibly brought on through fear, the lack of food and water and extreme temperature which is common in the Southern California region.

The man who found Teddy realized from the painted toenails and well-groomed appearance that it wasn't an average desert dog and took the tag from the collar and called the owners to let them know he'd located their pet. He left the Tillman's a message when he didn't get an answer at their home. The Los Angeles County Sheriff's department assigned a deputy to check the couple's home on February 8 after friends and business associates became concerned when Tillman didn't keep appointments and weren't answering their home phone. The deputy found no sign of foul play and assumed the couple had taken an unannounced trip. The next day two friends went into the house and after hearing the phone message about the couple's dog made contact with the caller. The San Bernardino Sheriff's office was notified and a short time after sunrise on Thursday, February 10, 2000 investigators unearthed the bodies of Tillman and his wife. Had it not been for Teddy, police said it's quite likely the victims would never have been discovered.

Joni was still wearing the robe and investigators found a number of items buried with them, including a bed sheet from the couple's home and some towels. On Friday, February 11, a day after the bodies were found, the couple's Durango was located by a Los Angeles Police officer in the vicinity of Community Street and Haskell Avenue, a working class neighborhood in Van Nuys, one block north of Roscoe Boulevard. Investigators spent painstaking hours through the years without coming up with an answer to the extremely puzzling case. Their hope now is that someone has information about the slayings and will come forward to provide details to identify the killer. The Tillman's were an average couple who had moved to LaCanada from Glendale, California only a few months before they were killed. Both had grown children from previous marriages but no one was living with them. Neighbors and friends described them as wonderful people and they cannot imagine them having enemies. They said he was kind and Joni very charming and full of life.

Martha Toms
Anchorage, Alaska

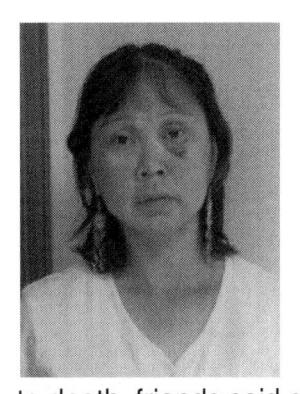

A 35-year-old native woman was sexually assaulted and beaten to death in Lion's Mountain View Park in Anchorage, Alaska. Found unconscious under a picnic table at the park on Mountain View Drive and North Pine Street on Thursday, September 22, 2005, Martha Toms died the next day at the Alaska Regional Hospital. For a few years prior to her death, she has had problems with alcohol and frequently travelled from her home area in Nome to Anchorage. Days before being beaten to death, friends said she had secured a job as a housekeeper at a Nome hotel and was making plans to travel there. Homicide investigators from the Anchorage Police Department don't have a clear picture of the victim's movements for a few days up to the time she was found and are still hoping to speak with people who saw her during that period. A reward has been posted by the Anchorage Crime Stoppers program to help police garner information that will solve this killing. Family members and individuals associated with Native organizations through the years have attended memorial services and other rallies to focus attention on a number of homicides that have taken the lives of aboriginal women in Alaska. They never want the community to forget these victims or consider them as "throwaways" because of their social status.

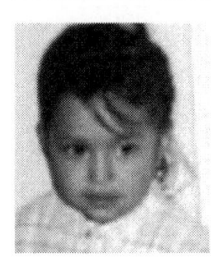

Daniella Torres
Phoenix, Arizona

A four-year-old girl was shot to death when armed attackers forced their way into an apartment unit in Phoenix, Arizona. It was at 9:50 p.m. on Friday, July

26, 2002 when Daniella Torres was shot after four men barged into the family apartment in the vicinity of South 21st Avenue and West Lincoln Street. The intruders armed with a rifle and handgun demanded to see someone, but the parents said no one by that name lived with them. At that moment the suspects began firing and Daniella was shot as she sat watching television. The Phoenix Silent Witness program has posted a $1,000 reward for information leading to the arrest and indictment of the girl's killer.

Joseph Anthony Torres
Philadelphia, Pennsylvania

A 36-year-old man was shot to death following a quarrel over a ten dollar debt in Philadelphia, Pennsylvania. It was around 1 a.m. on Sunday, October 28, 2007 when an assailant followed Joseph Torres from the Latin Room bar on North 8th Street at West Lycoming Street and shot him in the head. The man had earlier demanded ten dollars that the victim owed him, but Torres said he didn't have the cash and would pay him the following day. He was shot just outside the bar and died before reaching the hospital. Torres, who was known to everyone as Papo, had lived in a house two blocks from the bar for more than 35 years. He worked as a chef, was the father of a teenaged boy, and looked after his aging mother. His sister, Sonia Torres-Johnson described him as the backbone of the family. Investigators, who traced the victim's final footsteps before the killing, said he left his house on North 8th Street around 12:30 a.m. and walked to the bar. This was a bit out of character since his sister said Torres wasn't a person who would normally go to a bar in the evening, but detectives have theorized he may have gone to meet someone. He had a car radio with him and may have been trying to sell it to get money to repay the loan. The Pennsylvania Crime Commission and members of the victim's family have raised $5,000 for a reward to encourage anyone to tell police the name of the killer.

Vicki Toups
Des Allemands, Louisiana

A 38-year-old woman was beaten to death and dumped on a roadway in Des Allemands, Louisiana. The body of Vicki Toups was found around 7:30 a.m. on Saturday, October 11, 2003 on a portion of State Road 632 between Highway 90 and Old Spanish Trail. The victim was last seen around 2 a.m. some seven miles away in Boutte. At the time she was wearing denim shorts and a white shirt. Investigators from the St. Charles Parish Sheriff's Department were told a man in a white car had been driving around the Boutte area looking for Toups about six hours before her body was located. He was described as being white, with thick dark hair, long sideburns, thick eyebrows and a horseshoe style moustache which was parted under the nose and drooped on both sides of his mouth. Detectives said they would like to interview the man who they say is a person of interest and not a suspect in the homicide as well as talking to other people who saw Toups anytime on Friday evening or early Saturday. A reward has been posted by Crime Stoppers for the tip that leads to the arrest and indictment of the woman's killer.

Duc Tran
Fort Worth, Texas

A 23-year-old man who vanished after leaving a family-owned business was murdered and his body set on fire in Fort Worth, Texas. Relatives identified the victim as Duc Tran from tattoo markings on the body which was discovered around 1 a.m. on Thursday, May 8, 2003 on a two lane bridge spanning the West Fork of the Trinity River on the north edge of Gateway Park. Homicide detectives from the Fort Worth Police Department learned Tran went missing two days before his body was found while driving from Elite Nails, a family owned business in Decatur to his Arlington, Texas home. The killers set the victim's body ablaze after dumping him from the car and it was another two days before Tran was positively identified through the letters T and R tattooed on the back of his neck. A visual identification wasn't possible because the victim was so badly burned.

Tran, who was known to family and friends by the name Jason, was born in Vietnam on July 19, 1979 and brought to the United States by his parents, Diep Van Tran and Liem Hong, His father set up a tailoring business in Arlington and worked hard to look after his wife, five sons and two daughters. Diep Van Tran died in May 1998 and some of the children, including Duc Tran, began working at the nail business their mother had opened in Decatur, some 55 miles north of Arlington. His sister, Vy Tran, told investigators they left the store on the evening of May 6, 2003 and were driving in separate cars to their home. About 15 minutes down the road she spotted a police patrol car and called her brother, who was somewhere behind her, to warn him not to speed. That was the last time she heard his voice. There are a number of possibilities as to what happened, but one theory is that the victim was confronted by attackers somewhere along the route. Investigation has shown Duc Tran was fatally shot before his body was dumped on the bridge but they have no idea where the murder happened. They also don't know if the assailants had targeted the victim believing he was carrying money from the business or if it was some sort of random attack. There were no ransom demands and nothing to indicate Duc Tran was held captive for any length of time. Investigators were not able to determine the victim's whereabouts from the time he vanished until his body was found and are hoping someone will come forward to fill in the details. Anyone who doesn't feel comfortable talking directly to homicide detectives can contact the Tarrant County Crime Stoppers program which has posted a reward of up to $1,000 to help solve this killing.

Fakhur Uddin
Philadelphia, Pennsylvania

A college student was executed during a robbery while looking after his ailing father's variety store in Philadelphia, Pennsylvania. It was sometime after 9 a.m. on Wednesday, August 20, 2008 when Fakhur Uddin was overpowered by gunmen who entered the Rahman Body Oils, Beads and Variety at 5711 Germantown Avenue across from Vernon Park between East Price Street and East Chelten Avenue. The 20-year-old victim was forced to a storage room at the rear of the store where he was tied up and attempts made to coerce him into opening a small safe. While on the floor one of the attackers shot Uddin in the back of his head. A native of Bangladesh, Uddin was studying at the Community College of Philadelphia and hoped some day to become a lawyer. His ankles and wrists were bound with tape and cord and a gag placed over his mouth.

A $3,500 reward has been posted for information leading to the arrest of those responsible for Uddin's death. Investigators said it appears the killing occurred during a robbery but they are keeping an open mind and looking into all other possibilities. Relatives said Uddin, who came to the United States in 2002, was well liked and didn't have any enemies. They described him as a peaceful person. After Uddin was tied up investigators said it appears the bandits made their way through the store and took a little over $300 from a cash register and a small cash box. It's not known if Uddin was shot immediately after he was tied up or if the men returned to the storage room after taking cash from the till. His father, Syed Alam, who opened the store in 1994, said he cannot think of anyone who would harm his son and can't imagine why someone would kill for such a small amount of money.

Travis Villa
Anchorage, Alaska

Homicide detectives are trying to determine what led to a shooting that left one man dead and another critically wounded in an Anchorage, Alaska apartment. Travis Villa died when a number of shots were fired around 10 p.m. on Tuesday, September 9, 2008 in a third floor unit at the Contempo 1 Condominiums at 261 McCarrey Street between Chena Avenue and Kenai Avenue. Both men were shot in the head and chest. Twenty-two-year-old Villa died before paramedics arrived but the 20-year-old man who shared the apartment was taken to hospital for life saving surgery. Police have been unable to determine a motive for the slaying and haven't named possible suspects. Several people who were nearby heard the gunfire and saw two men getting into separate pick-up trucks after running from the building. The witnesses were able to provide only a sketchy description indicating the gunman was a Polynesian or light-skinned black, in his 20s and between 5-feet, nine-inches and five-feet, eleven-inches.

One suspect drove off in the wounded man's pick-up truck, a 2004 grey Toyota Tundra, which was set ablaze after being abandoned in the parking lot at the Mountain View Lion's Community Park, about four blocks from the shooting scene. Villa, a father of two sons, was born in Anchorage on August 2, 1986, but grew up in community of Soldotna, 150 miles away. Family members described him as a person with a big heart who was loved by many. While in Soldotna he enjoyed skateboarding and playing hockey. After graduating from high school he took a course on computer aided design and moved back to Anchorage. Records show he was arrested for disorderly conduct and forgery. The wounded man does not have a criminal record. Investigators said they would like to hear from anyone who knows anything about the murder or has knowledge of people the victims may have associated with in the weeks prior to the shooting. Police did indicate it's possible one or both of the victims may have known the attackers. The local Crime Stoppers program is offering a reward of up to $1,000 for information that helps police make an arrest.

Kathryn Vitagliano
Fairfield, California

A retired psychiatric technician was stabbed to death in her home in Fairfield, California while preparing food for a Thanksgiving dinner she was hosting the following day. The body of Kathryn Iola Vitagliano was discovered by one of her daughters around 8:35 p.m. on Wednesday, November 26, 2003 on the living room floor at the home where they lived on Robin Drive, a block long street running between Nightingale Drive and Meadowlark Drive. The 55-year-old victim had been stabbed multiple times. Investigators from the Fairfield Police Department said there was no sign of a forced entry and it's possible Vitagliano was confronted by her killer when she answered the door. The woman had lived at the home with her two adult daughters for a little over a year and detectives have never determined a motive for the slaying. It's a relatively quiet street lined with single family homes and neighbors said the area was virtually free of violent crime. Vitagliano had worked for years at the Napa State Hospital but didn't uncover anything in her work life that could have led to her murder. A $50,000 reward was authorized by California Governor Arnold Schwarzenegger for the arrest and conviction of Vitagliano's killer. The Solano County Crime Stoppers is offering a $1,000 reward for anyone wishing to provide anonymous information that leads to an indictment in this case.

David G. Wahoske
Porter, Indiana

He was in the middle of divorce proceedings when someone came into the kitchen of his Porter, Indiana home and shot him twice. It was around noon on Wednesday, October 11, 2000 when David G.

Wahoske was found dead on the floor of the tree-shrouded house at 1153 West Beam Street, between Highway 20 and North Mineral Springs Road. He had been shot with a large-caliber weapon on the head and stomach. Investigators said the 34-year-old victim was preparing a strawberry pie when the assailant entered the home through an unlocked front door. A man, who rented a room at the house, called emergency services after finding Wahoske face up on the floor in a pool of blood. The victim was last seen when he withdrew money from a local bank around 10 a.m. and after returning home made a telephone call at 10:30 a.m. to a friend. Neighbors heard what sounded like muffled gunshots at 11:11 a.m. but police were never able to confirm it was gunfire. They have put the time of death sometime between 10:30 a.m. and noon, but are interested in talking to anyone who saw or heard from Wahoske anytime after 8 a.m. on the day he died.

The victim had recently been fired as a pit boss at the Majestic Casino in Buffington Harbor, some 24 miles away in Gary, Indiana, but going through a labor hearing to get his job back. Investigators said it appeared Wahoske had been targeted for death, but they haven't been able to determine a motive or identify a specific suspect. Wahoske married Janet Hinchey in Newton County, Texas on February 29, 1988. He was 22 at the time and she was almost 10 years older. They lived in various parts of the U. S. before settling in Porter, a community of some 5,000 people on the southern tip of Lake Michigan just north of Interstate 94. Janet left Wahoske and moved with their seven year old daughter to White Oak, Texas about a year before his murder. She now lives in Fillmore, Oklahoma.

The gun used to kill Wahoske is believed to have been a six shot Strum Ruger .41 caliber revolver and investigators have issued appeals to anyone who might have information about an individual with this type of weapon. There is also indication the killer was driving a 1990 white colored Dodge pick-up truck with duel wheels at the rear. It may have had an Oklahoma license plate.

An individual who roomed with Wahoske and his wife for about a year prior to their break-up was driving a similar type vehicle registered to Janet Wahoske, but police were unable to link the man to the slaying. The Porter County Crime Stoppers program has offered a reward in this case and police are hopeful someone will come forward with a key piece of information that will assist them in solving the killing.

Thomas C. Wales

Thomas Crane Wales
Seattle, Washington

A federal prosecutor who spent 18 years putting people behind bars was shot to death while sitting at the computer in the basement of his Seattle, Washington home. The person who killed 49-year-old Thomas Crane Wales stood in the backyard around 10:40 p.m. on Thursday, October 11, 2001 and fired a number of shots through the window of the wood frame home in the city's Queen Anne district. Wales received bullet wounds to his neck and upper body by the gunman who fired three, four or possibly five shots. Bleeding profusely and unable to speak, the victim grabbed the phone beside his computer and dialed 911 for help. He was barely alive when the first police officers arrived and was pronounced dead at 1:15 a.m. while undergoing emergency surgery at the Harborview Medical Center.

As well as being a tough prosecutor, Wales was an ardent advocate for gun control and investigators haven't been able to determine if the slaying was related to his work or his passion to prevent people from owning weapons. An investigative task force, comprised of agents from the Federal Bureau of Investigation and detectives from the Seattle Police Department, have spent thousands of hours interviewing individuals and tracking down leads without finding specific evidence to identify the killer. The slaying has all the earmarks of a professional hit and it's obvious Wales had been deliberately targeted. The gunman selected a heavily shadowed area in the small back yard which gave him an unobstructed view of Wales while concealing himself from people in homes nearby. Police found several casings from the semi-automatic pistol in the backyard and identified the weapon as a

9x18mm Markarov, originally designed by the Soviet Union with specialized cartridges that couldn't be fired in weapons carried by soldiers of other nations. The gun that killed Wales was manufactured by one of the Soviet bloc countries around 1968 and underwent special modifications, including a replacement barrel that allowed it to fire 9mm bullets, before being distributed in the United States by the Federal Arms Corporation of America. Investigator tracked down more than half of the weapons that had been purchased in the United States but didn't locate the actual weapon used in the killing.

Investigators are still hoping to find the gun and trace its ownership over the years. They also have a sketch of an individual who was seen in the neighborhood around the time the shooting occurred. He is described as white, in his late 30s or early 40s, five-feet-seven to five-feet-ten-inches, with black hair and tobacco stained teeth. His front tooth was chipped and he was also described as being slim, about 140 to 165 pounds.

The contents of an anonymous letter mailed on January 23, 2006 in Las Vegas, Nevada to the FBI office in Seattle have also been released in hopes of turning up details that will assist in solving the slaying. Although the 308 word message, purportedly from the person who killed Wales, doesn't contain any information that hasn't already been made public, profilers from the FBI's behavioral science unit in Quantico, Virginia believe the author could have a connection to the homicide.

The name "Gidget" was written on the back of the envelope along with a return address that turned out to be a business which had no link to the prosecutor's murder. However, it is possible the letter writer may have used the term "Gidget" or has gone by that nickname and agents are interested in hearing from anyone who knows an individual who has used that reference since they could have a connection with the killing. There are what agents describe as factual inconsistencies and unrealistic claims in the letter, but investigators are still anxious to identify the individual in hopes they have additional details that will assist in solving the slaying.

This is the version of the letter that was released by the FBI with specific items omitted to ensure the integrity of the investigation:

Re: Thomas C Wales
OK, so I was broke and between jobs I got an anonymous call offering $xxxx to shoot the guy, so I drove to Seattle to do the job. I did not even know his name. Just got laid off from a job. Nice talking lady, I didn't know her name, she called me, talked to me by name, and asked if I needed some money. I agreed to pursue the matter, hell, I was going bankrupt.
Go to Seattle, heck I lived there once, no big deal. Hang out in this guy's backyard, she even gave me the address. Stop off at a place, pick up our gun, and drop it off at a specified location when you are done. THEN, you will be directed to where your money is. The wife was out of town, I had no witnesses here, I was curious about who knew me so well. I used cash to pay for all my expenses to avoid an audit trail. No cell phone. I was directed to a place to pick up the gun, they wanted me to use, and an address. The gun was there.
I drove to the address, and then parked some distance away, north of downtown. I kind of camped out in the backyard of this house, and waited for the guy to settle in at his computer. Once he was there, I took careful aim. I shot two or possibly more times, and watched him collapse. I absurdly waited a few minutes and then left. I was sure he was dead. Retracing my steps, I dropped off the gun, found my money, and returned to Vegas. I feel bad about it, but I needed the money, and there were no witnesses. I really don't know who fronted the money, but the $xxxx was there, and I sure needed it.

Wales, the father of two children who were studying in London, England at the time of the slaying, was divorced from his wife, Elizabeth Mueller, in 2000 but maintained a cordial relationship. She worked as a literary agent but was in England visiting her two children at the time of the slaying. Since separating, Mueller used the office during the day but the victim had ownership and full use of the house. On the night of the murder, Wales arrived home around 7 p.m. and did a bit of renovation work in the almost century old home before heading to the basement office to complete some reports and prepare a fundraising letter for Washington CeaseFire, the gun-control organization he was heading.

Wales was going to have dinner and spend the evening with his girlfriend, Marlis DeJongh, but cancelled the arrangements so he could complete some work. He went to the office shortly after 10 p.m. and at 10:24 p.m. sent an email to DeJongh. The killer avoided sensors that activated lights which illuminated the back yard and after firing the shots that claimed the life of Wales walked across a grassy area at the side of the victim's home and sped off in a car parked nearby.

Wales, who was born in Boston, got his law degree from Hofstra University in New York City after undergraduate studies at Harvard. He served with the firm of Sullivan and Cromwell in New York before being hired in 1983 as a federal prosecutor in Seattle. He had been a staunch proponent of gun control since his teens when a fellow student shot and wounded two people at the high school he attended in Southborough, Massachusetts. Apart from people who were vehemently opposed to his anti-gun position, investigators also compiled a lengthy list of individuals who may have wanted revenge from court cases through the 18 years he served as an assistant United States attorney.

Members of the federal task force are continuing to track down leads in this case and a one million dollar reward is available from the United States Justice Department to anyone who provides information which results in the arrest and conviction of the person responsible for the murder of Thomas Crane Wales. Crime Stoppers of Puget Sound in Seattle is offering a reward to anyone who provides anonymous information on their tip line that solves the slaying.

Debra A. Walton
Lincoln Park, New Jersey

The body of a 34-year-old prostitute was found near an industrial complex in Lincoln Park, New Jersey about eight miles from where she was last seen a week earlier. It was around 12:20 p.m. on August 2, 1995 when a passerby spotted Debra A. Walton face up in some tall brush just off Frassetto Way, a dead end extension from Borinski Road which runs off Ryerson Road. Detectives from the Lincoln Park Police Department said Walton was likely picked up by someone around 2 a.m. on July 28, 1995 in the vicinity of Passaic Street and Cianci Street in Paterson, New Jersey and driven to the area where she was found. It's not known where she was killed, but an autopsy showed she died as a result of blunt trauma inflicted during a beating.

Since the site where she was found is quite remote, investigators suggest it's possible the killer is someone who was familiar with the area. Police said they still hope to talk to anyone who has information about the killing or who saw the victim with anyone shortly before she vanished. At that time she was wearing a pink sleeveless v-neck sweater, black skirt, pink six-inch platform shoes, a rolled scarf across her forehead like a headband and carrying a black purse with a long strap. A $1,000 reward is available from the Morris County Crime Stoppers program for anyone who can assist police to solve the murder.

Melissa Michelle Ward
Chattanooga, Tennessee

Police are still trying to determine a motive for the murder of a 33-year-old prostitute who was last seen getting into a pick-up truck in Chattanooga, Tennessee. Melissa Michelle Ward wasn't wearing shoes when she climbed into the vehicle around 7 p.m. on Friday, October 29, 2004 at the Bi-Lo parking lot on East 23rd Street between Holly Street and Huff Place. At the time Ward, who was only five-feet, one-inch and 90 pounds with blue eyes and brown hair, was wearing a blue dress. The vehicle she got into was described as a late model red Ford pickup truck with a white camper top and the driver was a white male in his 50s with salt and pepper hair. Ward's badly decomposed remains were found on Sunday, December 5, 2004 almost nine miles away on the east side of the Tennessee River in a remote wooded area off Cash Canyon Road near O'Grady Drive.

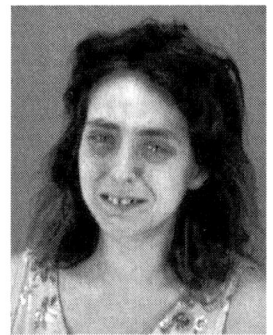

Investigators confirmed she had been murdered, but haven't revealed the cause of death. Records at the Chattanooga Police Department show Ward, who was born April 12, 1971 had been arrested on drug and prostitution charges and had associations with the criminal element. Homicide detectives with the Hamilton County Sheriff's Department indicate it's possible someone she knew is responsible for her death, but so far investigations have uncovered nothing that could be considered a reason for her murder. Chattanooga Crime Stoppers has authorized a reward of up to $1,000 for information leading to the indictment of the person responsible for the killing of Ward. Investigators said they would like to speak with individuals who remember seeing the victim around the time she vanished or know who Ward was with just before she was killed.

Richard Warner
Lexington, Kentucky

Moments after chatting briefly with his cousin, a 36-year-old man was shot to death outside a Lexington, Kentucky church. Richard Warner, a day laborer, had just started walking home on Georgetown Street at 1:53 a.m. on Saturday, September 11, 1999 when a man approached and fired several shots. Police found the victim collapsed on the sidewalk outside the Church of God in Jesus Name on Georgetown Street at Bright Avenue. He was pronounced dead a short time later at the University of Kentucky Medical Centre from a gunshot wound to the head. Carol Warner feared for her safety when she heard the gunfire and ran off, not realizing her cousin had been shot. Homicide detectives from the Lexington Division of Police still haven't determined a motive for the murder and want anyone with information to contact them. Crime Stoppers is also offering a reward of up to $1,000 to anyone who calls in the tip that allows police to arrest the killer.

Michael G. Watkins, Jr.
Tampa, Florida

Homicide detectives have been stymied by the refusal of eyewitnesses to identify gunman responsible for the shooting death of a 22-year-old man a short distance from a Florida nightclub that has become known as the killing fields. It was around 3 a.m. on Saturday, January 12 when Michael Watkins was shot multiple times after leaving the Apollo South Lounge at 5110 North 40th Street just south of Conover Street in central Tampa. Crime Stoppers is offering a reward of up to $1,000 for the arrest of the gunman. The one storey yellow flat roofed building that houses the bar which specializes in black music is on the west side of the six lane street, about half a mile north of East Dr. Martin Luther King Boulevard. It stands next to Custom Cabinetry and Millwork Incorporated and across from Gary Adult High

School. Through the day the dilapidated neon sign is the only hint the building houses a nightclub, but in the late evening and early morning hours the parking lot is jammed with vehicles and quite often a line-up of patrons trying to get in. There are usually four security guards and those entering must pass through metal detectors to ensure they are not carrying weapons.

Since 1998 at least half a dozen people have been killed, most after arguments inside the club turn into gun battles outside. In 1998 a 20-year-old man was fatally shot in a fight over a woman and more recently a 56-year-old man and a 29-year-old mother of four were shot dead when rival groups exchanged gunfire. A number of other people have been shot but survived their wounds and police said there have been arrests in some of the homicides. Following one violent encounter a manager said they try to keep things calm but the bar seems to breed death. "You try the best you can for entertainment and it turns out to be a killing field," he said. The victim had just left the club at closing time and walked through the parking lot onto Conover Street when he was confronted by two or three black males. There is no indication the men said anything to Watkins. Investigators said it appears the suspects stood near the victim and began firing numerous shots. Watkins was pronounced dead a short time later at a local hospital.

A graduate of King High School where he was captain of the football team, Watkins was 5-foot, 10-inches and just over 210 pounds. Born on January 22, 1977 in Tampa, he worked for a local electric firm and was married a short time before being murdered. He is survived by his parents, Michael Watkins Sr. and Janice B. Crews, brothers Ahmad Watkins and Reginald Burns and three sister, Erica L. McCall, Candice M. Jackson and Angie Burns. The message from police to anyone with information in the slaying of Watkins: You can help bring to justice those who have taken the lives of others.

Anthony White,
New Orleans, Louisiana

A man who came to help rebuild New Orleans after Hurricane Katrina was killed during a carjacking. The 51-year-old victim, Anthony White, an engineer with a Baton Rouge, Louisiana a contracting firm, was shot in the head after stopping his car around 3 a.m. on Thursday, July 26, 2007 in the 8400 block of Panola Street in the Carrollton area.

Deputy Police Chief Marlon Defillo said White was a gentleman who did not deserve to die. "He was a man who was helping rebuild this city," said Deputy Defillo. "As a community, we owe it to this man to find the person or persons involved."

The New Orleans Crime Stoppers program has a reward totaling $10,000 for information leading to the arrest and indictment of White's killer. Initially Crime Stoppers posted $5,000 but the amount was increased with a $5,000 donation from White's employer. The victim had just arrived at the rented home where he was living when confronted by at least one person. White was shot in the head and the gunman drove off in his blue 2002 Jeep Liberty.

Homicide detectives from the New Orleans Police Department said White was pulled from the vehicle after being shot and the gunman ran over the victim's body as he drove off. Police are urging anyone with information, no matter how trivial, to come forward and help solve the slaying.

Christina Marie Williams
Seaside, California

A young girl who vanished while walking her newly-acquired pet dog was found dead seven months later in a wooded area of old Fort Ord in Monterey County, California. Christina Marie Williams was last seen around 7:30 p.m. on Friday, June 12, 1998 when she set out from her parent's modest duplex in the vicinity of Nijmegen Road and Gigling Road on the site of the sprawling former U.S. Army facility that officially closed after serving for years as home to the 7th Infantry (Light) Division. It was on Tuesday, January 12, 1999 when the skeletal remains of the 13-year-old girl were discovered by a botany researcher from the University of California on the northern rim of the former base. The location, just south of Marina, California, some six miles north of her home in Seaside, was an out of the way piece of land covered with small bushes that easily concealed Christina's body. An autopsy failed to confirm the cause of death because the remains had deteriorated during the seven months they were exposed to the elements. Forensic investigators have retained samples to conduct further tests whenever advancements in scientific analysis become available.

Christina, the youngest child of Michael and Alice Williams, had just graduated from Grade 7 at Fitch Middle School. She was a good student and participated in the school's choral group. Like all young teenagers she enjoyed popular music and loved animals. She got her own dog, Greg, a month earlier and spent every moment she could with him. It was the dog that first alerted the family that something was wrong when he came home dragging his leash without Christina. Her father immediately notified police who mounted a massive search of the neighborhood but found no trace of the missing girl. In the days following hundreds of volunteers, including military personnel from the region and members of various law enforcement agencies combed the 10,000 acres of the former base property as well as adjacent areas. A $100,000 reward was offered for her safe return but now $20,000 is available for the capture of those responsible for the killing.

Christina had a bright and bubbly personality, and her father said there couldn't be a better daughter in the entire world. He said she was shy but polite and, like many girls here age, was obsessed with horses, the Spice Girls and Beanie Babies. She also hoped to someday become a veterinarian. When last seen Christina was wearing jeans, a striped t-shirt, a black Oakland Raider's jacket and blue Adidas sports sandals.

Police are still hoping to find out what happened while Christina was out with her dog. There are suggestions two men driving a late 70s to early 80s Ford Granada or Mercury Monarch with blue or primer gray paint who had been hanging around the town for three or four weeks may have some knowledge of the disappearance. Police were never able to find the individuals, but investigators said they are people they would like to question. The men had Asian or Pacific islands features and one much heavier than the other. The last reports of people seeing the vehicle was in the vicinity of where Christina's remains were eventually located.

Neighbors told police they noticed a car matching that description occupied by a skinny male on a nearby dirt road about a week after the girl vanished. The man was young, thin with a dark complexion and long hair. Some people told police about the boxy sedan at the time, but there was no sign of the girl when searchers checked the area, a natural reserve system owned by the University of California. Staff and students who live in the various gray-and-brown stucco homes about a quarter mile from where the body was found said it's a thickly wooded area and it would be quite easy for someone to conceal something among the bushes. Investigators even hypnotized one of the people who saw the vehicle in hopes in a trace-like state he could recall the license plate number or some other significant details.

The search for Christina became the Federal Bureau of Investigation's highest-priority missing persons cases in the United States and a number of celebrities came forward to make appeals for her safe return. They included Mariah Carey, the girl's favorite singer, baseball legend Reggie Jackson and Oakland Raiders running back Napolean Kaufman. Carey videotaped a public service announcement begging for Christina's safe return and the sports stars made public appeals through the media. Her Dad, a Navy chief petty officer and meteorologist, also issued pleas several times during the seven month ordeal urging the abductors to set his daughter free. Now Michael and his wife, Alice, continue to pray that those responsible for their daughter's death will be brought to justice. "I am praying to God that whoever took our daughter will get caught," Christa's mom said a short time after the body was found.

Shawn Louis Williamson
Greenville, North Carolina

A flamboyant nightclub owner and entertainment promoter was fatally shot at his Greenville, North Carolina apartment. The body of Shawn Williamson was found by police on Monday, March 24, 2008 when officers answered a burglary alarm at the Peed Drive condominium building in the city's southwest area.

The 41-year-old victim owned Club Dynasty and Escalades nightclub complex on North Greene Street, just north of the Tar River, and was known as Shawn Mack when doing double duty as dee-jay at the 42,000 square foot facility.

Investigators do not have a motive and haven't pinpointed a suspect. Williamson, originally from Jacksonville, Florida, was well liked and respected by a lot of young people who enjoy hip hop and rap music. Through the years he brought a number of well known performers to Greenville, including 50-cent in 2003. A $5,000 reward is available to anyone who can help police identify the killer.

Brandon David Wilson
Anchorage, Alaska

Four days after escaping a fire in his Anchorage, Alaska apartment, the 29-year-old man's charred remains were found when firefighters were called to put out a second blaze. The victim, Brandon David Wilson, was found Saturday, January 26, 2008 while firefighters were sifting through the debris trying to find a cause for the fire which gutted the apartment in the 55-unit building at 6135 East Tudor Road. Homicide detectives from the Anchorage Police Department said the blaze broke out around 6:20 p.m. and appears to have been deliberately set. They were not able to determine if Wilson had been killed elsewhere and his body dumped at the apartment or if he was killed there and the blaze was set to destroy any evidence.

Wilson and his wife had been forced to flee the apartment shortly before 4 a.m. on Tuesday, January 22, 2008 when a fire broke out in their bedroom closet. Wilson's truck was found in the parking lot of the two-storey apartment building between McKlean Place and Baxter Road and it's possible the victim may have encountered his killer when he went to the complex to retrieve some items. His body was so badly burned that initially investigators were unable to determine if the victim was a man or woman.

Tenants in the building described Wilson and his wife as a quiet couple and neighbors weren't aware of anything that could result in someone being murdered. Shortly after the homicide the Anchorage Crime Stoppers program offered a $1,000 reward for any information that will bring Wilson's killer to justice.

Christopher Wolfe
Jacksonville, Florida

A 911 call about shots being fired in the vicinity of a Jacksonville, Florida apartment building led police to the body of a 20-year-old man. It was just before midnight on Tuesday, October 29, 2008 when there was some sort of disturbance in the Grand Court complex at 7610 Blanding Boulevard, about half a mile north of Collins Road on the outskirts of Orange Park, near the Mike Shad Ford Mercury dealership. On arrival Jacksonville police found Christopher Wolfe outside his residence, apartment unit 719. He had been shot several times.

Homicide investigators from the Jacksonville Sheriff's Office found no witnesses; couldn't determine a motive and have not been able to make an arrest. First Coast Crime Stoppers is offering a reward of up to $1,000 to the person who helps solve this case.

The victim's mother has become an active anti-gun violence advocate and said it now breaks her heart over again when she hears of young people being murdered. She has campaigned against the right for people to have weapons in their homes for self defense and says her son wouldn't be dead if there wasn't a gun in the hand of whoever pulled the trigger. She hopes to find ways to fight gun violence by changing laws, educating people and encouraging individuals to warn young people not to carry weapons. "Squeezing the trigger of a loaded gun kills people," she said. "A life can never be replaced." She also said even though she wants justice for her son she doesn't want a life for a life.

Susan Leigh Wolfe
Austin, Texas

Walking to her friend's house the 25-year-old victim was dragged into a car and never seen alive again. The following morning on Thursday, January 10, 1980 the partially clad body of Susan Leigh Wolfe was found in an alleyway running behind homes on the south side of East 17th Street in Austin, Texas. Shortly after leaving her home at 212 Franklin Boulevard to walk the 10 or so blocks to a house on East 49th

Street at Rowena Avenue a witness told police two men forced the woman into a car. The victim had arranged to spend the night with her friend because her own frame home had to be fumigated because of a problem with roaches. The attackers, wearing trench coats, struggled briefly with the woman and pushed her into a 1971 or 1972 maroon two door Dodge Polara with a white vinyl top. The vehicle also had extensive damaged to the passenger door. Her body was found at 8:34 a.m. in the alleyway between Poquito Street and Alamo Street by someone checking a rental property. An autopsy showed she'd died from a single gunshot wound. She had also been raped. Homicide detectives from the Austin Police Department are hoping someone will come forward or call Crime Stoppers with information that will help them find the killers.

Larry W. Wray
Fort Wayne, Indiana

Neighbors heard his cries for help but the victim died before police arrived. It was just before 11 p.m. on Friday, June 3, 2005 when a resident of the Regency House apartments at 2440 Fairfield Avenue near Meyer Avenue in the Williams-Woodland Park District of Fort Wayne, Indiana called 911 after hearing a man screaming in apartment 206. Police arrived at the three-storey building minutes later but Larry W. Wray had succumbed to his injuries. Investigation indicated the 57-year-old victim had been savagely beaten about the head and body and died as a result of blunt force trauma. Greater Fort Wayne Crime Stoppers has made various appeals for help to solve this case, but so far no suspects have been identified.

Robert Wunderle
Rockaway Borough, New Jersey

Shortly after complaining to reporters about possible union corruption, a 45-year-old supermarket chain executive was shot to death gangland-style in Rockaway Borough, New Jersey. The body of Robert E. Wunderle was found at 9:10 a.m. on Thursday, November 16, 1989 in a muddy ditch beside an unpaved section of Beach Street, which at the time was a secluded roadway about half a mile south of exit 37 leading onto Hibernia Avenue from Interstate 80. Wunderle served as the vice-president in charge of labor relations at the Supermarkets

General Corporation based in Woodbridge, New Jersey and one of the firm's key spokespeople. He lived with his wife, Sue and their two sons, Max and Sam, in Westfield, a community of 29,000 residents, some eight miles from the company's headquarters. Wunderle focused his efforts with Pathmark Food which operated a chain of 141 supermarkets under the corporation's umbrella and was a management negotiator on contract issues with various unions. The company's chairman, Jack Futterman, described Wunderle as an esteemed and valued colleague who worked tirelessly on behalf of Supermarkets General Corporation and the food industry as a whole. A Rockaway Borough Department of Public Works employee found the victim's body in the drainage ditch beside an area now known as Firemen's Field when he brought some heavy equipment to do some excavation work in the vicinity. The victim was wearing a business suit and raincoat, but his wallet was missing. Investigators from the Morris County Sheriff's Department got the victim's name from a business card in his pocket. They also learned he had been shot once in the heart and in the head above his left ear. Investigation showed the killer stood almost directly in front of Wunderle and fired a bullet into his chest and after he fell to the ground put the gun close to his head and pulled the trigger.

Wunderle was last seen by a colleague leaving his office around 8:45 p.m. on Wednesday, November 15, 1989. He was scheduled to attend a business dinner in Mountainside, New Jersey, some 10 miles away, but didn't arrive. It's likely the victim was confronted by someone after getting into his vehicle at the company's headquarters or somewhere along the route he was driving to the meeting. Police haven't determined if Wunderle was the victim of a professional killer hired by someone who wanted to eliminate him or some sort of robbery that ended with his death. The victim's company-owned vehicle, a new four-door, gray-colored Mercury Grand Marquis, was found Monday, January 22, 1990 in a parking garage in New York City. It had been there since the early morning hours of November 16. Police haven't recovered the murder weapon.

A native of Canton, Ohio, he had served as chairman of the New Jersey Alliance for Action, a non-profit business coalition and a trustee of the Community Food Bank of New Jersey. He was also a lobbyist for the food industry and often called on by the media to comment on various issues. Just prior to his death he had discussed a problem with contaminated food shipments from Chile and was vocal about pressure being exerted on some of the company's stores and their employees by a large union that had already been implicated in criminal activity, including extortion and murder. Although police probed the possibility of a link with certain labor unions, investigators have never found any direct evidence to charge anyone. The case is described as an active homicide investigation with all possible avenues being explored. The Morris County Crime Stoppers program is continuing to offer a reward for any information that helps police solve this killing.

Machelle Renea Wynn
Goldsboro, North Carolina

The 17-year-old girl headed off to school in Goldsboro, North Carolina on Tuesday, August 29, 1995, but she didn't make it. The body of Machelle Renea Wynn was found just off Birch Street at the edge of a wooded area on an unpaved portion of Retha Street, one block from George St. in the city's southwest area. The five-foot, three-inch, 115-pound girl was last seen in the vicinity of a housing project on Slaughter Street near Lincoln Drive where she had stayed overnight at a friend's home. At that time she was heading to Goldsboro High School located some 15 blocks away on Beech Street between North Herman Street and North Jackson Street. It's possible she may have accepted a ride with someone. The school is north of the housing project where she was last seen, but her body was located at a spot 10 blocks to the west. There are a number of businesses along the section of George Street, between West Wayne Avenue and West Jenkins Road, but the site where she was found is quite isolated with trees and shrubs blocking the view of any people who might be in the vicinity. An autopsy showed the teenage girl was strangled but authorities have not indicated if she was sexually assaulted.

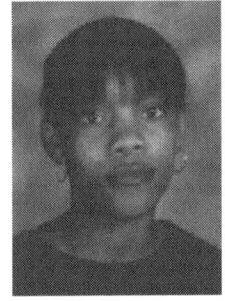

The victim's father has set up a web site and has issued several appeals through the years as well as putting up posters asking for help to find his daughter's killer. Eddie Wynn believes that two people may be responsible for Machelle's death. One who killed her and another who stood by, possibly keeping watch. He refers to her killer as a "low life creep" and mourns that his daughter was too young to die. She had her whole life ahead of her. They took it away. He said they also took all of her dreams and her hopes for the future.

Eddie said they also shattered a family forever and created an emptiness that cannot be filled. His daughter had hoped someday to be a lawyer and someone who could help people. She realized it would have been difficult for her family to finance her dreams through university, but she was hoping to join the United States Army and enroll in a program that could help fulfill her aspirations. Her father asks people to put themselves in his shoes and think of the pain and anguish you would go through when someone you know is murdered.

He urged people to come forward and call the Goldsboro Police Department or Crime Stoppers if they have any information about Machelle's slaying. Eddie said there are rumors that some of her friends know what happened but for whatever reason haven't yet provided the information that will help solve the killing. A $5,000 reward is available and her father still hopes someone will come forward either to collect the money or just to do the right thing and identify those responsible for Machelle's death. The Goldsboro-Wayne County Crime Stoppers program has appealed several times for assistance to solve this case.

Tammy Zywicki

Tammy Zywicki
Lawrence County, Missouri

She was a young woman traveling alone to Grinnell College when she was abducted and killed after her car broke down on a stretch of Interstate 80 between Ottawa and La Salle, Illinois. It was on Tuesday, September 1, 1992, nine days after she vanished, that the body of

Tammy J. Zywicki was discovered wrapped in a red blanket on the shoulder of Interstate 44 in a rural area of Lawrence County in Missouri near Sarcoxie, a community of some 1,200 residents, between Springfield and Joplin. The site is almost 500 miles south of where Tammy was abducted. Investigation showed the 21-year-old senior bled to death after being stabbed once in the arm and seven times in the chest. The victim had left her parent's home in Marlton, New Jersey, 16 miles southeast of Philadelphia and driven Daren, one of her three brothers, to Northwestern University in Evanston, Illinois and then set out in her white 1985 Pontiac for Grinnell, Iowa where she was in her final year of college. Around mile marker 83 the car broke down and Tammy was stranded on the shoulder of the highway, less than two miles from exit 81 which leads to East 8th Road and a major truck stop. A motorist who was driving by between 3:10 p.m. and 4 p.m. on Sunday, August 23, 1992 recalled seeing a young woman beside a car with the hood open. He also saw a tractor trailer a short distance behind and assumed the driver had stopped to give assistance. That was the last time police have talked to anyone who saw Tammy alive. An Illinois state trooper noticed the car sitting abandoned several hours later and the next day the vehicle was towed to an Illinois State Police compound in the area. Missing from the vehicle were the victim's 35 mm Cannon camera and a tune playing wrist watch with an umbrella on the face. Even finding these items could assist police in tracking down her killer.

When Tammy didn't call home to let her parents know she'd arrived at Grinnell, her mother, JoAnn, alerted police that her daughter was missing. The call to police came only hours after they had towed the girl's car so it was quite evident something sinister had occurred. Police in Iowa and Illinois began a full scale search and Tammy's description was flashed to news outlets from Chicago to Des Moines and beyond. Fear also gripped the campus of the small college where Tammy was to join the 1993 graduating class with the hope of some day becoming a Spanish teacher. Students realized how vulnerable it was to travel alone from their homes. Police combed ditches and bush areas for a couple of hundred miles on both sides of Interstate 80 as well as checking motels, gas stations and restaurants to see if they could locate anyone who saw the young woman anytime after she left her car abandoned at the side of the highway. Almost unbelievably investigators learned from the Missouri State Police that a body matching Tammy's description had been found in a blanket bound with duct tape several hundred miles away. She had also been raped prior to the murder. Investigators believe the killer likely pulled off Interstate 80 at exit 79A and traveled southbound on Interstate 39 to link up with Interstate 55 just outside Bloomington, Illinois. It's possible he drove through Springfield, Illinois and then to St. Louis, Missouri where he connected to Interstate 44 a direct route to Tulsa, Oklahoma. Police have no idea when the victim was murdered but the killing may have occurred at one of the numerous rest areas or interchanges along the 490 mile distance from where her car was discovered to the site where Tammy's body was eventually discovered. A task force involving various state police agencies and the Federal Bureau of Investigation was set up but so far no one has been charged. A $50,000 reward has been put up by the FBI and Tammy's family members are still hoping someone will come forward with the killer's name.

Tammy's mother and her husband, Hank, moved to Florida after he retired from his civil engineering job, but thoughts of their daughter flash through their minds at random moments. Her mom sees her daughter frozen in time as a 21-year-old girl with long blond hair and glasses. She sees her smile, her green eyes and radiant skin untouched by make-up. To her mom Tammy was the epitome of the all-American girl. She stood only five-feet, two-inches and was 120 pounds, but active in sports and enjoyed playing soccer. The couple kept mementos at their home as a reminder of their life with Tammy and they also celebrate special occasions such as her birthday. The family remembered Tammy as someone with many interests and qualities and they set up a scholarship in her memory at Grinnell. Although a good student she recognized grades were not the most important aspect of college life and family members want the recipients to be people with similar dreams and goals as Tammy. She was someone who worked and played hard, someone who was always willing to try new things, but also wanted to be successful in every endeavor. She enjoyed photography and thought she might make that her life's work. Tammy also loved her family who today still live with the hope that her killer will someday face justice.

Find My Killer

Chapter 8 – Canadian Cases

Delia Adriano

Delia Adriano
Oakville, Ontario

The disappearance and subsequent murder of Delia Adriano occurred in Oakville, Ontario, considered one of the safest communities in Canada and today the case continues to be a complete mystery. She was only steps from the sanctuary of her home when abducted in September 1982, the year the country's first Crime Stoppers program was launched in Calgary, Alberta. Her body was found six weeks later.

It was around 9:30 p.m. on Saturday, September 26, 1982 when Adriano's fiancé, Danny Dutra, dropped the 25-year-old woman off at the home where she lived with her parents in the affluent community on the northern shore of Lake Ontario midway between Toronto and Hamilton. He drove off after watching her walk up the driveway and toward the side door of the house on Wildwood Drive in the vicinity of Morden Road and Spears Road. She didn't enter her home and an hour later a woman matching Delia's description was seen arguing with a man and then being forced into a sub-compact vehicle around Mary Street and Slade Crescent, some three blocks away. Witnesses also saw some sort of struggle going on inside the car as it drove off without lights. Delia's purse was found a short distance away and that's the last time the young woman was seen alive.

Six weeks later on Saturday, November 6, 1982, a 35-year-old handyman, Del Parchem, discovered the victim's naked and decomposing remains in a secluded woods off Twiss Road at Third Sideroad in Campbellville, a hamlet 20 miles north of her home. Investigators from the Halton Regional Police Service have spent hundreds of manhours delving into the murder of Adriano, but were never able to identify a suspect. Through the years police have renewed appeals for information and the family has made public pleas through the media to help solve the case. Adriano was only five-feet-one with a slight build. Police said an assailant would have no trouble overpowering her.

This crime occurred before internet communication became popular and investigators had to rely on the media to keep the case alive through the 80s. Today victim's families will create web sites to issue worldwide appeals for assistance, but in the years after Adriano's slaying the media reach delivered the appeal to residents living in various municipalities throughout Southern Ontario. Investigators said it is possible someone living in another area of Canada or elsewhere in the world might have some vital information even today that will assist in solving this case.

Halton Regional Police, like many other law enforcement agencies, has implemented a cold case squad and posted details of the Adriano murder as well as other unsolved slayings on their web site. They have submitted evidence to the crime lab in hopes modern technology, including upgrades in DNA comparisons, will identify a suspect. Investigators feel it's also important to paint a personal picture of the victim to ensure she doesn't end up becoming a faceless statistic and fade from public memory. Adriano graduated from Gordon E. Purdue High School and had worked four years as a secretary in the Toronto offices of Wear-Check International, a firm that monitors oil quality in equipment and vehicles used by companies around the world.

Delia's parents, Augusto and Carman Adriano, made repeated pleas for their daughter's safe return when she went missing and through the years have joined her sisters Zelia, Lynn and Elena in making impassioned appeals to find her killer. They were a close knit family and even called in psychics and private detectives, but no additional evidence was ever turned up.

The person who was seen struggling with Adriano was described as a white male, between five-feet, seven-inches and five-feet, nine-inches with a medium build and brown hair feathered back to the neck. He was driving a dark blue 1970 Chevrolet Chevette or similar two-door vehicle with an automatic transmission. There were three stripes along the side and the car had Ontario license plates. In recent years police have gone word-by-word over statements and investigative reports as well as studying photographs and other evidence painstakingly collected by the original investigators who began the hunt for Adriano after her disappearance and subsequently the probe into her murder.

People who knew Adriano described her as a popular and well-liked person. She had brown eyes and short brown hair. She vanished only a few days before her 26th birthday and a few months before she was to be married. Delia was quite social and very outgoing with lots of friends, most affiliated with the local Portuguese community. Some 1,500 people attended her funeral. Today Halton's Crime Stoppers program has a $2,000 reward available for anyone who can provide information that will lead to the arrest of her killer.

Theresa Allore

Theresa Allore
Compton, Quebec

The teenager's death was initially classified as a drug overdose suicide, but the case was reopened some 24 years later and is now officially listed as an unsolved homicide. It was on Friday, November 3, 1978 when Theresa Allore disappeared while making her way from Champlain College, a boarding school in Lennoxville, to the residence where she was living in Compton, some 10 miles away. The 19-year-old had missed the 6:15 p.m. bus from the campus and would either have to wait until 11 p.m. or hitchhike to the isolated village where she was living. It was a more innocent time and she'd also lived a sheltered life with her parents and two brothers in St. John, New Brunswick before enrolling in a science program at the college, five miles south of Sherbrooke, Quebec. No one noticed she was missing during the weekend and it wasn't until Wednesday that classmates became concerned and called her family. There was no sign she'd been at the residence but when her parents arrived a week after she vanished, school officials hadn't organized any type of search and police refused to initiate a full-scale investigation suggesting their daughter was most likely a runaway.

Family members issued personal appeals and distributed flyers as well as hiring private investigators, but there was no sign of their daughter until five months later. It was on Friday, April 13, 1979 when a trapper discovered Theresa's body in a creek running beside a cornfield off a county road only a few miles from her Compton residence. She was face down in four inches of water and clad only in underwear. She was also wearing a watch. It had stopped at 11:55 p.m., possibly the time she was dumped into the creek, on the day she vanished. An autopsy didn't reveal how she died, but the pathologist indicated she was the victim of a violent death of undetermined nature. Marks on her body prior to a full post mortem were indicative of strangulation but that couldn't be confirmed through pathology. There were no signs she'd been in any type of struggle and no evidence of a sexual assault. Toxicology tests also turned up no traces of drugs in her system.

In addition to the medical evidence which weighs more toward homicide than any other cause of death, the victim's scarf was found in a nearby field and a week later her wallet was located in a ditch on a county road some seven miles from where her body was discovered. Despite those facts, the investigator looking into Theresa's death filed a report indicating suicide from a drug overdose. His report told of students from the college attending a party where LSD was freely available on the Friday she went missing. Police were told Theresa wasn't at the party, but the investigator concluded the young people knew more than they were saying and probably had knowledge she had wandered off after taking drugs. Even after the case was listed as an unsolved homicide, the initial investigator, who retired several years ago, still insists the victim died from a drug overdose. It was Theresa's brother, John, who convinced authorities to consider the case a murder after finding numerous inconsistencies with the investigative reports and the autopsy results. He was 14 at the time his sister was killed but vividly remembers the frustration his parents went through as they struggled to get assistance from law enforcement agencies and others who were reluctant to consider the disappearance of their daughter anything more than a runaway situation.

The media also played a key role in focusing attention on Theresa's death and two other cases in the vicinity which have gone dormant. Ten-year-old Manon Dube disappeared in Sherbrooke on Friday, January 27, 1978 while walking home with her eight-year-old sister. Two months later her body was found face down in a stream near Ayer's Cliff, less than four miles from where Theresa's body was discovered. Police said the little girl was probably struck and killed by a hit and run driver who then took her body and dumped it in the waterway to conceal his crime. On Saturday, March 19, 1977, Louise Camirand disappeared after leaving her Sherbrooke apartment and her body was later found in a snow bank at Magog, a rural community 20 miles to the southwest. An autopsy showed the 20-year-old woman had been raped and strangled but her killer has never been caught. Theresa's relatives wondered if the same person is responsible for the deaths, but when investigators made efforts to recover DNA evidence in the three cases, they learned all material related to Allore and Dube had been discarded. Today police admit there is little hope of solving these cases unless someone comes forward and identifies those who may be responsible.

Dana Bradley

Dana Bradley
St. John's, Newfoundland

Hitch-hiking may have led to the brutal slaying of a 14-year-old girl who was heading from a friend's house to her grandmother's home in St. John's, Newfoundland. After school on December 14, 1981, Dana Bradley spent a little more than an hour with three friends and called her grandmother at 4:30 p.m. to say she'd be arriving within the hour to attend a birthday party for her mother. Around 5:15 p.m. two men selling Christmas trees noticed a girl matching Dana's description hitch-hiking near the Tim Hortons coffee shop on Topsail Road. Within moments a 1973 to 1976 Dodge Dart or Plymouth Valiant stopped to give her a ride. Four days later at 3 p.m. on December 18 the girl's body was found in a brush area off Maddox Cove Road just east of Cape Spear Road. She had been killed with blows to the head from a heavy object.

Dana, described as a bright and very social individual, had planned to take the bus to her grandmother's home, but on the way to the bus stop put out her arm in hopes someone would give her a ride. Although St. John's is the largest community in Newfoundland, it was considered in 1981 as an extremely safe place and everyone seemed to know everyone else. It wasn't unusual to see young people soliciting rides, but police and school officials were trying to discourage the practice because of the risk. When Harry Smeaton spotted Dana hitch-hiking, he pointed her out to his brother from their Christmas tree lot about 25 feet away and commented that it was risky for a young girl to get into a car with a stranger. When Dana failed to show up at the birthday party, her parents realized something terrible must have happened and immediately called police thinking she may have been involved in an accident or something. Members of the Royal Newfoundland Constabulary determined Dana attended classes through the day at I. J. Sampson Junior High School and at 2:50 p.m. went with three friends to a local convenience store and then to a friend's house. She made the phone call to her grandmother from that home and left a short time later.

Detectives said it was around 5:15 p.m. when Dana was last seen alive. She stepped from the sidewalk and went over to a car that had stopped in the driving lane adjacent to the turn-in for buses at the bus stop. After briefly chatting with the driver through the open window Dana had trouble with the door and the man reached over and pushed it open. In addition to describing the car as a Dart or Valiant, witnesses said it was a four door model, a yellow, green or beige color with a dark roof and rust spots along the bottom and around the fenders and doors. The driver was a man in his late 20s, around five-feet, eight-inches with a slim build and dirty blond or brown unkempt collar-length hair. Apart from being spotted on Topsail Road, the vehicle was also observed around 8 p.m. the night Dana vanished stopped in the vicinity of Maddox Cove Road near where her body was discovered four days later just outside St. John's. Detectives are still hoping someone will come forward with information that will help identify the killer and the Newfoundland and Labrador Crime Stoppers program is offering a reward of up to $2,000 for anyone who calls in an anonymous tip that helps police to solve the girl's slaying.

Thelma Clapham
Hamilton, Ontario

A 79-year-old woman was beaten to death in her ninth floor apartment in Hamilton, Ontario. The body of Thelma Clapham was found at 11:30 a.m. on Thursday, December 2, 2004 after people were unable to contact her. There was no sign of a break-in at the apartment at 226 Rebecca Street where the woman had lived alone for the past four years. The victim received blunt force trauma injuries and although no weapon was found, investigators believe they know what was used to beat the woman. They also said it's possible a female was involved in the killing. Homicide detectives with the Hamilton-Wentworth Regional Police obtained a great deal of forensic evidence and have been able to paint a partial picture of what occurred, but they hope individuals will come forward who can assist with the investigation. A $5,000 reward has been offered for anyone who can provide information that will lead to the arrest and conviction of the killer.

Edwardo Daley
Toronto, Ontario

His dream was to be a police officer but his future was stolen when murdered by a gang of men who burst into his sixth-floor Toronto, Ontario apartment. The lifeless body of Edwardo "Eddie" Daley was found by his mother at 5:27 p.m. on Saturday, February 15, 2003 when she returned to unit 604 from the laundry room at the Willowridge Road apartment building. Daley had been shot and stabbed. Police described the 24-year-old victim as an "intelligent, kind and God-fearing man" who attended church regularly and worked at the Salvation Army hostel to help those who are less fortunate. Investigation showed the attack occurred during a 12 minute period when the victim's mother left the apartment to collect some clothes from the laundry room located in the basement of the high rise in the Martin Grove Road and Eglinton Avenue area in the city's west end. She found blood all over the place and signs of a violent struggle when she opened the door of the apartment where she lived with her husband, a daughter and Edwardo. Her son was on the floor and she could see he was gravely wounded.

Emergency crews arrived within minutes and raced the victim to a trauma centre but he was pronounced dead at 6:51 p.m. Toronto Crime Stoppers produced a video and offered a reward of up to $2,000 for information about the slaying but no one ever came forward to help police solve Daley's killing. The re-enactment which was broadcast on local television stations showed several men forcing their way into the apartment and confronting the victim. Detectives from the Toronto Police Service homicide unit have indicated it's possible the assailants went to the apartment with the intent of killing the victim, but there's also the likelihood they were going after money which his mother collected on a weekly basis for her church. Officially investigators haven't specified a motive.

After questioning hundreds of people in the vicinity investigators were able to produce a composite drawing of an individual described as a person of interest but so far no one resembling the sketch has been located. The Toronto Police Service posted a $50,000 reward for the arrest and conviction of those responsible for the killing of Daley, but still no one has come forward with vital information that will allow homicide investigators to resolve the case. Detectives are convinced someone living in the vicinity knows who killed Daley and the reason the killers came to the apartment.

Detectives believe the parents and girlfriends of the individuals who killed Daley are aware they committed murder but are not prepared to turn them in. They said these people manage to go about their lives, worrying about their children, working and even attending church while being haunted by a horrible secret of knowing one of their family members killed another human being and wreaked havoc on the Daley family.

Through the years police have made periodic appeals in hopes someone will have the courage to provide information that will allow them to make arrests in this senseless slaying. Detectives said the killers were covered with blood when they left the apartment and there were likely many people around who saw them, but are maintaining a code of silence to protect murderers rather than showing compassion to someone who was preparing to dedicate his life to the service of the community and his church.

Crysta Lynn David
New Westminster, British Columbia

The 20-year-old woman was last seen alive leaving a New Westminster, British Columbia nightclub with a blond haired man. Four days later on Wednesday, March 25, 1992, Crysta Lynn David was found dead in the basement apartment where she lived. An autopsy showed she had been smothered.

Detectives from the New Westminster Police Department's Major Crime Unit learned she left a bar formerly known as Dreamin around 2 a.m. on Saturday, March 21, 1992. She had turned 20 two weeks before her body was found.

Police hope there are people who remember seeing Crysta at the nightclub or know who was with her in the days prior to her body being discovered. The Metro Vancouver Crime Stoppers program will pay a reward up to $2,000 for information that helps solve this case.

Morag Davies
Sarnia, Ontario

Scientists have successfully utilized enhanced forensic technology to obtain the DNA profile of the individual who killed a 45-year-old real estate agent in Sarnia, Ontario, but police haven't linked the evidence with a suspect. Morag Davies was stabbed to death on Tuesday, August 23, 1988 in a home on Retlaw Drive where she's lived for less than a month. Investigators from the Sarnia Police Service criminal investigations division said the killer slashed himself during the vicious attack in the woman's bedroom and lost a considerable amount of blood. Samples of the blood were recently submitted to the Ontario government's crime lab where new technology allowed experts to produce a comprehensive generic fingerprint that will positively identify the suspect once an arrest is made. Davies had worked as a real estate agent with Canada Trust in Sarnia for about three years after a lengthy career as a nurse in Toronto and Sarnia. She divorced from her husband and moved to the Retlaw Drive home where she was living alone. A co-worker visited with Davies until sometime between 10:30 p.m. and 11 p.m. on August 23 and went back to the house with another realtor around noon hour on Saturday, August 25, 1988 after Davies failed to come into the office for a couple of days. They discovered the victim dead in her bedroom. She had been stabbed numerous times.

Since there was no sign of a forced entry, investigators suggest Davies may have known her killer, but detectives are exploring all possibilities. Friends and relatives described Davies as a friendly and professional person and there is nothing in her background that would make her a target for murder. Detectives have tracked scores of leads through the years without identifying a suspect and hope someone will come forward soon with information that will help them solve this case. Sarnia's Crime Stoppers program is offering a reward of up to $2,000 to anyone who calls in anonymously and provides the tip that leads to an arrest. The appeal from Crime Stoppers says anyone may have the one piece of information that could tie the investigation together.

Thera Johanna Dieleman
Innerkip, Ontario

Detectives have a DNA profile that will identify the killer of an 80-year-old woman in Innerkip, Ontario but so far have no idea who committed the murder. Thera Johanna Dieleman was found dead in her home at 806093 Oxford Road 29 in this community of 800 people located eight miles north of Woodstock around 2:40 p.m. on Friday, September 16, 1988. An autopsy showed she'd been beaten and strangled. Investigators said it appears the victim, who lived alone, put up quite a struggle with her attacker. A neighbor spoke to Dieleman early Thursday evening and there was no hint at that time she was in any danger. Another individual noticed a large red flat bed stake truck parked near the victim's home around the time police believe Dieleman was murdered. The vehicle was a one or five-ton truck with dual wheels and white lettering on the door of the cab. It also had a black headboard protector. Detectives from the Ontario Provincial Police Criminal Investigation Branch have never been able to establish a motive and have not identified any possible suspects through the course of their investigations. They did compare the DNA profile with samples currently on file in the national databank but didn't turn up a match. A $50,000 reward is being offered by the Ontario government for information leading to the arrest and conviction of the woman's killer and the Oxford County Crime Stoppers program has posted a reward of up to $2,000 for anyone wishing to anonymously provide information about the homicide to the tip line.

Rhona Margaret Duncan

Rhona Margaret Duncan
North Vancouver, British Columbia

A 16-year-old girl was raped and strangled near her North Vancouver, British Columbia home after returning from a late night party. Sometime around 3 a.m. on July 16, 1976 neighbors heard what appeared to be a couple arguing on the street. The following morning the partially-clad body of Rhona Margaret Duncan was found behind a neighbor's garage in some long grass. Investigation showed the victim had attended a house party on East Queen Avenue with some 60 friends from her school. She and a girlfriend, Marion Bogues, left the party with two boys sometime after 1 a.m. to walk home. Along the way, the boys went in separate directions toward their homes and the girls continued to Bogues' house which was about five blocks from Rhona's home. After saying goodnight to her friend around 2:45 a.m.

the victim headed home. She was confronted by someone three doors from her house and it was probably the noise of her struggle with the killer that the neighbor thought was an argument between a young couple. The neighbor did yell out but when the noise stopped, he went back to bed. An autopsy showed the teenager died as a result of manual strangulation. Police did locate DNA evidence but comparisons cleared males she knew from school and others in the neighborhood. Investigators from the Serious Crime Section of the Royal Canadian Mounted Police North Vancouver detachment are hoping someone knows who is responsible and will come forward with the name of her killer. The Vancouver Crime Stoppers program has also offered a reward of up to $2,000 for anyone providing anonymous information that leads to an arrest in this case.

Alban & Raymonde Garon   Marie-Claire Beniskos

Alban and Raymonde Garon & Marie-Claire Beniskos
Ottawa, Ontario

A retired federal judge, his wife and a family friend were bound, gagged and then murdered in a luxurious high-security condominium building in Ottawa, Ontario. The bodies of Judge Alban Garon, 77, his wife, Raymonde, 73, and friend, Marie-Claire Beniskos, 78, were discovered around 10:30 a.m. on Saturday, June 30, 2007 in the 10th floor apartment unit at 1510 Riverside Drive south of Highway 417. The victims had been beaten to death, but investigators from the Ottawa Police Service have been unable to determine a motive. Garon's brother-in-law went to apartment 1002 in the 27-floor building when telephone calls went unanswered. He notified police after spotting the victims. The couple was last seen alive on Thursday evening when they attended a former neighbor's birthday party. They left around 10:30 p.m. to go home. Beniskos moved into the building after her husband died and became close friends with Garon's wife. Other residents said the two women were like sisters together and would often be at each others apartment for coffee and conversation. Homicide detectives said the killing occurred sometimes between 9 a.m. and noon on Friday, June 29 while Beniskos was visiting. However, the couple may have come face to face with the killer the day before after answering a knock at their door. During the birthday party, Garon's wife told of being startled by the man at the door who identified himself as a delivery person. He told the couple he was supposed to deliver a package to them, but didn't have it with him and would return the next day. A person matching the description of the delivery man was seen in the elevator of the apartment building between 10 a.m. and 11 a.m. on the day of the triple homicide.

Detectives said there is nothing to indicate the person was responsible for the murders, but they have been unable to locate him and cannot rule him out as a possible suspect. He is described as white, in his early 40s, about five-feet, eight-inches and 180 pounds with short close-cropped black hair with some gray. He was clean shaven with a broad nose and at the time wearing a white short sleeve shirt with blue vertical stripes and dark pants. Police prepared a composite drawing of the individual but no one in the building ever remembered seeing him and nobody has been able to identify the person from the sketch. Police have recovered images from security cameras and questioned the building's security guards in an attempt to gain as much information as possible about the man seen in the elevator. No one can explain how he got into the building which has guards at the entrance and is protected by a high-tech security system that requires visitors to announce their arrival to occupants before being allowed through the main doors and onto the elevator. A $100,000 reward has been offered for information leading to the killer and police said the case remains a high priority investigation.

Beniskos was described as a very religious woman who volunteered at the church and a local hospital. She moved into the building because she didn't feel safe being alone in her home after her husband died. She also loved golf, going on outings and sharing dinner with friends. Both Beniskos and the Garon couple attended Nativite de Notre-Seigneur-Jesus-Christ Roman Catholic Church and often went together on Sundays. The Garon couple didn't have children but media reports indicated they had looked after a Latin American girl as a teenager and treated her daughter as their grandchild. Garon's wife retired from nursing many years ago but he continued serving on the bench until his retirement in November 2004. Friends described Judge Garon as a gentle, gracious and charming man. A priest who knew the judge wrote a public letter to the killer. Father Gerard Marier, who studied at the seminary of Nicolet with Garon and a friend for some 55 years, said the day he learned of the killings he prayed for the victims and the person who took their lives.

"With an extreme violence, you have killed two women and a man," he wrote. "We can presume that it was the man that you had in your sights. An ex-judge of 77 years, who during his entire life always refused to resort to violence to defend the law. I knew him well. I was his colleague. The news of his murder disturbs me." Father Marier, a former professor, continued his message to the killer: "After sadness, I haven't felt anger toward you. The very day I heard the news, I celebrated mass for your three victims and for you, too. I asked for heaven for them, but I didn't ask for hell for you. For you, I only asked for prison, not to punish you, but so that they can remove the means for you to start again. Your actions are irreparable. The life of Alban, of Raymonde and their friend has no price. What else could you do than to regret your actions, to suppose even that you had the courage to do it." He finished the letter by saying: "I'm looking for the man in the criminal…and that's what is letting me not lose hope in you."

Nadine Gurczenski
Vineland, Ontario

She was a 26-year-old exotic dancer who was last seen alive less than 24 hours before her body was discovered in a ditch off a lonely stretch of roadway in Vineland, Ontario. Nadine Gurczenski, who used the stage name Marilyn while dancing, lived in Toronto and had been separated from her husband for a couple of years. Her body was found Saturday, May 8, 1999 along a stretch of Victoria Avenue, a two-lane paved roadway, between Seventh Avenue and Eighth Avenue, 20 miles west of Hamilton. The roadway is bordered by farmland on both sides. It's also sparsely populated with very little traffic during the evening and overnight. A group of cyclists spotted the victim's body in the early evening hours and police said she'd been dead about a day. When found, Nadine was face up and wearing only knee-length stockings and some jewelry consisting of a large hoop earring, a small nose ring and a gold ankle bracelet. Detectives from the Niagara Regional Police Service have never revealed the cause of death, but did confirm she was the victim of a homicide. The night before her death, she was performing at a Mississauga strip club just west of Toronto and may have left with a man who had chatted with her on a number of different occasions. A composite drawing produced by police matched an individual who was arrested years later for the killing of two sex trade workers in the same area but he was never linked to Nadine's death or the murders of two other women. They are Dawn Stewart, 31, of Niagara Falls, a pregnant mother of two young boys, who was found in a wooded area September 27, 1995 in the village of Pelham, six months after she vanished and Margaret Jeannette Jugaru, 26, also of Niagara Falls, who was found dead July 9, 2004 in the parking lot of a Niagara Falls elementary school. She was last seen alive a day earlier.

Gurczenski came to Canada from Jamaica in 1992 and lived for a couple of years with her husband, Paul, before separating. He took custody of their young daughter while Nadine moved into an apartment on Weston Road in Toronto. She also started working as an exotic dancer at clubs in the Toronto area. Investigators said they are anxious to hear from anyone who has information about Nadine's death or the slaying of the other women. Niagara Crime Stoppers will also pay a reward of up to $2,000 to anyone who calls anonymously with information that helps police solve any of the cases.

Renata Hanelt

Renata Hanelt
New Westminster, British Columbia

Detectives from the Major Crime Unit are convinced there is someone who knows who fatally stabbed a 56-year-old woman in her New

Westminster, British Columbia apartment unit. The body of Renata Hanelt was found Thursday, May 17, 1990 in the third floor apartment at 209 Carnarvon Street between Elliot Street and Merrivale Street. The Greater Vancouver Crime Stoppers program is offering the standard reward of up to $2,000 for anyone who provides information that solves this slaying.

Shon Hart
Oshawa, Ontario

The 31-year-old victim was stabbed during a possible robbery attempt on a bicycle pathway in Oshawa, Ontario and bled to death after making his way to the apartment building where his mother lived. A short time earlier during the evening of Sunday, July 2, 2006 the victim, Shon Hart, was involved in an altercation with someone at the YMCA building but left after learning police had been called. He walked to Rotary Park off Centre Street and began traveling along a bike path that follows the Oshawa Creek toward Lake Ontario.

Homicide detectives from the Durham Regional Police Service found evidence showing Hart was stabbed in the neck after being confronted on the pathway about 150 yards north of Mill Street. He ran towards the apartment building at Mill Street and Centre Street but bled to death around 9 p.m. while attempting to smash his way through the patio door of the superintendent's ground floor unit. Durham Region Crime Stoppers produced a video reenactment of the attack and are offering a reward of up to $2,000 for information that helps police make an arrest. Detectives said they are interested in identifying an individual who had robbed a number of people on the bike path earlier in the evening who is described as being white, about 19 with a skinny build, brown hair and eyes. He was riding a brown and green stunt bike and police said he had a tattoo on his neck.

Chien Ju "Danny" Ho
West Vancouver, British Columbia

He was a 21-year-old mobster who got on the wrong side somebody in Vancouver, British Columbia. Chien Ju "Danny" Ho left a gambling table at a club on Fraser Street, between East 23rd Street and East 24th Street around 11 p.m. on Tuesday, September 17, 1996, to meet someone outside. He didn't return and the next day, at 10 a.m. his semi nude body was found on Highway 99, two miles north of Horseshoe Bay, and some 17 miles from the club. Police didn't indicate how he was killed but confirmed his death was a homicide. The car he normally drove, a black 1994 Mercedes 420E, was found on a residential street near Memorial South Park in Vancouver two days after the killing. Ho, who frequented numerous gambling and karaoke clubs in the Vancouver and Richmond, was associated with individuals linked to various organized crime groups and was involved in the illicit drug trade. The West Vancouver Police Department are continuing to pursue the investigation into Ho's death and want to speak to anyone who knows why he was killed and the identities of those who are responsible. The Greater Vancouver Crime Stoppers program will also pay a reward of up to $2,000 for information leading to the arrest of his killer.

John Horvath

John Horvath
Welland, Ontario

A 75-year-old retired teacher was likely murdered after confronting burglars at his Welland, Ontario home. The body of John Horvath was discovered in a pool of blood at the bottom of steps leading to the basement on Monday, January 4, 1999. He had been beaten and his skull was fractured. The rear door of the home at 156 Norway Avenue between First Avenue and Lillias Street had been forced open and investigators from the Niagara Regional Police believe at least two people were involved in the break-in. Evidence indicates the victim was killed a couple of days before his body was found. The former E. L. Crossley Secondary School shop teacher, who kept in touch with many of his students, had spent the Christmas holiday in Thunder Bay with his daughter. He returned home earlier than planned and homicide detectives believe burglars, who thought the home was going to be vacant through the holidays, unexpectedly came across Horvath after they broke in. At that point one of the individuals grabbed something and began beating the victim. The autopsy confirmed Horvath had blunt force trauma injuries. Even though years have passed since the killing, investigators said the perpetrators, especially if they knew Horvath, have been filled with guilt and hope one will find the courage to come forward and allow police to close the file on the homicide. Niagara Crime Stoppers is offering a reward of up to $2,000 for anyone who can provide anonymous information that helps police to arrest the individuals responsible for Horvath's death.

Jane Johnson   Cathryn Johnson

Jane and Cathryn Johnson
Turner Valley, Alberta

A 36-year-old pregnant mother and her eight year old daughter were found slain in their Turner Valley, Alberta home that had been set alight to cover up the murders. Firefighters discovered the bodies of Jane Johnson and daughter Cathryn on Tuesday, September 3, 1996 at the home on Royalite Way in this village of some 2,000 people 45 miles southwest of Calgary. It was first believed the pair had died as a result of smoke inhalation, but autopsies showed they were victims of homicide. The mother was stabbed to death, but police have never disclosed how the girl was killed. They had been living with Johnson's boyfriend for some time, but returned to the home so Cathryn, a Grade 3 student, wouldn't miss the opening day of classes at Turner Valley School. Homicide investigators from the Royal Canadian Mounted Police don't believe the killing was random or an act of violence committed during a burglary. Examination of the fire-gutted home showed the killer was familiar with Johnson's movements and seemed to know the day-to-day routine of the mother and daughter. Sometime during the late evening or early morning hours one or more individuals made their way into the house and proceeded to kill the victims. The murders were deliberate and planned but investigators have been unable to find a motive or pinpoint a specific suspect. There are a number of individuals who police believe could be responsible, but they do not have evidence to conclusively eliminate or implicate them. Her ex-husband, Sam, who remarried and was the father of a newborn son at the time of the killings, can't imagine why someone would want to take the life of an innocent little girl. Through the years Sam has made appeals and distributed posters in an effort to find the killer. His ex-wife's boyfriend, Henry Reichert, doesn't have answers but is adamant he isn't the killer. They were together four years and Reichert who was 37 at the time of the killing said Jane was a beautiful person who didn't deserve to die. She was five months pregnant with his child.

Investigators probing the homicides have theorized the pregnant mother knew the person who plunged a knife into her. Police compiled a "persons of interest" list which includes individuals who knew or were friendly with the woman. Once the killer murdered Jane and her daughter, a blaze was set that smoldered for some time before engulfing the home. It was neighbors who called the fire department after spotting flames shooting from the windows. They last saw the mother and daughter the day before the fire at an annual block party for residents of the street to celebrate the end of the summer holiday. They had just arrived home after spending a considerable part of the school vacation at Reichert's home, 10 miles east in farm country between Black Diamond and Okotoks. Both Jane and her daughter enjoyed horseback riding and there was lots of opportunity near Reichert's rural property. With the summer over and her daughter in school, Jane had plans to return to her job working with special needs children at the Millarville Community School in Millarville, seven miles to the north of her home. Investigators continue to appeal for information about the killings and rewards totaling $125,000 have been posted through the years in an effort to find those responsible for the murders of Johnson and her daughter. Police have also received profiles detailing the type of person they should be pursuing as possible suspects from the Federal Bureau of Investigation in Quantico and profiling experts in Ottawa. At this point they are now waiting for the final piece of the puzzle in their hunt for the killer.

Pamela Kosmack
Ottawa, Ontario

A pair of glasses from a middle-aged male could be a vital clue in identifying the killer of a 39-year-old Ottawa, Ontario woman. The victim, Pamela Kosmack, was found beaten to death at 6:15 a.m. on Wednesday, June 4, 2008 beside a bicycle path off Howe Street near Poulin Avenue, just over a mile from the apartment where she lived. A woman walking her dog found the half naked body only hours after the slaying. Kosmack, the mother of two children, a 15-year-old daughter and an 11-year-old son, had battled drug addiction since her early 20s but in the days before her death made a decision to get her life back on track. She was on a waiting list to get help at a treatment facility and may have left her third floor New Orchard Avenue apartment during the early morning hours to go for a walk along the Rideau River when she was attacked. She had lived in that area for some five years and would often go for walks or sometimes take the bus to a mall.

In the months before her murder, neighbors noticed she had lost weight and it was obvious she had started taking drugs again. Kosmack knew she needed help and talked to her mother and sister about her plan to get off drugs and move her life forward. She desperately wanted to be a good mother. Life started out as a struggle for Kosmack. She was born prematurely and as an infant required surgeries to sustain her life. Her childhood and teen years were spent living in a public housing project with other families who received welfare cheques to pay for food and clothing. Dropping out of school in Grade 10, she began experimenting with drugs and as a young adult was hooked on cocaine.

Her family wonders what life would have brought for her if she had the chance to kick her drug habit. She was dreaming of the life she would have as a mother looking after her son and daughter. There was so much hope, but everything was taken away by a killer on a lonely bicycle path in the middle of the night. In her youth she had enjoyed painting and could have been quite an accomplished artist. She was also very protective of her younger sister and wouldn't allow her to be bullied in the tough west-end Ottawa neighborhood where they grew up. When her children were younger she got herself drug free and worked for some time at a nursing home. But in the last couple of years of her life she again fell in with the wrong crowd and began relying on drugs to get through each day.

After the murder family members described Pam as a loving Mom and a wonderful person who had come under bad influences. Friends said she was a person with a great smile and a bubbling personality. At the time of the killing some other women had been assaulted but Ottawa Police Chief Vern White said investigators had found nothing to link the cases. However, he did stress that people should be careful when out walking and told women to be aware of what's going on around them and not put themselves into risky situations. Investigators from the Ottawa Police Service major crime unit are continuing to appeal for people to come forward with information. The brown frame Foster Grant reading glasses may turn out to be the piece of the puzzle that solves the case and detectives want anyone who knows someone who lost their glasses around that time or someone who stopped wearing glasses when Kosmack was killed. Calls can be made anonymously to Ottawa's National Capital Area Crime Stoppers program which is offering a $2,000 reward for information that solves the case.

Ralph Wayne Lange
New Westminster, British Columbia

Robbery may be the motive for the stabbing death of a 62-year-old man in New Westminster, British Columbia. The body of Ralph Wayne Lange was discovered by his son on Wednesday, December 8, 2004 in his ground level apartment on 11th Street. It was the day before his 63rd birthday and the victim hadn't been seen since November 24. Friends told police Lange enjoyed playing poker and may have been followed home after winning a large amount of money, but a check of security tapes from local casinos didn't turned up any images of the victim. Investigators from the Major Crime Unit of the New Westminster Police Service would like to hear from anyone who remembers seeing Lange at any time up to the day his body was found. Police have been told that the victim, who lived alone, was a friendly outgoing man who walked his dog on a regular basis and would stop for a coffee at the local Starbucks before going back to his condo. A $10,000 reward has been offered by the city and Crime Stoppers has made available $2,000 for anyone wishing to anonymously provide information that leads to an arrest.

Yan Jan Liu   Walter Chen Zhang   Zhu Xia Lin

Yan Jan Liu, Yan Walter Xiao Chen Zhang & Zhu Xia Lin
Markham, Ontario

Mystery still shrouds the shooting deaths of two women and a man at a Markham, Ontario massage parlor. The victims, Zhu Xia Lin, 41, Yan Jan Liu, 35, and Yan Walter Xiao Chen Zhang, 40, were shot around 12:50 a.m. on Sunday, February 8, 2004 at the Mirage Spa at 7170 Warden Avenue, a block and a half north of Steeles Avenue, the street that serves as the boundary between Toronto and York Region. After the execution-style slayings the killers wrapped the three victims in towels and sheets and put them in the rear of Zhang's sport utility vehicle. Around 4 a.m. the red 1999 Ford Explorer was driven some 10 miles north and left in a parking lot behind the Victoria Square United Church at the southwest corner of Woodbine Avenue and Elgin Mills Road.

Homicide detectives from the York Region Police Service believe at least two people were involved in the murders but investigations so far have failed to establish a motive. It's believed Zhang, a friend of both women, was shot first and Lin, the spa owner was forced to watch her employee, Liu, being murdered before she was put to death. Lin, who used the names Rita and Julie, claimed refugee status in 1997 after paying a criminal organization some $40,000 to smuggler her from the seaport city of Fuzhou in southeast China to Canada. She likely paid off part of her debt by working in a couple of Toronto area body rub parlors and earning extra money by offering sexual favors to customers. Investigation showed she had been friendly with some underworld characters and may have borrowed money to establish the massage parlor where she was killed.

Although police don't have a motive they are convinced Lin was the target of the gunmen and the other two were killed to make sure there were no witnesses. The killers also took precaution to make sure they didn't leave fingerprints or other evidence. It's possible they even made arrangements with someone to make sure the building's video surveillance system was turned off hours before they arrived on their murder mission. Lui, who used the names Judy, Amy or Sally with her various clients, was married but enjoyed the lifestyle she could afford with money earned through prostitution.

Zhang came to Canada with his parents at the age of 17 and was an engineer, but spent time at the massage parlor whenever Lui was there. When the women were with customers he would sit with his laptop completing projects for the company where he worked. Police described him as an innocent victim and someone who just happened to be in the wrong place. Investigators said there seems to be no explanation as to why the bodies were moved and are hoping someone who knows the killers or who has overhead a conversation about the murders will come forward and reveal whatever information they may have. The York Regional Police Service is offering a $100,000 reward for information leading to the arrest and conviction of the killers and York Region Crime Stoppers has a reward of up to $2,000 for anyone who anonymously calls the tip line and provides information that leads to an arrest.

David John Malloy
North Vancouver, British Columbia

A Yellow Cab driver died two days after being stabbed during a robbery in North Vancouver, British Columbia. The attack occurred at 9:39 p.m. on Sunday, March 17, 1996 after David Jon Malloy picked up a passenger at Seymour Street and Robson Street in Vancouver's west end. The Royal Canadian Mounted Police received a 911 call about a man bleeding in an alleyway in the 700 block of West 20th Street, a residential neighborhood on the fringe of Mosquito Creek Park. It was a 10 mile drive from where the man got into his taxi. Emergency crews found the 44-year-old victim in severe shock with multiple stab wounds and before they arrived he told people who came to his aid that he'd been robbed and his cab stolen.

An alert was issued to all police and taxi companies throughout the Greater Vancouver area and 10 minutes later another cab driver spotted the vehicle in the 100 block of West Hastings Street in downtown Vancouver. He attempted to follow the taxi but lost it in traffic before police had the opportunity to close in. A short time later the stolen cab was found abandoned at Dunlevy Avenue and Cordova Street, a few blocks from where the vehicle was last seen.

Police said forensic tests failed to provide any evidence that would assist in identifying the killer. However, the cab driver who tried to chase the vehicle along West Hastings Street said the lone occupant was a dark skinned man with a goatee, wearing glasses and a white baseball-style hat. He also assisted police in preparing a composite drawing of the individual.

Malloy who received 24 stab wounds to his neck, head, back and left hand, lingered for two days in critical condition at Lions Gate Hospital. He died March 19. Investigation showed the cab driver began his shift at 2 p.m. and was primarily working in the west end. After picking up the passenger, Malloy drove through Stanley Park on Stanley Park Causeway Road and then over the Lions Gate Bridge into North Vancouver. Police believe he was attacked at that point with the suspect stabbing him repeatedly before grabbing the cash and his wallet. People in the area reported hearing some sort of crash and spotting a cab just before the victim was found. Before losing consciousness Malloy was able to tell police his attacker was a black male in his late 20s and the location where he'd picked him up. The Greater Vancouver Crime Stoppers program is offering a reward of up to $2,000 for any information that leads to the arrest of Malloy's killer.

Joseph Marsala
Niagara Falls, Ontario

Police are trying to determine if a contract killing was behind the murder of a career criminal in Niagara Falls, Ontario. The body of Joseph Marsala was discovered around 1 a.m. on Friday, November 3,

1995 dumped on Kalar Road between Chippawa Creek Road and Brown Road. He had been shot several times. Detectives from the Niagara Regional Police said Marsala, who lived on Monrose Road, about two miles from where his body was dumped, had a criminal record dating back to 1972 for drug trafficking, weapons and other charges. The 47-year-old victim would sometimes visit the AA Auto Wreckers which is located on Kalar Road midway between Brown Road and McLeod Road. Investigators said they have traced Marsala's movements and know where he was up to 11:30 p.m. but have no idea of his whereabouts or who he was with within the last 90 minutes in his life. A white Oldsmobile was found near the body, but police haven't connected it to the slaying. Investigators were also told about two vehicles travelling at high rates of speed southbound on Kalar Road shortly before the body was discovered, but nothing has been turned up to link them with the slaying. Niagara Crime Stoppers will pay a reward of up to $2,000 for information leading to the arrest of Marsala's killer.

Corporal William McIntyre

Corporal William McIntyre
Oakville, Ontario

An undercover police officer who was shot in his Oakville, Ontario apartment is believed to have been on duty when killed. Corporal William McIntyre was an Ontario Provincial Police officer who had spent a good part of his career posing as a bad guy and getting evidence to put criminals behind bars. The body of the 32-year-old officer was discovered Saturday, April 21, 1984 in the locked Marlborough Court apartment unit off Trafalgar Road on the southern fringe of the sprawling Sheridan Community College campus. He had been shot, execution style, with a .22-caliber revolver. A resident of the apartment building saw McIntyre leaning over the balcony of his second-floor apartment in the mid afternoon talking to someone with a motorcycle helmet tucked under his arm. It was five hours before the body of the police officer was discovered. Police distributed a drawing of the individual on the sidewalk, described as someone in his late teens or early 20s, but the person was never identified. Detectives from the Halton Regional Police Service don't know if this person is connected with McIntyre's murder, but they would like to interview him in hopes he can shed light on the killing.

McIntyre was a police officer for 12 years and during that time was actively engaged in undercover investigations and electronic surveillance of motorcycle gang members, drug dealers and organized crime figures. Sometimes he'd pose as an outlaw biker and share a jail cell with a felon in hopes of gleaning information about their involvement with criminal activity. Investigators said there is a long list of people with a motive to kill McIntyre, but they are still working to find the person responsible. It's believed he may have invited an informant to his home in hopes of getting additional information on some criminal activity. A $50,000 reward is available for the arrest and conviction of the cop killer. Crime Stoppers of Halton is also offering a reward of up to $2,000 for anyone providing anonymous information that helps identify the individual who murdered McIntyre.

Robert Minor
Mattawa, Ontario

A 46-year-old man was stabbed to death and a $50,000 reward has been offered for help in identifying those involved in the killing. The body of Robert Minor was found Friday, January 11, 2002 at him home in Mattawa, Ontario, a community of 2,200 residents some 40 miles east of North Bay and 200 miles northwest of Ottawa. The reward was posted by the Ontario government but the Ontario Provincial Police says anyone with information is eligible collect a reward of up to $2,000 from the Near North Crime Stoppers program if they want to remain anonymous. Investigators have not released a great deal of information about the victim or the circumstances involved in the slaying, other than describing Minor's death as an incident of violence. The OPP's Criminal Investigation Branch is aggressively exploring all leads and re-interviewing witnesses in hopes of gaining additional details that might help pinpoint the killer. Detectives have recently submitted samples taken at the time of the murder to the crime lab in hopes of turning up DNA evidence that will be vital in linking an individual to the homicide once suspects are identified. OPP Commissioner Julian Fantino said advancements in technology could play a critical role in helping solve this case.

Ernest Uno Ozolins & Lisa Michelle Chamberlain
West Vancouver, British Columbia

A former Hells Angels chapter president and his girlfriend were shot to death at their West Vancouver home. The bodies of Ernest "Ernie" Uno Ozolins, 41, and Lisa Michelle Chamberlain were discovered around 8 p.m. on Monday, June 2, 1997 at the house on Wildwood Lane, a street that runs parallel to the Upper Levels Highway between 11th Street and Westcot Road.

The killings were described as execution style and occurred as outlaw bikers in British Columbia were embroiled in a fierce gang war. Ozolins was also actively involved at the time in drug trafficking and was arrested twice before his death for cocaine and heroin possession. Following the murder, the Haney Hells Angels chapter released a statement confirming Ozolins had served as the group's president but had retired from the Hells Angels Motorcycle Club for personal reasons in October 1996.

He had served as the chapter's secretary and as a Sergeant at Arms on the provincial executive. Reports indicated Ozolins was involved in a network that smuggled drugs from Columbia to Canada and was implicated in an attempt to smuggle about 53-pounds of cocaine worth $480,000 from the United States in a vehicle that was hauling music equipment for singer Sarah McLachlan. Two North Vancouver men were convicted of trafficking and conspiracy to import cocaine. The investigation also showed McLachlan was not in any way involved.

Detectives from the Criminal Investigation Section of the West Vancouver Police Department are looking for any information someone might have to help solve the killings of Ozolins and Chamberlain. Investigators have interviewed many people and obtained a great deal of forensic evidence but are looking for a couple of pieces of key detail to complete the puzzle. The local Crime Stoppers program is also offering a reward of up to $2,000 to anyone who anonymously provides information that leads to an arrest in this case.

Frank Perry
Niagara Falls, Ontario

A 62-year-old man was beaten to death during a robbery at his Niagara Falls, Ontario home. Frank Perry, who was actively involved in the sale of illegal alcohol and tobacco, was found dead at 9:08 a.m. on Thursday, August 27, 1992 when a friend went to visit. Although he lived with his wife, the father of five adult children was alone when the attack occurred. Investigators said someone crept into the bedroom while he was sleeping and struck him several times on the back and side of the head with a blunt object.

A box containing cash and jewelry was stolen and detectives from the Niagara Region Police Service indicate robbery was the motive for the murder. Many people knew Perry, a retired City of Niagara Falls employee, was actively involved in selling smuggled alcohol and cigarettes and investigators said it's likely the killer would have known he kept large amounts of money at home. Niagara Crime Stoppers has offered a reward for information leading to the arrest of Perry's killer.

Randy Rankin

Randy Rankin
Morewood, Ontario

Koo-Koo the Clown may have been murdered in Morewood, Ontario because he knew too much. Sitting at his computer just before 5 a.m. on Monday, February 12, 2007, Randy Rankin was shot in the head with a bullet fired through the basement window of his home at 13380 Thompson Road, a rural property, a little over a mile south of the village of Morewood and 30 miles south of Ottawa. Eighteen-year-old Amanda rushed downstairs and held her father in her arms as he took his last breath.

Apart from being a clown who entertained everyone from the Prime Minister of Canada to children in the small rural community where he lived, the 46-year-old Rankin had a passion for harness racing and was a crusader to keep corruption out of the sport. At six-foot-four and some 350 pounds, he was also someone who was easily recognized. Rankin was a regular contributor to a web site for harness racing enthusiasts and using the name Big Daddy identified owners and trainers he suspected had doped horses. He also gave evidence about doping, race-fixing and other corruption to investigators from the Ontario Provincial Police during a probe in 2004 they were conducting on behalf of the Ontario Racing Commission into irregularities at an Ottawa area racetrack. The allegations were not substantiated but the commission acknowledged some deficiencies with management processes.

A week before the murder, Rankin revealed he was getting ready to identify a number of well known owners who were regularly doping horses. He was already facing a now dropped $6.5 million lawsuit from earlier accusations and was hoping his latest allegations would force the Ontario Racing Commission to call a public inquiry and have members and others from the Ontario Harness Racing Association give evidence under oath about medications administered to horses at various race tracks. It was 4:52 a.m. when he signed onto the harness driver's web site but he didn't post his explosive information. A few minutes later while he was reading some of the messages posted by others, a gunman fired a shot from the backyard and through the basement window of Rankin's home. Detectives from the OPP's criminal investigation branch uncovered evidence showing the gunman had hidden in the darkness at the rear of the victim's home and shot Rankin moments after he sat at the computer with his back toward the window. The home is situated slightly less than a mile west of Moffat Road and there were no nearby neighbors.

Rankin had received some death threats and after moving into the bungalow-style home about a year earlier, he tried to keep his address secret by having mail sent to a post box at the town's general store. At the same time he ran for mayor of the community and most residents would have had no trouble directing anyone to the home where the clown, who recently changed his name to Lunch Box Louie, was living. Investigators have not publicly announced if they have a motive and have not indicated if they think the murder was a professional hit, but relatives believe Rankin was killed because of his controversial allegations about people in the harness racing world. A $50,000 reward is available for anyone who can provide details that lead to the arrest and conviction of the killer and the local Crime Stoppers program is offering up to $2,000 for an anonymous tip that leads to an arrest.

Patrick Jay Santos
Toronto, Ontario

A 21-year-old man went out partying with friends in Toronto, Ontario and ended up dead in the backyard of his parents' home. The father of Patrick Jay Santos found his son's body around 7 a.m. on Sunday, September 17, 2006 near the back entrance of his home on Bridlington Street in the Bellamy Drive and Ellesmere Road area. Toronto homicide detectives have not revealed how Santos was killed, but said his death was a murder. The victim lived and worked in the Brampton area, some 33 miles away, but would often visit his parents. Investigation revealed Santos, who graduated from St. Augustine Secondary School and was employed at the Turtle Jack's Sports Bar in Brampton, spoke to his girlfriend around 5 a.m. She asked where he was, Santos said: "I'll get back to you. I love you babe." It's believed he was with some male friends at a downtown Toronto nightclub. His girlfriend was at another club a block away, but they didn't meet that night.

Police have been trying to trace the victim's movements through the evening and up to the point where his body was found. His mother, Juliet, has issued passionate appeals through the media begging people to come forward with information. "Someone out there knows what happened. I need to know. I have no idea how my son got killed." She is convinced someone has information that will solve her son's murder but haven't come forward to give details to police. "I'm begging anyone who knows anything about the murder to call Crime Stoppers." Homicide detectives said the killer probably knew Santos and also was familiar with where he lived, but they have no idea why anyone would want to kill him. Toronto Crime Stoppers is offering a reward of up to $2,000 for anyone who provides information leading to an arrest.

Brandon Saville
Oshawa, Ontario

Only days after a 22-year-old man was murdered in Oshawa, Ontario, his mother made an emotional plea for someone to identify the killer. Brandon Saville, the father of a three-month-old son and a person police described as an experienced drug trafficker, was shot to death on Thursday, June 2, 2005 beside a pathway near the Erie Street foot bridge crossing the Oshawa Creek in Cordova Valley Park east of Malaga Road. He died from massive head trauma. Joy Clements called on his friends to give police the evidence they need to catch his killer. "Stand up for him now," she said. "He needs your help. Cowards who commit these atrocities in our society must be held accountable. You people, his friends who were out there, can help solve this horrific crime."

Detectives from the Durham Regional Police homicide squad are still trying to trace his movements during the last 24 hours of his life and who he may have been with. Investigators said it appears obvious he knew the individuals he met because he willingly went to an isolated location. As a drug dealer, police said he was extremely cautious and would never meet someone in a poorly lighted or out of the way area unless he was familiar with them. Saville was an associate of a local gang known as the BBCC and it's possible he was killed by a rival gang or by someone who wanted to rob him of drugs and money he would have been carrying.

Prior to the homicide the pathway in the park was a popular spot for people to sell crack cocaine since it was easily accessible location for young people living on both sides of the MacDonald-Cartier Freeway, a major highway running through Oshawa and carrying traffic from the Detroit Windsor area with eastern Ontario communities and Montreal. Investigators are confident there are people who know who killed Saville but are reluctant to come forward. The Durham Crime Stoppers program is offering a reward of up to $2,000 to anyone who calls in and anonymously provides the name of the killer.

Randall Servant
Timmins, Ontario

A 31-year-old man was shot to death in Timmins, Ontario possibly after arranging to meet someone near the city's water pumping station. The body of Randall Servant was found around 2 p.m. on Monday, February 2, 2004 on Vipond Road between Timmins and the community of Schumacher, two miles to the east. Servant was shot in the head and died almost instantly. Detectives from the Ontario Provincial Police criminal investigation branch said it appears the victim was targeted by the killer but they haven't established a motive. Police said Servant was associated with some local criminals and had links to an outlaw biker gang involved in the distribution of drugs in the Northern Ontario area. The victim was seen around noon having lunch at a local restaurant and shortly before his death was spotted driving along Vipond Road toward the pumping station. About 15 minutes later a motorist spotted Servant's body on the roadway. The Ontario government has offered a $50,000 reward for information leading to the arrest and conviction of the killer and Crime Stoppers is offering up to $2,000 for anyone who provides an anonymous tip that leads to an arrest.

Justin Shephard
Toronto, Ontario

His dream was to become a star with the National Basketball Association, but early one morning in Toronto, Ontario his life ended with two bullets to his head. Nineteen-year-old Justin Shephard was making his way to Glen Road via the Howard Street foot bridge at 1:20 a.m. on Saturday, June 23, 2001 when someone stood in front of him and fired the shots. He died instantly. Justin was at home with his mother, Audette and girlfriend, Latanya Langford, when sometime after midnight he received a call on his cell phone from someone who wanted to meet him. He left the apartment saying he'd be back in a few minutes. It appears he left the St. James Town apartment and walked north to Howard Street and then to Glen Road before heading over the walkway spanning Rosedale Valley Road and connecting with the another section of Glenn Road which runs through a neighborhood of multi-million dollar homes.

Hours before the shooting Justin had received an offer to attend a preparatory school in Maryland on a basketball scholarship. He could have left that day but wanted to spend the weekend with his mother and girlfriend. It was his opportunity to follow in the footsteps of his step-brother, Jamaal Dane Magloire, now with the Miami Heat, but at the time of the murder, a center with the Charlotte Hornets. From an early age it was evident Justin and Jamaal were natural basketball players.

Justin stood six-feet-five and his step-brother is six-feet-eleven and 265 pounds. His plan was to get accepted at the University of Kentucky where Jamaal played when drafted by the National Basketball Association. Justin was just starting to live his dream but everything ended on the pathway leading to the area with million dollar houses. Investigators determined the victim wasn't linked to any gang activity or drug dealing, but they are still trying to uncover the motive for his killing. There is every indication he was lured to the foot bridge and executed. Detectives believe some of his friends likely know who is responsible for the death but are maintaining a code of silence.

Justin was born on February 21, 1982 and was raised virtually by his mother after she broke up with his father a year after the birth. Although he didn't see his father often, Justin and his step-brother were inseparable especially if there was a basketball court anywhere near. After high school his step brother, who is four years older, got a scholarship to the University of Kentucky and in 2000 was a nineteenth round pick in the NBA draft, signing with the Charlotte Hornets. Justin was hoping to follow a similar education path and hoped someday to play on the same NBA team with Jamaal.

Since the slaying Audette helped set up a support group for mothers of other murder victims in Toronto called UMOVE, an acronym for United Mothers Opposing Violence Everywhere. She also became a director on the board of the local Crime Stoppers program but the high profile image hasn't helped produce any further leads in the murder of her son. Toronto Crime Stoppers offered a $2,000 reward for anyone who calls the tip line and anonymously provides information that leads to an arrest. The Toronto Police Service authorized a $50,000 reward for the arrest and conviction of the killer which was doubled through a donation by Justin's step-brother. Detectives said they are convinced someone has information and are urging them to come forward and provide justice to the family.

Therena Adelina Silva
Winnipeg, Manitoba

A recently divorced 36-year-old woman who earned money through prostitution to care for her two sons was found dead several months after being reported missing in Winnipeg, Manitoba. Investigators said Therena Adelina Silva vanished in 2002 sometime between April 11 and June 19 when she was officially reported missing by her family. Her skeletal remains were discovered on Sunday, December 15, 2002 in a field off Templeton Avenue near Richie Street in the northwest region of the city by a man walking his dog. Authorities have not revealed how she died, but police did confirm the death was the result of a homicide. Since 1987 some 17 sex trade workers have been murdered in this city of 700,000, but investigators haven't uncovered evidence indicating the slayings were the work of a serial killer. Even though the bodies of two prostitutes were dumped in the same barren area where Silva was found, police made an arrest in one of the cases but didn't find anything to link the individual with other deaths.

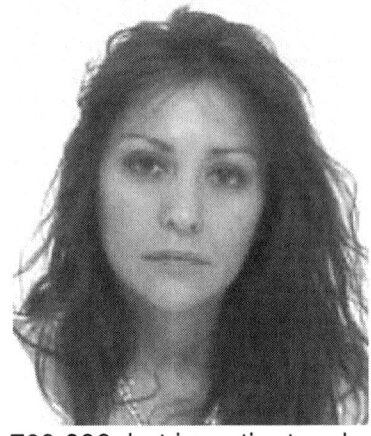

One of the last times Silva was seen alive was when she was arrested on April 11, 2002 for offering sex to an undercover officer near the corner of Toronto Street and Ellice Avenue in the city's downtown core. She was supposed to show up in court in June, but failed to appear. After the victim's remains were discovered, homicide detectives from the Winnipeg Police Service began an effort to trace Silva's final footsteps and determine who she may have been with around the time she was killed. Investigators said they encountered a great deal of difficulty in identifying people because many of the individuals who use prostitutes are reluctant to come forward. Winnipeg Crime Stoppers has offered a reward of up to $2,000 for an anonymous tip that helps solve the slaying, but detectives are still hoping they will be able to find people who are willing to provide evidence and testify in court to get a conviction once the killer is arrested. Therena's mother, Geraldine

Silva, is also hoping an arrest is made soon and will not bury her daughter's ashes until her killer is brought to justice.

Some of those linked to the sex trade industry who have been killed since 1987 include: Fonassa Lynn Bruyere, 17, August 30, 2007; Aynsley Kinch, 35, July 15, 2007; Tatia Ulm, 39, on May 9, 2005; David Joseph Boulanger, 28, alias Divas, November 3, 2004; Stephanie Ann Buboire, 30, May 24, 2004; Nicole Hands, 32, October 2, 2003; Moira Erb, 36, September 17, 2003; Simon Riley Bloomfield, 27, also known as Renee, July 14, 2002; Noreen Taylor, 32, August 15, 2001; Charmaine Sanderson, 22, March 18, 2001; Tania Marsden, 18, September 29, 1998; Evelyn Stewart, 25, March 20, 1998; Andrea Attwood, 19, April 3, 1996; Jamie McGuire, 20, March 17, 1994; Susa Holens, 15, April 13, 1989; Charlene Orshalak, 17, May 23, 1988 and Cheryl Duck, 15, December 5, 1987. Arrests were made in the deaths of Attwod, Buboire and Kinch, but rewards are available from Winnipeg Crime Stoppers for information that solves any of the other murders.

Mark Lincoln Smith

Mark Lincoln Smith
Toronto, Ontario

While driving home from a birthday celebration a 40-year-old man was killed in Toronto, Ontario when a person in a passing car opened fire on his vehicle. Mark Lincoln Smith died almost instantly at 4:14 a.m. on Monday, May 21, 2007 when his gold-colored Toyota Camry was sprayed with bullets while traveling southbound on Weston Road at Imogene Avenue. A 36-year-old passenger was shot in the upper arm and leg but recovered from her wounds. The pair had been at a ritzy party at the Pine Valley Banquet Hall, two-and-a-half miles away, on Vinyl Court where some 400 to 500 people had celebrated someone's birthday. The event has been held annually at the hall for a number of years and police found no evidence of anything happening during the evening that led to the shooting. However it's believed the gunman knew the victim and targeted the vehicle as he drove his companion home. When the first police units arrived Smith was slumped in the front seat and the passenger half way out of the vehicle sprawled on the ground. Investigators learned Smith arrived at the party shortly after 1 a.m. and left with the woman about three hours later. Detectives assigned to the Toronto Police Service homicide bureau are still trying to determine where the victim was earlier in the evening and if he had been involved in any type of dispute with any individuals. Numerous shots were fired and investigators said the gunmen used "cowboy tactics" in a callous and brazen attack. The windows of the driver's side of the car where shot out and it's possible the Toyota was rammed by the gunman's vehicle at some point during the incident. No weapons were found and there is no indication Smith had been armed. All the bullets came from one gun. Toronto Crime Stoppers has authorized a reward of up to $2,000 for information that solves this slaying.

Roger Smith & Wendy Haveron

Roger Smith & Wendy Haveron
Southwold Township, Ontario

It appeared a couple had died in a tragic farm house fire near St. Thomas, Ontario until pathologists determined the victims were murdered. Investigators said the attacker or attackers entered the home at 11553 Wellington Road, some four miles north of St. Thomas between 8:30 p.m. on Monday, February 1, 1999 and shortly before 7 a.m. the following day. Firefighters found the badly burned remains of 40-year-old Roger Smith and his 45-year-old wife Wendy Haveron in the gutted ruins. They had been called to the home at 6:52 a.m. when a passerby noticed the house engulfed in flames. Detectives from the Ontario Provincial Police criminal investigation branch have not released many details about the exact cause of death other than listing the couple as victims of a double homicide. Investigators did confirm the fire was deliberately set in an attempt to cover up the slayings and destroy evidence. Smith, described as a caring person, had spent years building up a highly productive dairy farm with a prize Jersey herd. His wife of 10 years was a frail woman and Smith had been caring for her during a lengthy period of ill health. Area residents told police the couple would not have put up much of a struggle when confronted by attackers and they cannot imagine why anyone would want to kill them. It's possible the motive was robbery but Smith wasn't known to keep a great deal of money at home. Investigators have worked through the years to encourage anyone with information to come forward and help solve the murders. They also enlisted the assistance of fire scene reconstruction experts from the United States Bureau of Alcohol, Tobacco and Firearms in hopes of coming up evidence in the debris that might identify the individuals responsible for the deaths. The Ontario government has posted a $50,000 reward to encourage anyone with information to come forward and give police the names of the killers and the St. Thomas Crime Stoppers program will pay up to $2,000 for anonymous information that helps solve this crime.

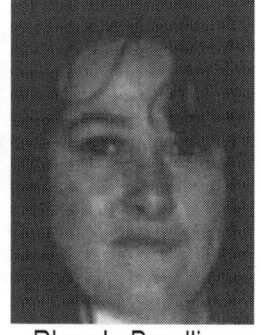

William Staples   Rhonda Borelli

William Staples & Rhonda Borelli
Hamilton, Ontario

A millionaire farmer and his 36-year-old daughter were found dead five months after they were reported missing in Hamilton, Ontario. The bodies of William Staples and Rhonda Borelli were found Monday, June 8, 1998 at a Park'n Fly lot on Dixon Road near Toronto's international airport. The victims were locked in the rear box compartment of Staples' white 1997 GMC Sonoma pick-up truck. They had been reported missing on Tuesday, January 20, 1998. Staples, who was 67 at the time of his death, was last seen around 7 p.m. at a corner store six miles from his farm home in the tiny village of

Binbrook, four days before the pair were officially reported missing to police. Pathologists were able to confirm Staples had been bludgeoned to death, but because of the advanced stage of decomposition they couldn't determine how his daughter died other than indicating signs of violence on the body. Before the bodies were found, police mounted searches for the couple and circulated their descriptions and details of their vehicle to police forces across Canada as well as to the local media. Even before the victims were located, police commenced a homicide investigation which included close scrutiny of family members, including Staples adopted son, Mark, who inherited the bulk of the family's $2.6 million estate.

Borelli had been married but moved back with her parents after her husband died. Staples wife died following a lengthy illness several months before he and his daughter were murdered. It was determined Staples was killed near the garage at the farm home on Sinclairville Road which runs between Hall Road and Haldimand Road 9 in Binbrook Township. Blood on the floor of a shed just to the rear of the home pinpointed the spot where Rhonda was murdered. No one has been charged with the killing and police have issued a $10,000 reward for anyone who can solve the murders of Staples and his daughter.

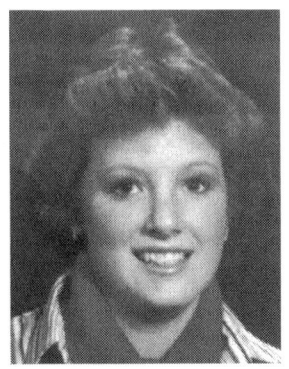

Nona Stephenson

Nona Stephenson
West Vancouver, British Columbia

A 17-year-old girl who had befriended people active in the sex and drug trade throughout the Vancouver, British Columbia area was shot and stabbed before being dumped in a 40-foot deep waterway. The victim, Nona Stephenson, was last seen alive around 7 p.m. on Friday, October 12, 1979 and her body found nine days later off Whytecliffe

Park with 25 pounds of chain wrapped around her. She had moved to the Vancouver area from Penticton a year earlier at the age of 16 and was living at a home on Triumph Street in Burnaby. She was supporting herself by working at a Vancouver restaurant but also spending a lot of time partying with people she met. Nona enjoyed the big city nightlife and the attention her friends gave her, but as an innocent small town girl, she had no idea she was being enticed into prostitution. She spent a lot of time at the Fat Cat's Club on Robson Street between Broughton Street and Jervis Street and a number of other nightclub locations in Vancouver. Investigators don't know if she had engaged in prostitution but they are aware of individuals who were attempting to recruit her. They also discovered that she was unknowingly sold for $1,000 to an individual at a pimp's party shortly before her death. Evidence shows Nona was shot and then stabbed four times in the heart before her body was wrapped in chain and dumped into the water near a marina at the park. Her killers thought the heavy chain would weigh the body down, but it floated to the surface within a few days. The homicide is now listed as a cold case file and detectives hope someone will remember something that will help them to solve the killing. The Greater Vancouver Crime Stoppers program is also offering a reward of up to $2,000 to encourage anyone with information to call the tip line anonymously.

Alma Teravainen
Thunder Bay, Ontario

A 67-year-old woman was stabbed to death at a small convenience store she operated in a Thunder Bay, Ontario apartment complex. Alma Teravainen was attacked around 6:45 p.m. on Monday, July 25, 2005 in the Harbour Terrace Variety Store on the west side of South Cumberland Street between Wilson Street and Water Street in the city's downtown area. The Thunder Bay District Crime Stoppers program described the victim as a well known and respected by the many tenants who knew her and have set a reward of $2,000 for a caller who provides information anonymously on their tip line that solves the case. They also described the murder as senseless and said it's unusual for the program to approve the maximum reward prior to an arrest, but considered this crime to be out of the ordinary.

"This is the type of crime that goes to the heart of Crime Stoppers and why it was established back in 1976 in Albuquerque, New Mexico," said a statement issued by the program after the killing. "Crime Stoppers has taken the extraordinary step of having a $2,000 reward pre-approved by our local committee. In other words, if you provide anonymous information that leads to an arrest in this homicide, Crime Stoppers will give you $2,000."

The Thunder Bay Police Service hasn't released too many details about the crime, but indicated the store is in a high traffic area and only two blocks from the Thunder Bay Charity Casino. Detectives said it's likely a number of people saw something related to the murder but don't realize it is significant to the investigation. They want anyone who was in the vicinity of the apartment complex to think back to the evening of the slaying and try to recall if they saw anything regarding a suspicious individual or something unusual that stuck in their mind.

Mahamed Adbi Warsame
Toronto, Ontario

A 16-year-old boy went out on Saturday night in Toronto, Ontario to see a movie, but a few hours later his savagely beaten body was found in the stairwell of a high rise apartment building. Mahamed Adbi Warsame was reported missing at 2 a.m. on Sunday, May 4, 2008 some 12 hours before his body was discovered on the ninth floor landing in the apartment building at 25 Cougar Court in Toronto's Scarborough district. He was the eldest of three boys who lived with their mother, Ayan Dahir, and an uncle in a subsidized apartment on Biggin Court, almost five miles away. The mother fled her native war torn country of Somalia to set up a new life in Canada and keep her sons from the clutches of warlords who would likely have recruited them as child soldiers. She didn't want them to die in wild gun battles that often raged between warring factions on the streets of Mogadishu. It isn't known if Mahamed ever went to the movie theatre of if he went directly to the apartment building which was the site of a homicide ten days earlier. Relatives described the victim as an average teenager who liked to joke around a lot. He also loved playing basketball. They said he was respectful of his mother and would always call if he was going to be late. He didn't call the evening he went out to the movies and by 2 a.m. his mother realized something was wrong and alerted police. She told them he had never stayed out all night. The Grade 11 student at Winston Churchill Collegiate Institute, a public high school, was a role model to his brothers.

Homicide detectives from the Toronto Police Service were called to the 22-storey apartment building in the Markham Road and Eglinton Avenue area at 2:16 p.m. when the boy's body was found by a resident in a pool of blood in the southeast stairwell. A post mortem showed death was caused by multiple blunt impact trauma consistent with a beating. Investigators have been unable to find any residents of the building who knew the victim and police are still trying to determine why he was in the vicinity. Police said they don't know how the victim got into the building since residents require digital cards to unlock the door and guests must be buzzed through by tenants. Detectives said they would like to speak with anyone who was with the young teenager or had plans to be with him during a 48 hour period prior to his killing. They are also anxious to speak with anyone who saw Mohamed in a 24 hour span before the body was discovered.

A 22-year-old man was stabbed to death on Thursday, April 24, 2008 but a suspect was arrested for that killing and police do not believe there is any connection with the Warsame homicide. Community organizers with the local ACORN group criticized the building owners for not beefing up security after the stabbing death and an earlier stabbing where a man was critically injured but survived. Toronto's Crime Stoppers program is offering a reward of up to $2,000 for information leading to an arrest in the slaying.

Christine Ann Woelk
Leamington, Ontario

A 49-year-old woman managed to telephone a relative before she was murdered in Leamington, Ontario. Christine Ann Woelk called from her van around 8:40 p.m. on Tuesday, May 18, 2004 with a chilling message that she was in trouble. She had finished her shift and had gone to visit a friend in the Oak Street area and was making her way home when some sort of encounter took place in her vehicle. It's not known if she picked up a hitch-hiker or offered to drive someone home that she knew. The individual who received the call immediately alerted police but they were unable to immediately find her van in this community of 30,000 people. Two days later Woelk's 1997 Pontiac van was discovered parked between two cottages just south of the Point Pelee National Park entrance. There was no sign of the woman, but blood spattering indicated there had been a violent struggle inside the van. Searches were conducted throughout the area and on Tuesday, May 25, 2004 the victim's body was found at Black Willow Beach, on the western shoreline of the park, about five miles south of the entrance.

Detectives from the Leamington Police Service teamed up with Ontario Provincial Police investigators but so far haven't found a motive for the slaying. Interviews with people who saw the mother of two children on the day she vanished indicates Woelk completed her shift at the Leamington District Memorial Hospital and stopped on her way home to visit a friend. One person reported seeing the woman arguing with a man inside her van travelling eastbound on Oak Street East around the time she managed to make the phone call.

An autopsy showed the woman's body had washed up on shore after being in the water for a week. There was no indication she'd been sexually assaulted but pathologists were not able to determine how she died other than listing the cause of death as homicide. The Windsor and Essex Crime Stoppers program made several appeals for help to solve the slaying after posting a reward of up to $2,000. The Ontario government has also offered a $50,000 reward for the arrest and conviction of the killer, but so far no one has come forward to provide information that would assist investigators in making an arrest.

Epilogue

Anyone with information regarding any of the cases in this book or other unsolved homicides is urged to contact the police or law enforcement agency responsible for the investigation. You may also contact the Federal Bureau of Investigation or your nearest police department and provide them with the details which will help solve the case. If you do not wish to contact the police directly, please call your nearest Crime Stoppers office and anonymously provide them with any information you may have regarding the murder. Your cooperation is vital to bring these cases to a conclusion.

A sequel to this book is currently in progress and the author is anxious to hear from any law enforcement agencies or relatives of homicide victims to highlight as many unsolved cases to the widest possible audience. Please email the author at – unsolvedmurders@gmail.com – to make arrangements to forward the information you have regarding the case and a photograph of the victim.

Made in the USA